LI*V*ING
VO**I**CES

**Proceedings of Common Ground:
A Conference on Progressive Education**

Edited by Peter Blaze Corcoran and Margaret Tatnall Pennock

Published by The School in Rose Valley and The Network of
Progressive Educators

Common Ground:
A Conference on Progressive Education
was held at Swarthmore College,
Swarthmore, Pennsylvania,
on October 25-26, 1992;
it was sponsored by The School in Rose Valley,
Moylan, Pennsylvania.

Design by Woodworth Associates
Portland, Maine

All photographs by Macarthur McBurney
except page 17 by Terry Wild Studio

Printing by Penmor Lithographers
Lewiston, Maine

Editorial Assistance by Simon Firestone

"Filling Station" from The Complete Poems 1927-
1979 by Elizabeth Bishop. Copyright © 1979, 1983
by Alice Helen Methfessel. Reprinted by permission
of Farrar, Straus & Giroux, Inc.

ISBN:
0-9635242-0-8

Library of Congress Catalog Card Number:
92-85544

© 1993 by The School in Rose Valley, Moylan,
Pennsylvania and The Network of Progressive
Educators, Evanston, Illinois

Printed on recycled paper.

I hope I can at least keep alive
the sounds of those living voices and not
lose them in something philosophical
and abstract.

Maxine Greene
Keynote Address at Common Ground
October 25, 1992

To Maxine, her powerful capacity to
listen and to speak, we dedicate this
volume.

PBC and MTP

Contents

Critical Reflection Upon Practice

Appendices

Foreword

The Context of Progressivism

Carol Montag, Director of The Cornerstone School, Ocala, Florida
Carol Ouimette, Executive Director, The Network of Progressive Educators,
Evanston, Illinois

Progressive education began over one hundred years ago in the heartland of America. It grew in simple rural schoolhouses before coming to public and private urban schools. In these more complex settings, progressive education flourished. With the start of a new century, other views of children's needs replaced the rigid, one-way-to-learn systems of the nineteenth century. Experiential and outdoor education as well as a new emphasis on social responsibility brought by the founders of the settlement houses infused progressive schools. Well-known educators such as John Dewey and Colonel Francis W. Parker created, for the most part, white middle class schools in urban areas. The twenties and thirties gave the progressive movement the smaller community-inspired private schools, such as The School in Rose Valley and The Putney School, under the leadership of Grace Rotzel and Carmelita Hinton respectively. They promoted the principle that the child's interest is the basic motive for all work.

The Progressive Education Association, founded in 1919, ceased to exist in 1955 and progressivism receded from the school scene. In the late sixties, the British Infant Schools acted as a catalyst for progressive ideas which began to spread under the name of open education or alternative schools. Once again there was an active interest in children as learners and a renewed faith in the educability of all children. The emphasis was on the social and political obligations of the schools, not solely on content or the techniques of instruction. The teacher was the knowledgeable guide and facilitator of learning. Progressive and alternative education, exemplified by many excellent schools, never became widely available to the majority of students in this country — yet it was widely blamed for the failure of American schools. In the seventies and eighties, as faith in public education decreased, standardization of curriculum increased, standardized tests grew as the measure of accountability, and conservative school policy flourished. Progressive education once again faded.

Now, the social reality of class, race, and gender is being confronted by all educators. Greater awareness and attention will have to be given to the democratic tradition of struggle that underlies progressive education and the social condition of the country. We must reclaim early progressivism by honoring differences among children, offering opportunity for children to learn through their strengths, and by making political impact on the educational institutions of the country.

A new wave of progressive education is now gathering momentum. It is grounded in the belief that students' interests, development, and ways of building knowledge are at the heart of learning, and that the rich, diverse texture of the lives of the community members, parents, and teachers must be woven into school culture. The Network of Progressive Educators is a stimulus to this new progressivism. Officially launched in 1989, The Network grew from a series of conferences which ended the isolation of progressive educators.

The Network connects members with one another through national and regional conferences, teacher reflection and research projects, local teacher-support group meetings, a national directory, and a newsletter. Path*ways: A Forum for Progressive Educators* provides a place to write about classroom experiences and speculate about practice. Most Network members are individuals working in classrooms, teacher educators, school board members, or parents. Institutional members include public and independent schools, child advocacy organizations, teacher education programs, teacher centers, and organizations that identify with progressive ideas and practice. These new voices have moved beyond the progressive education of the past. Today's progressives leave behind the idea that progressive education is only for the elite and found primarily in private schools. They reject the idea that there is "A Progressive Way," a definition that in the past has not necessarily honored the diverse values of the community which it serves. Many communities are forging new schools around the basic tenets of progressivism, confident that students will be at the center of classroom practice. Communities of teachers, students, and significant family members are working together to set priorities and provide the best education possible, to create and sustain what Joseph Featherstone calls "decent schools." Progressive educators bring a redefinition of progressivism, current knowledge of child development, new learning theory and curricular developments, and a renewed commitment to a just school society for all children. They bring a long history of shared experience with such currently publicized "new" programs as whole language, cooperative learning, alternative forms of assessment, integrated learning, and hands-on experiences. They come with classrooms and schools that have survived and, indeed, flourished as models of progressive practice.

As always, we struggle with hard questions. What, from our history of the past hundred years, do we proudly bring forward? What do we wish to change for the future? Frequently The Network of Progressive Educators is urged to delete the word "Progressive" from the organization's name. We are asked, "Couldn't a name be found that is less controversial?" The answer is a clear "no." We believe that we have a rich heritage, a willingness to redefine and expand our understanding of progressivism, and a commitment to decent schools for all children.

Educators, community members, and parents who met at *Common Ground* share that commitment and are hard at work making these ideas a reality. Progressivism continues to grow through conferences and publications such as *Living Voices*.

Introduction

Description of the Conference and of the Proceedings

Searching for common ground in philosophy and practice despite diversity of settings and students, over three hundred teachers gathered on the misty autumn morning of October 25, 1991, to begin a two-day conversation. This discourse took place across twenty conversation groups, thirty-seven workshops, six working groups, and countless interactions at keynote addresses, breaks, and social activities. The goal was to bring teachers from public and independent schools; from rural, suburban, and urban environments; from all grades and disciplines together — teachers who themselves represented cultural diversity — to capture the richness and tension of difference in an exploration of progressive principles as they apply to actual work.

The conference was designed to solicit the authentic participation of each teacher. As a matter of philosophy, it began with small conversation groups where each person could find voice in expressing why she or he had come. It then moved to the plenary to hear Maxine Greene's inspirational call towards common ground. Next, conferees again went to small, more intensive single-session workshops, or to three-session working groups. So it went for two days. The emphasis was on dialogue, participation, and the questions which arose in the conversation.

Every session was both tape-recorded and captured by a scribe listening for the voices of participants as well as presenters. This record is the basis for the document you hold. The elements of the text, therefore, are written from a variety of perspectives — one keynote and some working groups from that of a presenter, most working groups and workshops from that of an observer, and some workshops from that of a participant. Our effort was to capture the varied sounds of the ideas and exchanges. The proceedings are intended to provide a remembrance, record, and sense of the whole for the person in attendance, a sense of how the conference felt and of the ideas exchanged for the person who could not attend — and a source of further exploration for both.

We hope the book itself is consistent with a philosophy of progressive education; that it is participant-centered. We wanted the concerns of the participants to provide the organizing principle for this text. The conference proceedings include the ideas of all who participated in *Common Ground* — students, teachers, administrators, parents, as well as organizers and those formally on the program. Our desire to capture individual participants' ideas was reinspired by Maxine Greene's keynote address, with its emphasis on attending to "living voices." We realize that this diversity of voice can be challenging for the reader. *Living Voices* may be more of a cacophony than a symphony, but our aim was to listen, then organize a record of the event.

We used notes taken by members of conversation groups to discover what individual participants thought and felt during *Common Ground*. These conversation groups were informal times for the participants to articulate their goals, and later, to reflect upon their experience. The first step we took in writing this book was to read the written record of each conversation group and identify issues discussed there as they related to the conference purpose.

The following themes emerged from those conversations:

> There is a need for spaces where people of diverse backgrounds and experience can gather and engage in dialogue with each other. Those who construct such spaces must be aware of and respect differences between themselves and others. We identified this theme with the title of the conference, *Common Ground*.

> Everyone needs support. Learners and teachers need to feel safe, to be able to take risks that can lead to growth. Such support engenders self-discovery and enhances the prospects for change. Rapport between parents and teachers is vital for effective progressive education. We named this *Supportive Relationships and Environments*.

> We value children's experience. Classrooms can give students opportunities to direct their own educations. Teachers are responsible for creating caring environments where children's voices, concerns, needs, and questions can be honored. This theme is *Attending to Children*.

> Progressive educators believe that the way one arrives at the answer to a problem is more interesting than the "correct" nature of the answer. Learning is strengthened by excitement and direct experience; through experience we construct meaning. After John Dewey, we call this *Philosophy of Experience*.

> The final theme evokes the concept of critique. Educators ask themselves questions, examine their own work, recognize their achievements, and look for opportunities to grow. Such is *Critical Reflection Upon Practice*.

The proceedings are divided into sections according to these themes. Each thematic section is introduced by an explanation of that theme and by quotations from the conversation groups which illustrate it. Each section contains the keynote addresses, working groups, and workshops which spoke most strongly to the relevant theme. Descriptions are written from a variety of perspectives as noted at the beginning of each. Where names are provided we wished to credit those whose work was little-changed in editing.

We hope the structure of the conference provided space for conversation among many living voices. We hope the proceedings embody a philosophy of listening to many voices and that they faithfully capture some of what happened, some of what was said at *Common Ground*.

And we hope the experience of attending and/or reading about the conference will inspire further conversation in formal professional groups, in informal networks, in future conferences. The organizers of *Common Ground* seek to support and expand dialogue among practitioners because we believe in the importance of what each teacher, each parent, each student has to say.

Acknowledgments

Without the conference, there would have been no proceedings; without the Herculean efforts of The School in Rose Valley staff, the members of the Conference Steering Committee, and the student workers from Swarthmore College, there would have been no conference. There are, truly, too many of them to mention, but we must note the superb leadership of Lauren deMoll and Edie Klausner, and the dedication of Ken Landis to raising the necessary funds. We also wish to thank the Philadelphia Foundation for providing scholarship support to all administrators, teachers, and parents from the School District of Philadelphia, and an anonymous donor who provided significant additional scholarship support. Publication of these proceedings was made possible by a grant from The Pew Charitable Trusts; we thank the Trusts.

So many have contributed to the successful completion of this volume. Appreciation goes to the presenters and scribes who, in addition to their original work, reread, and sometimes helped us rewrite the pieces. We accept full responsibility and hope we have not misrepresented their work in any way. Appreciation is extended to three who guided us and contextualized this volume in the long and rich tradition of Progressive Education Conference Proceedings to which they have contributed so much — Carol Montag, Kathe Jervis, and Carol Ouimette. Again, we thank Edie Klausner and Lauren deMoll and, again, Carol Ouimette for serving as an informal, but highly professional editorial committee.

Peter especially wishes to thank his colleagues at Swarthmore College for providing the opportunity to pursue this project and his students at Swarthmore for their talented assistance, especially Macarthur McBurney for the photographs and Simon Firestone for editorial assistance. Great thanks go to Bates College for providing secretarial support for the manuscript, especially to Joyce Caron. Special thanks from Margaret and Peter to Simon for his inestimable contributions to the organization and refinement of the text.

PBC and MTP

Conference Opening

After making their way, on an uncharacteristically foggy autumn morning, across the bucolic Swarthmore College campus, participants were assigned to conversation groups based on the first letter of their first name. Each group was composed of approximately a dozen people including a designated facilitator. For an hour and a half, participants shared why they had come and their aspirations as to the conference theme of common ground. In this way, conference planners sought to provide an opportunity for each person to find voice, to experience a sense of community within the larger group. The conference also closed with an hour-and-a-half session in which the conversation included each participant sharing an idea, concept, or question gained at *Common Ground*.

Conferences, like classrooms, are more than places for the transmission of skills and information. They are opportunities for people to reflect, to examine the assumptions that shape their lives, to listen to and to chat with others who have similar hopes, frustrations, and experiences. Conversation groups were a chance for *Common Ground* participants to explore both what they share with and how they differ from others. They were a point of departure for discourse — a time for participants to find their place within a community that was created for the two days.

Following the initial meeting of conversation groups, Edie Klausner, principal of The School in Rose Valley, opened the first plenary gathering of the conference by acknowledging important contributions to the organization of the conference. She then continued:

"Many, many other people visible and invisible to you today made this conference happen. Thanks to everyone. I feel sure that the events of today and tomorrow will be reward in themselves without my naming names.

In 1981 Richard Mandel, then principal of The Miquon School, began to plan a national conference on Progressive Education in Philadelphia. The main idea for that conference was to see if anyone was out there...were there still some folks who remembered what progressive education in the early part of the twentieth century looked like? Were there any progressive schools still alive and well? Did they want to come together and think about the future?

Lauren deMoll, Mike Nowell, and I, from The School in Rose Valley, joined members of The Miquon School staff and a professor at the University of Pennsylvania, and we began the work. We wrote letters to schools asking them if they wanted to be conference sponsors along with us.

By the spring of 1983, 15 schools had agreed to be sponsors; Vito Perrone, Eleanor Duckworth, Brian Sutton-Smith, and Patricia Carini agreed to present major addresses; and the Miquon Progressive Education Conference *Reunion, Reaffirmation and Resurgence* became reality. Some 100 people from across the country came, mostly from independent schools. It was exciting for those schools and for those individuals who found one another and discovered common ground in their educational philosophies and practices.

But we knew then, right from the start, as we know now, that a strong future for progressive education must rest upon an equally balanced partnership that includes the diversity and access of public schools as well as the immediacy of response possible in smaller independent schools.

Here we are now, some eight years after the Miquon Conference. We have much distance to travel, but we also have accomplished a lot. Three national progressive education conferences and approximately a dozen regional conferences have taken place. Each national conference has included more diversity and more public school participation than the one that preceded it. One third of the participants at today's conference are from public schools in the Delaware Valley, many of those from the Philadelphia School District. As public and private schools in partnership, we increase our strength as we nurture the diversity that enriches all of us. This diversity is an absolutely essential element in the principles of progressive education. The roots of progressive education are deep, but much of the visibility and growing strength of the resurgent progressive education movement today has been nurtured by The Network of Progressive Educators, a small but ever-expanding organization that is growing daily. The mission of The Network is to support progressive principles, to connect educators and organizations both public and private, to encourage progressive classroom practices and democratically-organized schools, and to pursue diversity, equity, and inclusion for all children. The principles of the Network are:

• Students learn best through direct experience, primary sources, personal relationships, and cooperative exploration.
• The blending of students' interests and teachers' knowledge is the starting point for all work.
• Schools pay equal attention to all facets of students' development.
• Assessment is accomplished through multiple perspectives.
• The school and the home are active partners in meeting the needs of students.
• Parents, students, and staff cooperate in school decision making.
• Schools build on the home cultures of students and their families.
• Schools encourage young people to fulfill their responsibilities as world citizens by teaching critical inquiry and the complexities of global issues.
• Schools help students develop their social consciences and help them learn to recognize and confront issues of race, class, and gender.

If progressive educators are to stand tall and to advocate for children and teachers, public and independent schools *must* join together. We *must* be relevant to schools with a range of needs and gifts, schools with large numbers of children and teachers of color, schools with strong voices of respect for all learners, schools that celebrate cultural inclusion and recognize the realities of inner city, suburban, and rural life.

Of course we are all different, our teaching and administrative and parenting practices are different. They reflect our own experience, our individual uniqueness and personal strengths; but something obviously draws us together here. There is a reason why this conference, modestly advertised, was over-enrolled two weeks ago.

We are a passionate group — strongly biased in favor of our commitments to what is directly meaningful and important to the children we teach. We are here today to seek common ground. We are responding to knowledge, understandings, and intuition about children and schools that is critical to our lives and to our professional values. I hope we can continue the connections we find in this setting and develop these riches in our own regions.

I hope we are today both a continuation of history and the birth of new vision."

Edie's talk was followed by the introduction of Maxine Greene and her keynote address.

Chapter 1

Common Ground

Common ground is the ongoing conversation among parties who recognize that differences exist. It is created through mutual respect and each participant's genuine concern for learning more about both oneself and others. The making of common ground requires that differences should be celebrated and explored, not hidden or ignored. Learning, growth, and untold possibilities come from exposure to diverse perspectives.

From common ground, we establish new pathways.

I'd like the uneasiness to exist; we should recognize it, not cover it up.

We examine our values and assumptions when we are made uncomfortable with new perspectives.

People who are not alike have the most to say to each other.

We don't want to go away thinking that we all agree.

Perspective and Diversity: Towards a Common Ground

A Keynote Address by Maxine Greene,
Teachers College, Columbia University, New York, New York

Peter Corcoran made an introduction, as follows:
"Good Morning. Maxine Greene has taught at Montclair State College, Brooklyn College of City University of New York, and New York University, and is Professor Emeritus at Teachers College of Columbia University. She holds the William F. Russell Chair in the Foundations of Education. She is also a Philosopher-In-Residence at the Lincoln Center Institute, a program in New York City which brings public school teachers, their students, and artists together. She has taught literature, aesthetics, and philosophy. She continues to teach and lecture widely in her peripatetic and energetic retirement. She has served as President of the Philosophy of Education Society, the American Educational Studies Association, and the American Educational Research Association, and has twice been Phi Delta Kappa Teacher of the Year. She also was recently awarded the Teachers College Award for Teacher of the Year. She holds honorary degrees from several universities, and under *any* circumstances it would be an honor to welcome Maxine to Swarthmore. Under *these* circumstances where so many have gathered to seek common ground in how we see educational problems and in how we use philosophy to solve them, it is more — it is, I believe, a source of hope that we might indeed be guided toward a common ground.

"Maxine, in your award-winning book, *Teacher as Stranger,* we saw our existential dilemmas as teachers; in *Landscapes of Learning,* we felt the predicaments of women and gained courage to educate against the mainstream. Most recently, in *Dialectic of Freedom,* we were shown how freedom might be achieved and how despair might be resisted. Your voice has helped us not only to resist, but to affirm what we believe in and to imagine things as they might be.... In these books, and in your essays and lectures, we have admired your passion and your courage. Thank you for coming to talk with us today."

Maxine Greene began:
Thank you, Peter, and thank you, Edie. It's such a privilege to be here. Last night Peter was very worried about the stage set that was being built. He thought they might be building it while we were speaking. And then he started to worry about the height and I started to think about Albert Camus in the *Myth of Sisyphus,* who talks about suddenly the stage set melting away and — everything begins in a moment of wideawakeness tinged with amazement. So I hope something like that is happening here. I was in one of the conversation groups before, and people spoke to each other about their lived lives. I learned a lot. I was deeply moved by what I heard, and I was struck again by a difficulty. I guess none of us

can quite overcome that which is involved in moving from the sound of the personal voice, from the existential, to a speech. I hope I can at least keep alive the sounds of those living voices and not lose them in something philosophical and abstract.

This is a time of newly acknowledged diversity in American culture. Voices are becoming audible, faces are becoming visible; and we are realizing, some of us for the first time, how many silences there have been in the past, how many blank spaces in our history. We may have looked too long from monological points of view; we may have assumed consensus where it did not exist. Today we are being made sharply aware of multiplicity. We are discovering the range of perspectives that must be taken into account as we work to remake community, as we strive for the achieving of a common ground. Not only are we asked today to look through the lenses of gender and class and ethnic difference; not only are we provoked to pose questions to the "canon," the so-called tradition. We are being asked to recreate our "habits of the heart," to redefine our "habits of mind" and what we can communicate in schools.

Fundamental to a conception of progressive education, most of us would agree, is a conception of pluralism linked to a notion of a "great community." Concerned as John Dewey was about the "steadying and integrating office" of the schools, he never thought in terms of homogeneities or the kind of sharing that overwhelmed diversity. One of the ends in view where connectedness and cooperation were concerned was the release of individuality. He understood that situations have to be deliberately created if there is to be a play of difference, an expression of personal energy. At once he recognized that people abandoned to privacy and total self-reliance are unlikely to develop, to "become different," or even to achieve their freedom. Fabrics of care, networks, support systems, communication: all are needed for the growth of persons, for the pursuit of possibilities. He wrote one time that "only the voluntary initiative and voluntary cooperation of individuals can produce social institutions that will protect the liberties necessary for achieving development of genuine individuality."[1] He had choosing in mind, and new beginnings; and he knew very well the "social pathology" that stood in the way — the kind of pathology that stands in the way today.

In his words, it manifested itself "in querulousness, in impotent drifting, in uneasy snatching at distractions, in idealization of the long established, in a facile optimism assumed as a cloak, in riotous glorification of things 'as they are,' in intimidation of all dissenters, ways which depress and dissipate thought all the more effectually because they operate with subtle and unconscious pervasiveness."[2] This in many ways characterizes what we see around us today in this peculiar moment of self-righteousness and social neglect. As we speak about progressive education, we must not allow ourselves to put aside the dreary realities of contemporary life — the violation of children, the drug epidemic, the spread of AIDS, homelessness, the erosion of services, the racism, the homophobia, the privatism, the lack of care. Nor ought we ignore the perspectives, the vantage points of those suffering violation, exclusion, humiliation, and neglect. They are as important as the perspective so many of us unflinchingly oppose: the perspective of the positivist, the instrumental rationalist, the Pentagon spokesman who translates wounded civilians into diagrams on a chalkboard for all to see. I need to turn to literature to highlight what I am saying before going on. I think of Joseph Conrad's Marlow in *Heart of Darkness* talking to the Director of Companies, the Lawyer, and the Accountant about the Roman conquest of Britain and the Roman officials' confrontation with "the mysterious life of the wilderness." Sardonically conscious that he is speaking to latter-day exemplars of imperial greed, Marlow tells them: "'Mind, none of us would feel exactly like this. What saves us is efficiency — the devotion to efficiency.'"[3] How can we who are in education not be attuned to those who use efficiency as test and mystifier at once?

And then I think of the moment late in Fitzgerald's *The Great Gatsby*, when Nick Carraway realizes that Tom Buchanan's sending George to kill Gatsby seems entirely justified to Tom. "It was all very careless and confused. They were careless people, Tom and Daisy — they smashed up things and creatures and then retreated back into their money or their vast carelessness, or whatever it was that kept them together, and let other people clean up the mess they had made...."[4] There are few of us today who do not feel the cold blast of such carelessness in streets, schoolyards, emergency rooms, libraries; it too is part of the pathology. And then there is that remark in Albert Camus's novel *The Plague*, one I cannot but hope we people who care about progressive education take seriously. It is spoken by Tarrou, who is telling his friend Dr. Rieux about the vocation of true healing, which seems to him to be very hard. "'That's why I decided to take, in every predicament, the victims' side, so as to reduce the damage done.'" Later, Dr. Rieux acknowledges Tarrou when he speaks of how important it is to bear witness in favor of the plague-stricken people, and to state "quite simply what we learn in a time of pestilence: that there are more things to admire" in human beings than to despise. And lastly, there is Christa Wolf, whose woman narrator ponders in *Accident*: "...I was once more forced to admire the way in which everything fits together with a sleepwalker's precision: the desire of most people for a comfortable life, their tendency to believe the speakers on raised platforms and the men in white coats; the addiction to harmony and the fear of contradiction of the many seem to correspond to the arrogance and hunger for power, the dedication to profit, unscrupulous inquisitiveness, and self-infatuation of the few. So what was it that didn't add up in this equation?"[5] It may be our pedagogical responsibility to respond.

Moving from that reflection (generated, it happens, by the Chernobyl disaster of a few years ago), we might well think of the kind of critical intelligence (and, I would hope, critical dialogue) presumably fostered in progressive classrooms. In this case, there are implications for what Dewey called "social inquiry," what some of us — drawing out some of its strands — might call a form of ideology critique. Surely, given the persisting mystifications surrounding official formulators, men on platforms, and the rest, and adding to those the obvious desire for harmony and easy answers, educators have much to do in enabling the young to pose worthwhile questions having to do with what William Blake called "mind-forged manacles." There is clearly a bland coercion of consciousness going on that moves even adults to take short cuts, to avoid examination of their own assumptions, to blind themselves to the consequences of thoughtless (or careless, or manipulative) acts. Then, in addition, there is the implication for an encouragement of scientific literacy, linked to concrete experiences in what is thought to be "real" life.

Surely, the centrality of care in Fitzgerald's sense (and, probably, in the sense of feminist ethics) is connected with this. I am reminded of Dewey's discussion of mind in *Art as Experience*, where he says that mind ought to be thought of as a verb and not a noun. "It denotes," he wrote, "all the ways in which we deal consciously and expressly with the situations in which we find ourselves." He said mind is "care in the sense of solicitude, anxiety, as well as of active looking after things that need to be tended."[6] It was, for Dewey, an activity that was intellectual, volitional, and (as he put it) affectional; to be mindful in the most significant sense was to be responsive to norms, to take careful heed, to use intelligence in the funding of meanings, personally to attend. To speak this way is to abandon the enclaves of academic specialism as it is such values as detachment and "objectivity." The mindful individual is engaged in participant thinking in the midst of life. She/he is at the furthest remove from the spectator or the abstract observer or experimenter. For Dewey, and for progressive educators generally, the thoughtful person is not only grounded; she/he is given to relational thinking, contextualized thinking. Unlike the Buchanans, she/he cannot retreat, no matter how great the confusion; she/he is required to "stop and think,"[7] in part because she/he is in the world with others, connected with humankind.

That is why it as natural as "2+2 is 4" for Dr. Rieux to fight the plague in Camus's novel, because it "is his job." There is no likelihood that the plague can be overcome by medical efforts; but it nonetheless remains necessary, if one is a physician, to struggle against the pestilence. Similarly, in that novel, sanitary squads were in time organized by the citizens to play their part in the fight. Most of the townsfolk ignored the plague when it first arrived; they were so devoted to "cultivating habits" that they could not arouse themselves at first from resignation or indifference. The squads did finally enable those people to come to grips with the disease and convinced them that, since plague was among them, "it was up to them to do whatever could be done to fight it." Since it became in that way some people's duty, "it revealed itself as what it really was; that is, the concern of all."[8]

Now I realize it is extreme to assert that, in fighting for progressive education, we may well be fighting the pestilence. It is perfectly clear that the concerns I have been identifying are not part of the dominant discourse in education today. There is considerable pressure in many quarters (federal, corporate, even local) to orient education to the achievement of technical expertise. The end most often defined has to do with economic competitiveness or technological and military primacy in the world. Mathematical and scientific failures are lamented (as they probably should be) but not for reasons that have to do with young persons' understanding of their lived worlds. Rather, the reasons have again to do with extrinsic factors: the need for "world class" achievement in the interests of the nation; the importance of American leadership in an "undeveloped" world. The messages that come to young people have little to do with the values of extending their own repertoires or reducing their powerlessness. Almost nothing is said about the connections between mathematical and scientific literacy and ecological issues, health and nutritional problems, pregnancy, demographic matters, nuclear threats. Low test scores are made to appear a sign of disloyalty; the decline of functional literacy, evidence of impiety. There are suggestions, sometimes explicit, sometimes hinted at, that those who do not "pass," who do not "live up" or pull themselves up "by their bootstraps" will simply be left by the wayside. Several of the educational reports actually assert that society can no longer afford to support those who cannot cope with the new technologies.

Somewhat the same implications can be detected when people in official positions speak of "cultural literacy" and "what every American needs to know."[9] Overtly fearful of what is called "multiculturalism," there are many who try to legislate a predefined literacy, to encapsulate the "American heritage." They become protectionist — defending the canon or the tradition against the on- slaughts of multiplicity and perspectivism. There are those, in fact, who have begun associating problem-posing in the classroom, or what is conceived of as critical inquiry, with what is called "politically correct." We are seeing a reemer- gence of what used to be named essentialism in schools where the establishment of unified language communities is more important than young persons' thinking about their own thinking, reaching out from their own places to interpret and make sense of the world. Almost nothing is done to enable the young to deal thoughtfully and critically with the media. It follows that attitudes of passive receptivity are allowed, if not encouraged; consumerist and formulaic responses are taken to be the norms. Ironically, in the midst of all this, there are complaints that we are working to create communities of the competent rather than communities of citizens. In spite of this, few speak of educating what Dewey called an "articulate public." Few seem openly to want to break with what looks more and more like a monological mold.

There is certainly considerable agreement that progressive education does indeed break with that mold in its stress upon the dialogical, the experiential, the alternative possibility. If we do succeed in finding common ground, it will be one — it ought to be one — on which many voices can engage in dialogue, on which many perspectives are continually revealed. Questions about what constitutes the literacies required in the contemporary world ought to take us beyond considerations of purely functional literacy. We know something about the kind of learning that involves continuities and connections in lived experience. We know something about windows opening in consciousness, about what it means to look at things as if they could be otherwise. We learn more and more from Eleanor Duckworth, for example, about "wonderful ideas" and about questioning and about the uses of figuring things in complex ways, of "keeping it complex."[10]

We need to explore the ways in which the local and particular can feed into what we cherish as common, what we define and redefine as common ground. We need to discover how the particular can fertilize the common, how new perspectives and new visions can enrich the familiar landscapes, how the landscapes themselves can set off and highlight the new visions, enclose them in wider and wider frames. We may find that the crucial problems of cultural literacy can best be dealt with in such contexts, where diverse voices can be celebrated, where (as Marianne Moore once said) confusion itself can be celebrated. They may be dealt with in contexts where different voices join now and then in reciprocity, where they make contact in conversations stemming from dimensions of what they share. Confronting pluralism as seldom before, we have to ponder what it actually can mean for a common world to emerge from so many meaning systems, such a spectrum of "realities."

It is interesting to note the many voices, speaking in a range of idioms, concerned with overcoming fragmentation and incoherence in our nation today; and it is difficult not to hear them as voices of resistance to the plague. There are Robert Bellah and his colleagues calling for a transformation of the culture through a reconstitution of what they call the "social world." Like Dewey, they write of how individuals need the nurture of groups that carry a "moral tradition reinforcing their own aspirations."[11] The philosopher Richard Rorty, seeking a contemporary significance for pragmatism, writes both of contingency and solidarity.[12] Contingency refers to the variability of languages and identities that becomes clear when we recognize the dependence of points of view on biography, on lived situation in the world. It connects with what I am attempting to say about perspectivism: the relation between vantage point and sense-making; the role of standpoint when it comes to interpreting what comes into focus, what reveals itself before our eyes. Rorty speaks of solidarity as well as an alternative to objective certainties. For him, it implies a sharing of beliefs among those who share a community's story. Such sharing, such reciprocity may be the only reasonable goal at a moment marked by so much multiplicity. Certainly this coheres with the thinking of the ethnographic thinker Clifford Geertz, who writes of translation and intersubjectivity, and who raises what becomes for us a pedagogical question: "how separate individuals come to conceive, or do not, reasonably similar things."[13]

We find, wherever we look, an increasing interest in what is called "conversation." We find persons responding to the critic Mikhail Bakhtin and his explorations of the dialogical and the multiple voices engaged in sense-making, within personal consciousness and without.[14] Even in art criticism, in a book like Lucy Lippard's *Mixed Blessings*, we find a call not merely for respect for differences, but for an area between the familiar and the unfamiliar: a "fertile, liminal ground where new meanings germinate and where common experiences in different contexts can provoke new bonds."[15] All this connects for me with the notion of common ground, as it does with the nurture of learning communities, always in the making, always in process, like democracy itself.

There is a moral intention visible in the forming of such communities, and it has to do with solicitude and care, and with resistance to what is perceived as plague. Of course the tension is great, the afflictions multiple. The scholarly interest in dialogue and connection has not yet undermined the corporate and technicist oratory, nor the management ethos that has so little use for active citizenship or what Bellah and his colleagues call "communities of memory." Still, there *are* memories, and there are renewals. There are persons in education choosing themselves again, collaborating voluntarily in regard for the experiential, for the kinds of questioning that arise out of lived actualities in all their ambiguity and complexity.

The School in Rose Valley is an exemplar. We all know that, gathering here today. Thinking of the teachers here and in, I must say, kindred schools, I am reminded of Dewey again, writing in *Democracy and Education* about the fact that the self is not ready-made, "but something in continuous formation through choice of action." He associated the self with what he called interest and said that "the kind and amount of interest actively taken in a thing reveals and measures the

quality of selfhood which exists."[16] I imagine Edith Klausner and Peter Corcoran
forming their selves through their active interest in persons, in children, in consciousness, in experience, in dialogue, in community; and I know something remarkable is happening in many parts of the country, in small spaces, murmurous
spaces, totally in contrast to the plague-stricken hearings we have just witnessed,
in contrast to the places where heartlessness and efficiency rule.

We might summon up the names, the faces of numerous teachers and principals
resisting technical rationality as they refuse exclusion, breaking with the deaden-
ing consequences of traditional scheduling and specializing, trying for interdisciplinary vistas and forms. Many are deliberately creating small communities in
their schools: "family groups," collaborative teams among teachers and parents
(and sometimes with people from universities). Many are reaching beyond the
walls of the schools, as young people move out into their own neighborhoods to
work in child care or among the homeless or in tutoring centers or in places
where they can do field research, do interviews, take down stories, plant seeds.
There is Deborah Meier, who began her work at Central Park East in New York,
surely a place where progressive education occurs. There are small groups meeting there, dialogue of many kinds. Students are offered a "promise" that they
will be enabled to use their minds. It is necessary, realizing that, for us to picture
the urban environment in which this takes place — not only the treeless streets,
the litter, the traffic, but the worn-down housing projects, the drug salespeople,
the crack houses. And, downtown, we must remember, the constant beckoning
of an unattainable consumerist paradise. Ann Cook in the Urban Academy urges
her students on to many-faceted inquiries in the city, in museums, theatres,
sidestreets, hospitals. In Bronx Regional High School, cement-gray and graffiti-
scarred, young people came together to learn how to create a mural rendering
Rosa Parks's refusal — with their own faces in the windows of the celebrated
bus. In that school too, students took the initiative to learn how to construct a
shelter for their homeless classmates. They worked with construction men to
learn the crafts they required; their community was a working community as
well as a moral one; and they involved, as collaborators, the homeless youngsters
who were to be served — so, one of them said, "they won't be embarrassed."
There is, of course, Eliot Wigginton's remarkable work in Georgia, known to the
nation through the Foxfire books the students have written and prepared for
publication themselves. Their particular field research, their studies of strip
mining and health programs and union histories have opened new dimensions of
the common ground, especially as what is done in practice is made to radiate
outward to the thinking "complex things" Eleanor Duckworth describes and
recommends.

There are more, many more, in a largely invisible network of individuals held
together (I would guess) by a conception of some common ground. Strangely
enough, what they are saying in their small communities and, on occasion simply

to one another is affecting the language of what is called "restructuring," the latest wave of school reform. The emphasis on collaborative learning, flexible scheduling, work experiences, community activity, field research, and — perhaps most centrally — on what is called the "active learner" all are consonant with what has been said or is being said with respect to progressive education. This may be the case as well with newer approaches to assessment and evaluation, as portfolios are utilized in the place of multiple choice tests, as qualitative or naturalistic inquiries are used. We hear increasingly of "learner-centered schools," alternative schools, magnet schools, "site-based management," teacher autonomy; and it may be that those involved have the values of democratic education in mind. There is no assurance, however, that this is the case. There are too many examples left of sexist and racist practices, class discrimination, tracking, and bureaucratic controls. The so-called "free market" society still exists with its condemnations, its exclusions, its use of young people as means rather than ends. We might hope, however, that some of the new language in use and some of the new research feeding at some levels into school practice might provoke greater resistance, even as it enables more educators to see.

Some of the inquiries in the fields of psychology, philosophy, and literature seem to have become peculiarly relevant even for what we would like to think of as a rebirth of progressive education. I have in mind the attention being paid to narrative and story-telling as ways of knowing, ways of learning and sense-making. It connects at many junctures with the swelling interest in texts and textuality, as it does with the emphasis on dialogue. Jerome Bruner's interest in story-telling[17] as a way of knowing has drawn many kinds of attention; so has Charles Taylor's treatment of narrative as a mode of imparting meaning to experience and working out the moral purposes of human lives.[18] Martha Nussbaum's turn towards imaginative literature for images of how we ought to live those lives adds another level to this movement,[19] as does Rorty's recent insistence on the importance of poets and novelists as guides to the doing of philosophy.[20] Whether influence can be identified or causes and effects defined, all this seems to connect in some dimension to the work of Donald Graves, Donald Murray, James Britton, Jane Hansen, Lucy Calkins, and the many young women instrumental in forming what is called the "Whole Language" movement in the teaching of writing. This, along with the new approaches to reading and to "language-based classrooms" that distinguish what has been called the "new literacy," overlaps at many points with some of the basic concerns of progressive education.[21]

It is not accidental that one of the leaders in taking experiential approaches to reading and writing was Louise Rosenblatt, whose first book, *Literature as Exploration*,[22] appeared under the sponsorship of the Progressive Education Association. In recent years, her work has been widely recognized as instrumental in the development of what has been called "reader reception theory." This is an approach to literature very evocative of Dewey's *Art as Experience*,[23] in part because of its stress on the importance of any work of art becoming an object of a reader's experience if it is to be realized, and in part because of its acknowledgment of the importance of perspectives when it comes to the achievement of meaning. When we relate all this swelling reaffirmation of experience and point of view to the engagement with journal writing among children and adults, and to the attentiveness to lifestories and lived landscapes, we cannot but feel a gulf (perhaps a healthy gulf) between the preoccupation with behaviorisms and measurement and what might be called existential reality in all its variety. When we turn our attention at once to the life stories being disclosed in Women's Studies, to the probing of connectedness and relationality in feminist literature, we may experience a kind of meshwork among us, something that may bring the common ground in view.

If there are indeed distinguishable threads connecting those who share and are beginning to articulate progressive values and norms, they may resemble what Hannah Arendt had in mind when she spoke of the "web of relations" that forms when persons begin speaking to one another as "who, and not what they are" in their efforts to bring into being — among themselves — what Arendt called an "in-between," an "inter-est," perhaps a metaphor for what we are calling a common ground.[24] We may in fact try to render it continuous with some of the efforts being made, being chosen in democratic education. In any event, the themes of communication and articulateness appear and reappear; they are beginning to distinguish the most significant talk of our time. Suddenly, it seems that all sorts of persons are struggling to give shape to the flux of their lived experiences, reaching beyond where they are in response to their own puzzlements, their own shared questionings.

To wonder at all this makes some talk of the arts irresistible, especially as I try to think what is involved in achieving a common ground. Dewey certainly realized that inquiries can be freed and consciousness of judgment find deeper levels when persons involve themselves in some informed fashion with the several arts. He wrote, for example, that the function of literature, like the function of art in general, is "to break through the crust of conventionalized and routine consciousness."[25] He knew the importance of imagination when it came to rendering art forms objects of experience, enabling persons to break through the "crust" when they did. He knew too that imagination, which is a cognitive capacity, is what frees persons to look at things as if they could be otherwise. If young persons are to be aroused to come together in learning communities and open spaces among themselves, if they are to be awake enough to take heed of the pestilences in the world, they have to be aroused to stop and think on occasion. They have to be enabled to look through the windows of the actual, to perceive what might be, perhaps what ought to be. Imagination is the capacity to reach beyond in that manner. It is imagination that permits us to break with what

Virginia Woolf called "the cotton wool of daily life," the grip of the overly familiar — yes, and comfortable.[26] Only when imagination is released are people
likely to notice enough and risk enough to want to fight the plagues, to side with
the victims of pestilences. But in these days, what with the constant bombard-
ment of conventional television images, we can no longer rely on children becoming authentically imaginative, shaping "as/ifs" in their own particular ways.
This is another argument for early and continual exposure to the arts, which
cannot be realized without the ability to posit alternative realities. Even in elementary school, children are able — if introduced to paintings or melodies or
stories or plays — to create their own visions of experiential possibility. Gradually, as they grow, they become conscious of looking through unaccustomed
lenses; they begin to understand how and why encounters with art forms
defamiliarize what lies around. Things obscured by routines and habits surge
into presentness before them; and in some way they understand. Understanding,
they are awakened to pay heed.

A scene from *Romeo and Juliet* or *The Glass Menagerie* or *Gawain and the
Green Knight* may, if seriously attended to, reveal shapes and colors and nuances
of relationships never noticed before. Edward Hopper's rendering of a city "Sun-
day Morning," or Cezanne's "Lac d'Annecy," or Martha Graham's *Appalachian
Spring* will permit the appearing world to disclose more depths and shallows,
shades of movement, glimpses of passion than might ever have been suspected by
the one paying heed. Elizabeth Bishop's "At the Fishhouses," Toni Morrison's
Beloved, Tillie Olsen's *Tell Me a Riddle*, Jamaica Kincaid's *Lucy*: any one can
make a person "see" in her/his own memory, her/his own experience passages,
collisions, flashes, vacancies never noticed before her/his life was loaned to the
text. Perhaps, as Jean-Paul Sartre said with respect to literature, a work may
appeal to a reader's or perceiver's freedom. It may move her or him to choose in
some unpredicted fashion, to take action in a realm of possibilities, to try to
repair. There may be an abrupt awareness of the abandoned droop of someone's
hand, of an empty window like an eye socket in a burned out building, the
sadness of departing footsteps, the explosion of a child's red ribbon in the sun,
the tremulous sculpture of linked arms. Some persons will want to create, to
make, to bring something new into the world by shaping a medium: sound,
perhaps, language, clay, their own bodies in movement. Others may find suffi-
cient occasions for transformation in reading fictions or visiting museums and
concert halls. What is important is their realization that it is up to them to
achieve the works they encounter as meaningful, to transmute them into aesthetic objects for themselves.

These are, in many senses, private transactions; but they become increasingly
meaningful if they are talked about later on, if they can be shared. The play, the
novel, the painting, the sonata are, after all, emergent from human making in

other social contexts; they belong to a community stretching back in time. Attending, taking note along with others, persons cannot but find more doorways opening. Personal encounters may be complicated and enriched, the more they are opened to what others see and feel and know. "The Possible's slow fuse," wrote Emily Dickinson, "is lit/by the imagination." In classrooms thought to be progressive, thought to be educative, we need to open spaces of possibility. It is with the consciousness of possibility that persons experience their freedom. It is with such a consciousness that they are moved to engage in dialogue with others, to reach towards what is not, what might be — what seems decent, valuable, humane.

These are the kinds of spaces that may become public spaces, where diverse beings come together to articulate their concerns and, perhaps, to take action to make change. For Dewey, democracy had much to do with the bringing into being of such spaces, even as it had to do with a community in the making. This may be where the richest vein of progressive thinking is to be found. Today, particularly, it seems so deeply important to break with the silences of apathy, the silences of indifference and of powerlessness. When Dewey wrote of an "articulate public," he had in the mind the necessity for communication, for the kind of communion that sustains a common ground. Dewey would have been as appalled as we are by what he would call an "eclipse of the public"[27] that always leads to feelings of pointlessness and inertia on the part of many young people. The "eclipse" today refers not only to the widespread speechlessness and, yes, the anaesthesia with regard to wars and social ills and what some have called "the needs of strangers." It refers as well to a felt incapacity to exert power, to resist the diffusions of power, to make oneself felt by one's representatives, by anyone claiming authority.

For Dewey, publics are formed and public spaces opened when people associate with one another in response to perceived crises or deficiencies — homelessness, we might say, child abuse, street crime, AIDS — and find out how to speak up in such a fashion as to draw the attention of officials and representatives responsible for taking action to remedy such ills. To become a member of such a public, an individual has to be able to communicate as well as to reflect and to know and to imagine. Dewey wanted to see "the highest and most difficult kind of inquiry and a subtle, delicate, vivid, and responsive art of communication,"[28] something he knew depended upon atmospheres of cooperation, sympathy, and care. He surely would have understood and responded to the idea of the "sanitary squads" in Camus's *The Plague*. And I believe he would have seen the pedagogical implications of sanitary squads and opening public spaces, especially in times of public passivity, group antagonisms, consumerism, banality, and malaise. It seems to many that progressive education, with its conceptions of active learning, dialogue, and problem-posing, may be literally understood to represent public education at its best — education for the nurture of an articulate public reaching towards a common ground.

If more and more people can resist what Dewey called the "inertia of habit," if they can truly choose to take the side of the victims, if they can choose for vitality and action and critique, there may be a common ground emerging from a great diversity of vantage points. Persons have to be released to see and speak and imagine and think as situated beings; and situated beings look towards each other through their own distinctive perspectives, even as they look towards possibility.

The themes may converge and part and converge again as time goes on and the world keeps changing. Progressive education is and will be education for reflective practice and for wide-awakeness and for social concern. It will be carving out wider and wider spaces for freedom and the bite of possibility. Its relevance, like the common ground, continues to lie ahead. It can be, though, education for the resurgence of a public that may take a new responsibility for the world. Perhaps Vaclav Havel said it best, imagined it most ardently, when he was in prison before the revolution in Czechoslovakia with no clear idea of what was coming and little expectation of his own release. Havel wrote often about the human journey from the injunction to pay attention to the voice that everywhere calls persons to take responsibility, and what it means when such responsibility brings home the feeling of being alive. Wondering whether there were indeed any signs of an existential revolution (even as we wonder whether there are indeed signs of a firm progressive common ground), he wrote: "I can't help feeling that if you are open to hope, you can find timid signals in many things: in movements of youth in revolt such as have broken out periodically since the 1950s, in genuine peace movements, in varied activities in defense of human rights, in liberation movements (as long as they don't degenerate into mere attempts to replace one kind of terror with another)...in ecological initiatives, in short, in all the constantly recurring attempts to create authentic and meaningful communities that rebel against a world in crisis, not merely to escape from it, but to devote their full efforts — with the clear-sighted deliberation and humility that always go with genuine faith — to assume responsibility for the state of the world."[29]

Now I know Havel was not and is not a progressive educator; but the ground he stands on and the hope he acts upon are what many of us would choose to share. What he wrote in his own dark time seems consonant to me with what we are doing here — trying to choose ourselves as responsible, determining to fight the plague. He was showing forth the juncture between personal possibility and the public space; doing so, he was offering hope to anyone willing to make a commitment in the midst of multiplicity — a commitment to remake and remake again a democratic community. This is how we in our own fashion can rebel against a world of carelessness, a nation in crisis, as we reach out together towards our common ground and towards what we hope might be.

Endnotes

1   John Dewey, Democracy and Education. (New York: Macmillan Publishing Co., 1916), p. 115.

2   John Dewey, The Public and Its Problems. (Athens, Ohio: Swallow Press, 1954), p. 170.

3   Joseph Conrad, "Heart of Darkness," in Three Great Tales. (New York: Modern Library Press, n.d.), p. 221.

4   F. Scott Fitzgerald, The Great Gatsby. (New York: Charles Scribner's Sons, 1953), pp. 180-181.

5   Christa Wolf, Accident: A Day's News. (New York: Farrar, Straus, and Giroux, 1989), p. 17.

6   John Dewey, Art as Experience. (New York: Minton, Balch & Co., 1934), p. 263.

7   Hannah Arendt, Thinking, Volume One, The Life of the Mind. (New York: Harcourt Brace Jovanovich, 1978), p. 4.

8   Albert Camus, The Plague. (New York: Alfred A. Knopf, 1948), p. 121.

9   E.D. Hirsch, Jr., Cultural Literacy: What Every American Needs to Know. (Boston: Houghton Mifflin Co., 1987).

10 Eleanor Duckworth, "Twenty-four, Forty-two, and I Love You: Keeping It Complex," Harvard Educational Review, Vol. 61, No. 1, February, 1991, pp. 1-24.

11 Robert N. Bellah, et al., Habits of the Heart. (Berkeley: University of California Press, 1985), p. 141.

12 Richard Rorty, Contingency, Irony, and Solidarity. (New York: Cambridge University Press, 1989).

13 Clifford Geertz, Local Knowledge. (New York: Basic Books, 1981), p. 156.

14 Mikhail Bakhtin, The Dialogic Imagination. (Austin: University of Texas Press, 1981).

15 Lucy Lippard, Mixed Blessings. (New York: Pantheon Books, 1990), p. 9.

16 John Dewey, Democracy and Education, op. cit., p. 408.

17 Jerome Bruner, Actual Minds, Possible Worlds. (New York: Cambridge University Press, 1986), pp. 11-43.

18 Charles Taylor, Sources of the Self. (Cambridge: Harvard University Press, 1989), pp. 51-52.

19 Martha Nussbaum, Love's Knowledge: Essays on Philosophy and Literature. (New York: Oxford University Press, 1990).

20 Richard Rorty, Objectivity, Relativism, and Truth. (New York: Cambridge University Press, 1991).

21 John Willinsky, The New Literacy. (New York: Rutledge, 1990).

22 Louise Rosenblatt, Literature as Exploration. (New York: Appleton Century, 1938).

23 Louise Rosenblatt, The Reader, the Text, the Poem. (Carbondale: Southern Illinois University Press, 1978).

24 Hannah Arendt, The Human Condition. (Chicago: University of Chicago Press, 1958), pp. 182-4.

25 John Dewey, The Public and Its Problems, op. cit., p. 183.

26 Virginia Woolf, Moments of Being. (New York: Harcourt Brace Jovanovich, 1976), p. 72.

27 John Dewey, The Public and Its Problems, op. cit., p. 110.

28 John Dewey, op. cit., p. 184.

29 Vaclav Havel, Letters to Olga. (New York: Henry Holt and Co., 1983), p. 372.

Creating a Multicultural School Community
A Working Group Facilitated by Zara Joffe and Maxine Bailey,
Community Housing Resource Board, Media, Pennsylvania

Description by Zara Joffe and Maxine Bailey, presenters

> If we have multiple perspectives, what are we about together?
> — a participant

The Working Group
This Working Group explored strategies for building a school environment
which affirms and respects differences in race, ethnicity, gender, class, sexual
orientation, and ability. As facilitators, we were excited about working with a
group of progressive educators who had chosen to
devote the bulk of their time at the conference to
exploring these issues. We came to the session with
the belief that the progressive school tradition has
much to contribute to the discussion about school
diversity. The focus on each child as a unique individual, belief in a cooperative learning mode, and
the attention paid to process are all practices which can contribute to the creation of a multicultural school climate. However, in our work with the progressive school community, a number of issues around diversity have arisen with
startling regularity: attracting and retaining students and teachers of color; discomfort in talking about social identity, especially race; difficulties in establishing classroom behavioral norms which work for all students; lack of success
among faculty in reaching agreement about the goals and process for building
multicultural school communities.

**Clear thinking about multicult-
uralism is often inhibited by the
strong feelings evoked and
the self consciousness of people
when talking about topics that
have been taboo.**

The overall goal for the three sessions of the working group was to create a
supportive climate in which workshop participants could openly and honestly
discuss the issues related to cultural diversity and the creation of multicultural
school communities. The format was largely small group exercises, some facilitator presentations, and large group discussions. Our design was based on a few
key assumptions: 1) These issues are sensitive and hard to talk about. Because
our culture does not encourage such dialogue, and because the issues provoke
powerful emotional responses, taking time to create a climate for sharing is
crucial. 2) Clear thinking about multiculturalism is often inhibited by the strong
feelings evoked and the self consciousness of people when talking about topics
that have been taboo. Beginning with personal experiences allows participants to
get in touch with these feelings and to break the taboo. 3) Once people do some
personal work, it is more possible to examine oppressive systems — both the
wider societal systems and systems created within their own educational institutions. To talk about multicultural education, it is necessary to recognize power

disparities and the very real impact of systems of oppression. 4) With both the personal and institutional perspectives, it is possible to envision what a multicultural school community might look like and a process for getting there.

There were seventeen participants in the group — four African American women, one Japanese American woman, eleven white women, and two white men. Most were teachers, but there were two administrators, one parent, and one student. They were from both public and independent schools. We are a bi-racial facilitator team, one an African American woman, the other a white woman.

Personal Experiences: Race, Class, and Gender

We began with an exercise which allowed participants to reflect on their own social identities and experiences with difference and to gain some practice in sharing this information with others. Participants were asked to describe them-selves in terms of race, gender, and social class and to consider the difficulties and the strengths resulting from their backgrounds. During small group sharing, participants took turns responding to the questions. Group members were asked not to interrupt or question, but to practice listening carefully and being affirming. Once everyone had taken a turn, group members reflected together about the process of both thinking and talking about their backgrounds.

One participant talked about how anxious she had been before the exercise: her fear that she would be judged or misunderstood and that talking about issues of difference would create distance between the participants. She, like others, in-stead found herself energized and excited by the discussion. Time and time again, participants acknowledged that within their school communities, people who have worked closely together for years do not reach the level of intimacy, disclo-sure, and sharing that occurred within the working group.

A second exercise, on names, introduced latecomers to the group and allowed all participants to actively claim the power of their identities. While innocuous on the surface, talking in pairs about the significance of their names provided oppor-tunities to relate names to ethnic and racial identities, express feelings about the gender dynamics in naming (diminutives, marital names), and to talk about ethnic "safety" (different immigrant ethnic groups changing their last names to be more "American"). The full group discussion focused on what we have all lost through racism and assimilation — how the pride in who we are, our his-tory, and our ancestry is often taken away through "renaming." Sexism was discussed here, too. A number of women shared their feelings about taking on their husbands' names, with some experiencing a loss of family identity and a sense of being "property." Claiming your name can make a statement about roles you want to take on, not the ones imposed on you. As one participant observed, "There is power in how you name yourself."

Is It All Personal? From Race and Gender to Racism and Sexism

In telling their personal stories, people find that others have had similar, often painful experiences and that they are not isolated. A number of white participants shared stories of becoming aware that racism existed, and the feelings of confusion, guilt, or shame that accompanied those experiences. Some people of color talked about drawing strength from family and community to survive daily mistreatment — from racial slurs, to being rendered invisible, to having few people able to pronounce their names. One white teacher talked about feeling distanced by social class from her wealthy white students, yet complicit with them in some way by benefiting from racism. This provoked an emotional discussion about experiencing privilege on the one hand while being disadvantaged on the other.

The focus shifted when another white teacher said she found the discussion "unsettling," and that we should "focus on the positive and not dwell on the negative." While not dismissing her feelings, we were able to draw on the patterns

revealed by participants' sharing. Their experiences and wide range of feelings can be seen as products of systematic oppression, not isolated instances or coincidence. Mistreatment often appears "normal" or "natural," and is perceived as an individual rather than a social problem. Examples provided by participants included: sexual harassment of women in the workplace (sexism); the ban against gay men and lesbians in the armed forces (heterosexism); and the over representation of people of color in the prisons (racism).

Every individual and institution is impacted by these systems of oppression. In order to effect change, we must have some understanding of how these systems work. The next exercise, in which participants were divided into two groups, was designed to engage participants in thinking about two of these systems: one group was instructed to create an unequivocally racist society, the second a sexist society. Participants were to picture a community as real as possible with people, institutions, and laws; then to identify those aspects which made the society racist or sexist.

The group creating a sexist society decided that they would make men the targets and women the agents of sexism in their society. Men were to be denied formal access to power; have no right to vote or to own property; suffer restrictions on movement, schooling, and allowable occupations; and experience financial dependence on women. Their dress would be regulated and they would be chosen by women purely for their reproductive attributes. The tools of oppression to maintain this society would be media, propaganda, and psychology. Male children would be raised without warmth, taught to be passive, and would not resist their roles because they would internalize all the ideas of gender appropriate behavior.

The group was able to develop this picture of a sexist society in a very short time (about 15 minutes). Initially there was some discomfort on the part of the men and a sense of the thrill of power on the part of the women, who were clearly having fun with the exercise. After a while, however, the thrill began to diminish, the pace slowed down, and the women began to join the men in raising questions and expressing discomfort about what had been created. "In such a culture," one participant observed, "both men and women would be deprived." This provoked animated discussion within the group, and, later, in the larger group about all forms of oppression — do they hurt the perpetrators as well as the victims?

The group involved in creating a racist society did not generate as much detail as the sexist group, as a great deal of time was spent debating how to define the targets and agents within their imaginary society. The issue was tentatively resolved with the use of the terms "right color" and "wrong color" but was revived again in the larger group through a heated discussion between a white woman and a woman of color. The white woman advocated for the more abstract terms in order to see what would be created independent of current practices, while the woman of color insisted that the language had to reflect the historical realities of American racism. While the argument was not fully resolved, participants noted that there was, in fact, movement on both sides. "It made me realize," said one participant, "that not everyone experiences society in the same way."

The session ended with participants spending time reflecting on the thoughts and feelings that had been provoked. Many talked about how hard it was to confront the issues. Others shared how much was stirred up for them on a personal level in confronting their own feelings and in responsing to the emotional and heated nature of some of the discussions. Many expressed a sense that even though "the going had been hard" it felt like a tremendous relief to be able to disagree, express strong emotions and still be able to continue talking. As one participant explained, "We discovered in our racism group how important it is to allow people to define their own selves, free of assumptions... you have to get real before you can make change. Multiculturalism is very sensitive. It stirs up scary emotions, it touches the soul."

What Do Kids Have To Do With It?

If you can make it possible for children to talk openly and honestly about their diversity, incredible richness and depth emerges. Modeling an ease and willingness to talk by adults is crucial.

A question was raised about how to create such a classroom environment where children get to a level of depth without putting each other down. Some requirements for creating such an environment include:

• Be comfortable with yourself and your own social identity. You cannot really hear and appreciate others' stories if you have not dealt with your own.

• You have to encourage and value the uniqueness of everyone's experiences. For example, white children often feel they have no cultural history to share, yet the heritage they have lost and their sense of loss is a part of their story.

• Appreciation of diversity must become the fabric of everything you do in the classroom. The difficulty of it must be coupled with affirmation; the kids must see what's in it for them.

• You must make it possible for each child to locate the difference within her/himself. This is not just about the kids of color. For example, help all kids share their family history and background to discover all that they don't know about each other. The richness that workshop participants found in each other will be there in children, too.

Participants shared experiences in trying to make their classrooms more multicultural, and affirmed that having a level of personal ease with the issues was key. "Kids will be able to deal if you can," said one teacher. Some people expressed frustration at failed attempts to deal "on this level of self" within the faculty or staff in their schools. Can people from the same turf really be that open with each other? As facilitators we shared with the group our work with faculty and staff in many schools, and recommended that to begin the dialogue it is often helpful to have someone come in from the outside, because it is hard to be in it and on the outside at the same time. With some guidance, it is definitely possible for faculty to engage with each other, to see conflict as constructive, and to be able to support each other in building multicultural classrooms.

From Classroom to School Community

It is important to understand that multicultural change is a political process which involves strategic thinking and planning. In order to begin thinking strategically, participants again divided into small groups. This time the assignment was to generate a list of all the advantages and disadvantages of a multicultural school community. The lists were compiled and displayed. In the ensuing full group discussion participants were asked to consider several questions: Which list was longer? What did the two lists have in common? Were there different themes for each list and common themes between the two lists?

For many participants, the advantages were easy to generate. Included were: affective benefits (reduces fear, generates excitement); societal gains (reduces oppression, helps us get along in the real world); and cognitive growth through new expanded perspectives. The disadvantages list was shorter but provoked more internal struggle. It was harder to acknowledge the problems. In observing this difference, one participant raised the following question: "If we are so clear that there are so many more advantages than disadvantages to creating multicultural school communities, why haven't we done it?" A closer look at the disadvantages list was revealing. It quickly became clear that many of the disadvantages spoke to emotional issues related to fear: fear of conflict, fear of anger, fear of emotions getting out of control, fear that pain and anger would come up, fear that tensions between groups would be increased, and fear of confrontations. These fears, it was pointed out, often translate into statements such as: "It's too time and energy consuming." "There are too many differences in one place." "It's impossible to attract minority role models." "It's hard to start the process."

Some participants noted that a second level of fear had to do with a perception that some people or groups stand to lose something if a school community becomes multicultural. Issues of giving up or sharing power, concerns around exposing self, classroom, and school to input from the wider community, and questions such as "at whose expense do communities become diverse?" were prominent on the disadvantages list.

A third area of concern which was reflected on the disadvantages list centered around the impact of the move to multiculturalism upon people of color. There were concerns about trivializing or placing minority cultures on display: "reducing minority culture to dance, food, and art." There was also a concern that by promoting multiculturalism, schools would be increasing stereotypes about different groups.

As one participant noted, even if the advantages list was twice as extensive, as long as these fears are not dealt with, efforts on the part of advocates of multicultural school communities will be unsuccessful. To be successful, participants affirmed the importance of creating the opportunity and climate in which all members of the school community can talk openly and honestly about their personal feelings. In creating such a climate, "political correctness" was viewed as a major stumbling block.

The discussion illuminated the challenges in front of those interested in developing a process for change. Participants were eager at this stage to debate the definition of multiculturalism. Participants were asked to think about and be prepared to discuss (for the next morning's session) definitions for four key terms: "integrated," "desegregated," "multicultural," and "community."

The Language of Power and The Power of Language

A key assumption guiding our work as diversity trainers is that there is very little about language that is innocent. For example, "minority" is a convenient umbrella word usually used to talk about people of color but is often used to describe all oppressed groups. Implicit in the term "minority" is a sense of "less than." It reflects power relations and not just numbers. The term minority in American culture has become a shorthand term which wipes out the specifics of an individual's race, ethnicity, or cultural background. The dilemma of the use of the word minority is even more apparent when we consider that people of color are going to be in the numerical majority in this country at the turn of the century and are already the majority in the world. While the term minority appears, on the surface, to be useful and neutral, it actually serves to reinforce the normalcy of an oppressive system.

When asked for other examples of how language is related to power dynamics in our culture, one participant offered the following observation:

> In schools of the dominant culture, students of color are sometimes described as "successful" in a way that means that they have learned to get along in the dominant culture; that they are more "of the system" now; that they have transcended the "street culture." This sends a message to students that devalues where they came from.

Another participant noted that the term multicultural often provokes a hysterical response. "Rather than back away from the term," she concluded, "you need to realize that such hysteria means that you're dealing with much more than the issue as it seems on the surface."

There are many different notions of what multicultural education is. One participant expressed her view that integration represented little more than the wholesale movement of raced and gendered bodies to achieve a numerical goal that did little to change power relationships. Conversely, for her, a multicultural school signified a variety of perspectives and world views, not just a variety of bodies. "In fact", she conceded, "you can have a numerically integrated school in which there is no attention paid to perspective and you can have a multicultural school community which does not have to be a mini-United Nations in representation." Multiculturalism implies that the status of groups is as important as the individual.

By acknowledging the power of language and expanding the terrain for discourse, participants were able to move on and talk about highly charged dimensions of the muticultural debate including the question of proposals for all-male, all-African American academies, whether neighborhood schools in all-white or all-African American neighborhoods can offer multiple cultural perspectives, and whether separate and equal is possible and can also mean multicultural. While these deliberations did not yield definitive answers, the discussion gave participants practice in debating tough and complex issues within the framework of the politics of power.

There seemed to be a new level of excitement in the room following this discussion. Many remarked on the additional insights they had gained, including one participant who shared with the group that as a result of the discussion she now understood that her school's response to the question of multiculturalism, which was to initiate a campaign to recruit more students of color, was not really an adequate response for transforming the school community. Participants collectively were able to affirm that there are no "quick fixes," and that building multicultural school communities is a process which involves reviewing and rethinking all our assumptions, even those about common ground.

Are the norms of progressive schools only reflective of the norms of the dominant culture?

Where Is There Common Ground When There Isn't One Norm?
As participants reflected on the range of perspectives necessary for building multicultural school communities, a quandary about how to create school and classroom norms presented itself. The discussion was sparked by two questions: "Are the norms of progressive schools only reflective of the norms of the dominant culture?" and "How can you have uniform school rules if everybody is coming in with different norms?" The first step in unraveling this dilemma was recognizing that the norms for communication and behavior that are often defined as "normal" and "universal" are actually culturally specific, and they limit the full participation of everyone.

To help illustrate this, a teacher from the group shared the following situation:

> In our school we are really struggling with this idea, multiculturalism. Are we, by
> the nature of the kind of school we are, expecting all kids to act in one way that
> we have determined is the best way or a way that works best in a social setting?
> Like at circle time, kids are expected to sit still and be quiet and mostly kids from
> the Black culture seem to have a hard time with that. It was recently brought out
> that in their culture at home, turn-taking isn't thought as much of as it is in some
> other cultures.

Questions raised which helped her clarify her thinking and reexamine her assumptions included: "Who defined 'the best' way? Was this decided through a
collaborative process involving a wide range of perspectives, or was it assumed
that 'everyone knows' this is the best way?" "If something is not working for a
particular group of students, who is expected to change?" "What additional
information is needed? Is the reality that turn-taking in the Black culture is not
valued, or that the rules that govern turn-taking are different from the rules of
the dominant culture?"

The sharing of concrete, everyday situations, such as those offered by the teachers in the group, is an essential element in the multicultural change process.
Through the dialogue, it became apparent that reexamining the question of
whose norms are operating does not mean that you cannot have rules or standards of behavior; rather the process for determining those rules and standards
must be expansive and inclusive. For some participants this discussion was a
totally new way to look at their perspectives and classroom practices. As one
teacher commented:

> Well, it wasn't until this very moment that I began to realize that, "Aha! What
> I've been doing in my classroom isn't what you're talking about." I always felt
> that there's a certain kind of behavior that's acceptable in school — school type
> behavior — and I made the distinction between that and what you're comfortable
> with at home...It was not until this very minute that I began to think maybe
> JI'm not being respectful to different patterns of behavior of different children in
> my room.

The discussion again shifted when one participant noted that it was critical to
involve parents in the process of establishing school and classroom norms. A
second participant, however, cautioned that it is important not to place parents
of color in the position of representing all people of color or of taking on the
burden of teaching white teachers everything there is to know about their culture. "You need to take responsibility for your own learning and that doesn't
come just from reading a few books." As a final word of caution, we added that
individuals must never assume that they know everything about or are experts
on someone else's culture from a few limited experiences. Always assume that
learning to be multicultural is a lifelong process.

Collective Visioning For A Multicultural School Community

The final session was devoted to the challenge which had brought most participants to the working group: the creation of collective visions for multicultural
school communities. Small groups were asked to think about all aspects of
the school community: classroom, students, parents, faculty, administration, the
neighborhood, the school, and the philosophy, policies, rules, standards, and
practices of their schools. Participants were asked to think carefully about
the process for change; that is, not just what changes would occur, but the process that could be used to bring about such changes.

When the model school communities were presented, a comparison of the three
revealed several key assumptions shared by each group:
• Commitment from the school leadership is essential (both informal and formal
leadership structures need to be involved).
• The change process must include people from different cultures in deciding
what it will mean for the school to be multicultural. This may involve expanding
the definition and boundaries of the school community.
• Multiple opportunities for public dialogues need to be included. The hard
questions must be put on the table openly and a supportive climate for this to
happen must be created. All segments of the community must have an opportunity to define themselves in relation to the emerging school philosophy.
• Every area of the school's operation has to be examined and evaluated, including curriculum, recruitment practices, textbooks, hiring practices, teaching styles,
extracurricular activities, relationship with the neighborhood, school programs,
trips and cultural events, visual imagery, approaches to different learning styles,
mechanisms for parent involvement, places for student voices, and
empowerment...everything.

The spirited level of engagement within each group confirmed our fundamental
belief that individuals can be freed up to think creatively and positively about
the challenges of creating multicultural school communities and to find common
ground through an appreciation of diversity. Participants gained some clarity
about the meaning of multiculturalism, cleared out some of their personal barriers and were ready to engage in the task of visioning what might be. Most im-
portantly, participants approached the visioning task with heightened enthusiasm
about the prospects for multicultural change, a spirit of camaraderie, and free
flowing creativity.

Breaking Through to Deeper Connections: The Interdisciplinary Humanities Approach

A Workshop Presented by Susan Dean, Bryn Mawr College, Bryn Mawr, Pennsylvania, and Robert Templeton, Strath Haven High School, Wallingford, Pennsylvania

Description by Chris Verdecchia, scribe

Bob Templeton begins by reading two quotes, the first from Gregory Bateson's introduction to *Mind and Nature: A Necessary Unity.*

> Break the pattern which connects the items of learning and you necessarily destroy all quality...the pattern which connects. Why do schools teach almost nothing of the pattern which connects? Is it that teachers know that they carry the kiss of death which will turn to tastelessness whatever they touch and therefore they are wisely unwilling to touch or teach anything of real-life importance? Or is it that they carry the kiss of death because they dare not teach anything of real-life importance? What's wrong with them?[1]

The second quote is from one of Bob's students in his humanities course, it appeared in what is called a metacognitive journal — a journal in which the students reflect on and trace the patterns and trends of thought that have appeared throughout their journals on the course readings and discussions written throughout the first two trimesters of the year.

> I was looking at the word Humanities and found that by crossing out the first i, I had Human ties. I didn't tell the person next to me because I figured he would laugh at my stupid, simpleton discovery or just ignore it. Anyway, I think that's what we've been studying all year long — the connections between ourselves past and present, our classmates, our families, our teachers, our fellow Americans, our fellow human beings, and what we humans have created: art, literature, religion, science, and thought.

The humanities program grew from Bob's having taught high school for thirteen years at Swarthmore High School and Strath Haven High School. In listening to students, he noticed that while there may be individually good teachers and classes, the overall effect of high school on the students is stifling — they didn't make connections among what's being taught in science, what's being taught in math, what's being taught in English, what's being taught in social studies. When Bob went to the University of Pennsylvania to get his doctorate in education, he discovered some of the reasons for this lack of connectedness, and he was introduced to a number of works that were making the connections. "Why not create a course like that; if the school won't be interdisciplinary, at least one course can be interdisciplinary."

The course Bob created fuses not just art, literature, and religion, but also anthropology, philosophy, sociology, philosophy of science, and mathematics in order to show that all of these disciplines inform each other in various ways. The course emphasizes student sense-making; the students are encouraged to value and write about their ideas and experiences in and out of the classroom. Bob gives no tests or quizzes in this course. Instead, he asks the students to submit a journal every two weeks in which they make sense of the material and discussions. It is from these journals that the students write their metacognitive journal entries in which they trace the emergence and development of various thoughts and ideas; in this they also must note where their thinking has changed, consider why it's changed, and provide the specific context for that change. This leads students to valuable insights into the ways their thinking is shaped. The course emphasizes that meaning is constructed from the coming together of students and text, and therefore varies. There are as many meanings as students. Grades become irrelevant.

Susan explains the creation of her introductory course for the Katharine E. McBride Scholars Program for Women Beyond Traditional College Age, at Bryn Mawr College. The program is comprised of women who might be intimidated by the Bryn Mawr's reputation for high academic caliber. The college is known for giving a good traditional, classical education, yet it is also known for being politically liberal. Susan wants the McBride program to challenge and question the structure of the education itself. It is her goal to have students consider why people take the varying positions that they do on social issues. To begin to empower the women in the McBride program to be comfortable in criticizing the structure of their own education, Susan uses a piece by Liz Schneider which is titled, "Our Failures Only Marry: Bryn Mawr and the Failure of Feminism,"[2] which invites students to critique Bryn Mawr.

Susan then introduces an excerpt of a 1962 essay by James Baldwin to his nephew which addresses the issue of integration and how it has been spoken of by the mainstream culture. Baldwin writes advising his nephew on how to cope with integration and what it means to the "black man."[3] After giving five minutes to read the passage, Susan asks the following questions:

What images does Baldwin employ in making his point?

What makes these images "universal"? What is the effect of these "universal" images on the black reader? On the white reader?

Susan explains how this kind of essay made readers feel in 1963. Discussion then really takes off, and expands to include today's racial tensions in dealing with what has been coined the "angry black." The assumption that race is only relevant to the other, or the different is taken up.

Bob then chimes in to agree with this statement and says, "we as whites really don't have a race, and during the integration of the 1960s, the whites probably felt very betrayed by what was going on. The whites felt that they had done some great deed for the blacks, and that blacks reacted by blowing things up — whites felt betrayed."

Shirley, a teacher, then responds by mentioning Peggy MacIntosh and her essay on white privilege — "White Privilege: Unpacking the Invisible Knapsack"[4] "There are too many assumptions that we as whites make and take who we are for granted because we are in the position of privilege, and it is very hard for us to see how others are going to react to what we do."

Susan then goes on to say that reading Baldwin usually leads to discussions on social and economic issues, and also discussions on men's treatment of women and of the hierarchical structure of our society with regard to both race and gender. The idea behind this exercise is to create a window through which we can see connections between fear and race and gender, and that in many ways we all have the same feelings and fears.

The second exercise is a critique of Baldwin by a Caribbean writer, George Lamming.[5] This piece deals with language — he speaks about the problems of being a writer in an English colony in which his peers only wanted to be like the British and read Jane Austen rather than read something that dealt with their own lives. Colonization leads to the loss of peoples' mother-tongues in favor of the language of the upper-class of the colony. He says the problem is colonialism and not color. Lamming feels that Baldwin lost his culture in favor of the culture that allowed him to succeed. He treats Baldwin not as a liberator, but as a wounded man.

The point of the exercise is to be sure that her students are not blinded by their education. This exercise also leads to a sense of interconnectedness through Lamming's claim that the problem is not color, but colonialism. This is a problem that is the same for both the white and the black.

Shirley then asks Susan, "Have you ever encountered any objection to moving discussion off the issue of race to issues of class or sexism?" It is her experience that it is very hard for us to discuss issues of race, and we defer often to issues of class or gender because we are more comfortable with that particular arena than we are with the idea of race.

In response, Susan says, "My aim is to show the connections, and as we move from topic to topic, we should see the trend of a superior always needing to have an inferior."

This discussion then leads to the idea of the curriculum being skewed to the realization and that the problem often lies in the materials. The next turn in the discussion moves into the realm of blacks being afraid of education because they are afraid it will make them white. Susan responds to this by paralleling the scenario that Shirley has presented with the situation that a white person may find herself in as a result of having a college education, that of being unable to communicate with her family because of the difference in vocabulary and, possibly, awareness. Education can create casualties in anyone of any race, gender, or ethnicity.

Then, deep in thought, the group disperses.

Endnotes

1   Gregory Bateson, <u>Mind and Nature: A Necessary Unity</u>. (New York: Dutton, 1979).

2   Liz Schneider, "Our Failures Only Marry: Bryn Mawr and the Failure of Feminism."

3   James Baldwin, "My Dungeon Shook: Letter to My Nephew," from <u>The Fire Next Time</u>. (New York: Dial Press, 1963).

4   Peggy MacIntosh, "White Privilege: Unpacking the Invisible Backpack," <u>Peace and Freedom</u>, July/August, 1989.

5   George Lamming, "The Occasion for Speaking," <u>The Pleasures of Exile</u>. (1960).

Infusing Environmental Education: Why and How?
A Workshop Presented by Peter Corcoran and his students, Michael Rothbart, Brendan Kelly, and Eric Sievers, Swarthmore College

Description by John Bulavage, scribe

Peter and his fellow presenters hoped to give the participants a sense of the past, present, and future of environmental education. Peter began with the history of environmental education, with nature study, and early science education. Since many nature study writers focused on development of an affinity for nature as a result of childhood experiences, Peter asked participants to reflect on their own childhoods by experiencing a guided imagery. He encouraged the participants to relax — close their eyes, sit on the floor. Judging from the fact that more than half of the participants chose to stretch out on the floor, one might say that it was an easy-going, receptive, and enthusiastic group.

Peter encouraged the participants to go back to a place and time when they felt especially in touch with nature. He allowed plenty of quiet time for the participants to find such a place, asking them to "let their hearts wander" and to recall sounds and smells. After a few minutes, Peter asked the participants to "come back" whenever they were ready and to share their memories in clusters of three or four if they felt comfortable doing so. Someone related a story about an old house that she used as a fort when she was six or seven years old and its adjacent woods. Another person told a poignant story about a mud fight with a sibling in a backyard marsh. This person emphasized her sometimes adversarial relationship prior to the encounter and the laughter they shared afterward. She said the smell of the mud was particularly memorable. The stories were truly touching and the sharing seemed to be a bonding experience for the participants.

Peter asked the participants to reconvene as one large group. Many remained relaxed on the floor as he read two passages from *The Sense of Wonder* by Rachel Carson, whom Peter considers "one of the greats" among nature study writers.

> A child's world is fresh and new and beautiful, full of wonder and excitement. It is our misfortune that for most of us that clear-eyed vision, that true instinct for what is beautiful and awe-inspiring is dimmed and even lost before we reach adulthood. If I had influence with the good fairy who is supposed to preside over the christening of all children I should ask that her gift to each child in the world be a sense of wonder so indestructible that it would last throughout life, as an unfailing antidote against the boredom and disenchantments of later years, the sterile preoccupation with things that are artificial, the alienation from the sources of our strength.[1]

What is the value of preserving and strengthening this sense of awe and wonder, this recognition of something beyond the boundaries of human existence? Is the exploration of the natural world just a pleasant way to pass the golden hours of childhood or is there something deeper?

I am sure there is something much deeper, something lasting and significant. Those who dwell, as scientists or laymen, among the beauties and mysteries of the earth are never alone or weary of life. Whatever the vexations or concerns of their personal lives, their thoughts can find paths that lead to inner contentment and to renewed excitement in living. Those who contemplate the beauty of the earth find reserves of strength that will endure as long as life lasts. There is symbolic as well as actual beauty in the migration of the birds, the ebb and flow of the tides, the folded bud ready for the spring. There is something infinitely healing in the repeated refrains of nature — the assurance that dawn comes after night, and spring after the winter.[2]

Peter argued in favor of environmental education, saying that one cannot assume that children are having positive experiences in nature such as those recalled by the participants during the guided imagery. With video games, TVs, VCRs and computers, students are spending less time in nature.

At this point, one of the participants asked what one can do in an urban setting, considering that urban areas, for the most part, lack significant natural, undeveloped areas. Peter encouraged using what is available — the schoolyard, the view from the apartment window. Once again, Peter cited Rachel Carson, who states in *The Sense of Wonder*:

Wherever you are and whatever your resources, you can still look up at the sky — its dawn and twilight beauties, its moving clouds, its stars by night. You can listen to the wind, whether it blows with majestic voice through a forest or sings a many-voiced chorus around the eaves of your house or the corners of your apartment building, and in the listening, you can gain magical release for your thoughts. You can still feel the rain on your face and think of its long journey, its many transmutations, from sea to air to earth. Even if you are a city dweller, you can find some place, perhaps a park or a golf course, where you can observe the mysterious migrations of the birds and the changing seasons. And with your child you can ponder the mystery of a growing seed, even if it be only one planted in a pot of earth in the kitchen window.[3]

Peter admitted that in the harshest urban settings environmental education can be rather difficult, but he reminded the participants of local resources such as nature centers and arboreta. Cynthia Potter of State College Friends School remarked that "we are overlooking the most available resource...from which to draw concerning the environment and that is ourselves. We have an internal wilderness and we are creatures of this planet." She went on to discuss how we try excessively to control our environment and, in doing so, forget just how natural we are or, perhaps, should be.

Peter then returned to the history of environmental education. He talked about Johan Amos Comenius (1592-1670), whom Peter considers the "greatest educational theorist of the past three hundred years." Peter talked about Comenius as a proponent of the "object method of learning," which proposes that "instruction must begin with actual inspection, not the verbal description" of an object. Peter lamented that science education has moved too far away from "object methods" or "hands-on" learning. Next, Peter discussed Jean Jacques Rousseau (1712-1778), who, in *Emile*, advocated educating the child "according to nature." Rousseau felt "science was to be discovered by the child, not merely learned as facts." Rousseau also was in favor of having the child determine the order of learning. Heinrich Pestalozzi (1746-1827) is credited with bringing Rousseau's ideas to North America and was particularly interested in reform methodology. He wished to "replace catechism with thinking." Friedrich Froebel (1782-1852), known for his efforts in establishing kindergartens, suggested:

> Take your little children by the hand. Go with them into nature as into the house of God. Allow the wee one to stroke the good cow's forehead and to run among the fowl and to play at the edge of the woods. Make companions for your boys and girls of the tree and the barns and the pasture lands.

Froebel advocated studying not only an object, but also its environment, its ecology. Peter mentioned Anna Botsford Comstock (1854-1930) and Liberty Hyde Bailey (1858-1954), both of whom taught at Cornell University at the beginning of the twentieth century. Peter noted that Comstock's *Handbook of Nature Study* is the one book he would take to an island if he could take only one.

Eric began his discussion of current trends in environmental education with an attempt to define environmental education, admitting that environmental education is an ever-changing field. Since it is not yet a recognized discipline, it has not found a clearly defined space in the curriculum and, **The seminal work in the field was** as a result, often has no place at all. Nonetheless, it **written 4.5 billion years ago.** exists in "YMCA camps, Audubon reserves, in classes held outside rather than indoors, Outward Bound, and many others." It can teach students to question their lifestyles and the structures and system that necessitate such lifestyles or it can "bring the student in closer contact" with nature through active learning. Therefore, environmental education can be intellectual or experiential, or both. It can "empower some students to protest actively against traditional society and encourage others to change themselves internally." As a result, environmental education is sometimes seen as subversive. It lacks definitive boundaries or a recognized leader, and, as Eric joked, "The seminal work in the field was written 4.5 billion years ago."

The same urgency which empowers the environmental movement also drives the development of environmental education. There recently has been a greater desire for environmental education, which has led to exploration of diverse issues within the field such as deep ecology and ecofeminism. There is certainly disagreement about what is effective environmental education. Some say it is effective if it results in action, since its purpose is to save the natural world; others claim it is successful if the student is fulfilled. Although environmental education cannot be clearly defined and its effectiveness is gauged differently by different groups, it is taking place in more and more locations. Eric believes that "ultimately, all education came from environmental education. Before books and speech, there were stars and seasons."

Jane, a fourth grade teacher at Abington Friends School, voiced her concern about "proselytizing" when discussing environmental issues. She and her class studied wetlands and she was concerned that she presented just one of the many sides of the issue. She mentioned that perhaps she should have brought in developers so that a non-conservationist perspective could be heard. She admitted to having strong beliefs on the issues and said she noticed the same "sense of urgency" among the students, but she wondered if her presentations were somehow unfairly skewed by her own beliefs. Eric responded that many teachers are "partisan toward the environmental movement," yet have a genuine concern for the development of the child and an individual responsibility to be fair.

Eric led a group activity devised by Joseph Cornell called "Build a Tree." The participants acted as different parts of the tree. They represented heartwood, the taproot, lateral roots, sapwood, xylem, cambium, phloem, and leaves. The four people representing the heartwood, which provides support for the tree, stood with their backs to each other and locked arms. One person represented the taproot, which goes as far as thirty feet into the ground and also provides support, and a few represented lateral roots, which find water. All of the people who represented roots lay on the floor, radiating from the heartwood. Three people representing sapwood and xylem formed a circle around the heartwood by joining hands. The xylem lifts the water from the roots and was called "the most efficient pump in the world" by Eric. A larger circle of people representing cambium, the growing part of the tree, and phloem, which transports food manufactured by the leaves, formed around those representing sapwood and xylem. Finally, the few remaining participants pretended to be leaves and bark and scattered themselves on the outside of the formation. Upon hearing the command "Let's make food" given by Eric, the participants surged into action and took on their roles as parts of the tree. The roots pretended to bring in water and made "slurping" sounds while doing so. The xylem transported the water, moving up and down to represent the movement. Then, the leaves moved while making food and sent it down through the phloem, which also moved up and down to illustrate the action. Eric inquired about the purpose of the bark, and everyone agreed it was for protection. Eric pretended to be a pine-borer and attacked the bark, but the participants wisely responded by performing their respective functions in order to fortify the tree so that it could sustain the attack. They moved and made their noises and seemed to be enjoying themselves.

...all education came from environmental education. Before books and speech, there were stars and seasons....

Mike began his talk on the future of environmental education by explaining that current environmental education programs may help students learn about environmental problems, but do not really empower the students to devise and implement solutions. He attributed this weakness to the short-term goals of many environmental education programs. For example, Mike mentioned student letter-writing programs designed to save the Arctic National Wildlife Refuge in Alaska from development. Such a program may increase awareness among students, but the long-term problems created by a political system that does not highly value the environment are not solved. Mike believes that "teaching kids to turn off the lights and write letters is nice, but this action alone is not really enough... we need to change the whole paradigm, the whole system in which we

are living...to one that is more environmentally focused." He acknowledged that "children feel frightened, disempowered, and, often, even guilty for not doing enough to solve environmental problems."

Mike and Brendan talked about some emerging ideas in environmental education. Brendan began with the concept of "valuing aspects of our society that are often associated with females. In a culture where the overwhelming majority of the political power is in the hands of a select group of white males,...ideas such as nurturing, compassion, empathy, a sense of community, and a sense of a larger process are often significantly undervalued." There are connections between the "value allotted to females in our society and the secondary values allotted to the earth, and there is a connection between women and the planet." This philosophy has been called "ecofeminism," and ecofeminists believe that the "dominating, exploitive paradigm in our male-centered, patriarchal society" has led to a devaluing of both women and the environment. Ecofeminists feel that the liberation of women and the liberation of the earth from destruction brought about by humanity are interconnected.

More and more environmental education programs are incorporating Native American concepts of nature into the curricula. Many Native American communities, for example the Lenape tribe of the Delaware Valley, lived here in a sustainable manner for hundreds of years before Christopher Columbus "discovered" America. Brendan feels that they demonstrated their concern for the environment not only by leading a materially sustainable lifestyle, but also in their spirituality. Lenapes feel that the integrity of the earth should not be preserved simply because humans need it, but because humans are part of the earth. Brendan believes that Lenapes exhibit a feeling of sacredness for the earth that is sorely lacking in our society.

Mike briefly discussed the concepts of deep ecology and bioregionalism. Deep ecology is a philosophy which promotes biocentrism, the belief that all organisms are created equal. Deep ecologists believe that each life form is intrinsically valuable to all others, and, therefore, should be protected. Bioregionalism is a way of viewing a group of organisms and their environment as one ecosystem, a bioregion.

...the "dominating, exploitive paradigm in our male-centered, patriarchal society" has led to a devaluing of both women and the environment.

Bioregions are naturally determined by geography, and the ultimate goal of bioregionalism is to have the inhabitants of a bioregion live using the resources of its own ecosystem. One common thread among these varied environmental philosophies and practices is "an expanding sense of Self," a term coined by Norwegian philosopher Arne Naess to express and expand on consciousness to include the non-human world. Brendan said, "The future of Environmental Education may hold an expanded sense of cultural and biological self expanding to include the wisdom of many traditional societies as well as the connections between women and improving the condition of the planet, and biologically expanding in recognition of the importance of, and our intrinsic connection to, the non-human world."

Brendan closed the formal part of the workshop with a discussion on what he calls the "biological reality of the environmental crisis." He quoted Mustafa Tolba, Director General of the United Nations Environment Programme, "We face by the turn of this century an environmental catastrophe as complete and irreversible as any nuclear holocaust." He asserted that the challenge we face to create a sustainable society can either be "an empowering or depressing thought." He believes environmental education is essential, and that direct action in the form of protest and civil disobedience is necessary. Brendan considers actions such as picketing outside an incinerator both educative for others and self-educating because they stimulate others to evaluate their own views on the environment and force the participant to clarify and defend her or his views, to say, "I cannot live with the poisons from that incinerator, I cannot live without that redwood forest..."

Peter felt that since together the participants became a tree, they could become a forest, as well. He alluded to the theme of the conference, common ground, and asked the participants to join him in standing as trees of the forest on common ground as he read the following prose poem by Susan Griffin entitled "Forest — The Way We Stand."

> The way we stand, you can see we have grown up this way together, out of the same soil, with the same rains, leaning in the same way toward the sun. See how we lean together in the same direction. How the dead limbs of one of us rest in the branches of the others. How those branches have grown around the limbs. How the two are inseparable. And if you look you can see the different ways we have taken this place into us. And we are various, and amazing in our variety, and our differences multiply, so that edge after edge of the endlessness of possibility is exposed. You know we have grown this way for years. And to no purpose we can understand. Yet what you fail to know we know, and the knowing is in us, how we have grown this way, why these years were not one of them heedless, why we are shaped the way we are, not all straight to your purpose, but to ours. And how we are each purpose, how each cell, how light and soil are in us, how we are in the soil, how we are in the air, how we are both infinitesimal and great, and how we are infinitely without any purpose you can see, in the way we stand, each alone, yet none of us separable, none of us beautiful when separate, but all of us exquisite as we stand, each moment needed in this cycle, no detail unlovely.[4]

Fourteen women and three men attended the session; their ages varied greatly. Many of the participants remained long afterward to talk with the presenters and each other.

Endnotes

1   Rachel Carson, The Sense of Wonder. (New York: Harper and Row, 1956), pp. 41-42.

2   *Ibid*, pp. 88-89.

3   *Ibid*, p.49.

4   Susan Griffin, Woman and Nature. (New York: Harper and Row, 1978), pp. 220-221.

Resources

Carson, Rachel. The Sense of Wonder. New York: Harper and Row, 1956.

Cornell, Joseph. Listening to Nature. Nevada City, California: Dawn Publications, 1987.

Cornell, Joseph. Sharing Nature with Children. Nevada City, Calfornia: Dawn Publication, 1979.

Griffin, Susan. Woman and Nature. New York: Harper and Row, 1978.

Grover, Herbert. A Guide to Curriculum Planning in Environmental Education. Madison, Wisconsin: Wisconsin Department of Public Instruction, 1989.

Herman, Marina Lachecki and Passineau, Joseph, *et al*. Teaching Kids to Love the Earth. Duluth, Minnesota: Pfeifer-Hamilton Publishers, 1991.

Leopold, Aldo. A Sand County Almanac. New York: Oxford University Press, 1966.

Macy, Joanna and Seed, John, *et al*. Thinking Like a Mountain: Towards a Council of All Beings. Santa Cruz, California: New Society Publishers, 1988.

Nhat Hanh, Thich. A Guide to Walking Meditation. Nyack, New York: Fellowship of Reconciliation, 1985.

Robottom, Ian, ed. Environmental Education: Practice and Possibility. Victoria, Australia: Deakin University Press, 1987.

Sisson, Edith. Nature With Children of All Ages. Englewood Cliffs, New Jersey: Prentice Hall, 1982.

Van Matre, Steve and Weiler, Bill. The Earth Speaks. Warrenville, Iowa: Institute for Earth Education, 1989.

Chapter 2

Supportive Relationships and Environments

Support among parents, administrators, students, and teachers sustains creativity and energy; it facilitates growth. Learning involves vulnerability and best occurs in a caring milieu. The relationship between parents and teachers is especially complex and in need of support. Supportive environments allow individuals to clarify and implement new ideas.

To what extent do you feel common ground with your fellow teachers? Can you admit you have problems?

We have to recognize our common ground with parents... Progressive educators must recognize this. It will help with the conversation.

Learning becomes meaningful and less intimidating in cooperative situations. Anxiety seems to evaporate, confidence grows, risk-taking seems less scary.

To support something, parents need to understand it. It is important for teachers to educate parents. Rather than being experts, we need to redefine progressive education *with* our local communities.

There is a problem in people who feel certainty — they know the answers. It's good to see people who are wondering.

Helping Parents Have Confidence in Progressive Education
*A Working Group Facilitated by Penny Colgan-Davis, Friends Select School,
Philadelphia, Pennsylvania, and Karla Read, The School in Rose Valley,
Moylan, Pennsylvania*

*Description by Patricia Finley Hamdan, scribe,
and Simon Firestone, editorial assistant*

The goal of the workshop's facilitators, Penny Colgan-Davis and Karla Read,
was to work with the participants to create knowledge together. Penny and Karla
wanted to explore ideas about parent confidence in progressive education. The
perspective and experience of each person were integrated into the format, and
into the description of the working group.

First Session
Penny and Karla began by asking each person to report a significant personal
learning experience. The experiences tended to contain strong emotion tied to a
need for support from others and a feeling of confidence. One participant recalled becoming "fired up" in a high school biology class to go into a particular
topic in depth. She spent weeks in the library doing research, and was both excited about and proud of the report that she submitted. Unfortunately, the
teacher was so angry that he never read the report, because she had neglected her
other work. Years later, the student decided that teachers sometimes have more
power than wisdom, and that teachers' choices are not inherently better than
student choices. Her experience led her to seek another perspective in education.

Two people talked about learning physical activities. One discussed the pride
that is associated with teaching oneself, and the other commented on how
muscles provide one with immediate feedback; the latter had taught her sister
how to ride a bike. She was impressed with the idea of "letting someone go when
they didn't know it," that is, allowing others the freedom to learn and be competent when they are ready and confident.

Two teachers talked about learning from their students. One said that she felt
humbled by the strengths of children whose environment was economically
depressed. The other teacher mentioned her experience at a Prospect Summer
Institute in North Bennington, Vermont. She said that it had been her first experience of "an ongoing education that's personal" and a curriculum that is
planned anew each year.

On the basis of our own experiences, the working group concluded that certain
elements seemed to contribute to optimal learning. They included an emphasis
on student-directed learning where the teacher lets the students take personal

responsibility for their own education, and an emphasis on direct experience. Students should form their own questions as part of a personal quest for knowledge. Teachers should support students, rather than place pressures upon them which are harmful to individual confidence.

Penny then asked the participants to think of general definitions of learning that are representative of progressive education. Jed, a teacher at Green Acres School said that learning involves complexity, has an ethical dimension, and allows the student to understand or appreciate relationship. As a teacher, he finds that significant learning occurs when students try to teach each other. He thinks that Maxine Greene's citation of John Dewey's emphasis of "mind" as a verb was very significant. Joan, a teacher at Friends Select said,

> My learning was an issue when I became a teacher. Learning occurs in a context or a certain atmosphere. Respect for the learner is essential, as is openness. Everyone has something to learn. It's necessary to take the long view of learning with children — everyone is curious about something. Remember the suffering that takes place in school.

Patricia, of the Graduate School of Education at the University of Pennsylvania, asserted that,

> Learning relies on integration of mind, body, and emotions. Fragmentation of knowledge assumes that the mind can apprehend knowledge by itself, without experience if the fragments are small enough. Here is a metaphor — what would it be like to learn how to play the piano as a problem of eye-hand coordination, using random notes, without any melody? The melody provides meaning and order for the mind and pleasure for the senses.

Penny concluded the first session of the workshop by extracting the following themes from our perspectives on learning.
• We know that we've learned something when we can communicate it to someone else, or when our beliefs have changed.
• We need to be in an environment of mutual respect and openness in which people take a larger view of the meaning of education. A relaxed environment allows people to feel confident.
• Learning requires hard work and perseverance. It means growing through mistakes, and surviving failure in order to do better the next time around.
• All children can learn and want to learn. Learning is enhanced by personal interest. It involves seeing connections, appreciating complexities and layers of meaning.

Second Session
The second session was held at The School in Rose Valley. We were asked to consider the following questions about the classrooms that we saw: What evidence is there of the expectations or standards to which children are held?

What skills or content are displayed in the children's work? Betty, of The School in Rose Valley, observed from the displayed projects that the children were trying to understand the use of patterns in math. Others noted evidence of the diversity of approaches to teaching mathematics, even within the same classroom. In one display, measurements with non-standard measuring devices, such as shoes and pieces of string, were presented. It occurred to us that this display was a metaphor for the kind of assessment which progressive schools use with children, multiple non-standard measures.

The appearance of the rooms suggested that much of the work done by children was communal and cooperative. The rooms seemed to be designed to engage the children with both their environment and their own behavior. In one room there were charts that measured children's television viewing behavior with multiple approaches, such as time spent watching, quality and type of shows, and the presence of commercials. There was also evidence of the documentation of the children's personal histories in the form of their time lines, writing, and art.

In pairs, we examined samples of teacher reports to parents. For purposes of comparison, we were also given a traditional report card. Some participants remarked that a few of the progressive reports were explicit in their descriptions of curriculum and content, but others were vague. We were concerned that the use of terms such as "excellent" and "very good" were not very different than traditional As and Bs. We had hoped to see descriptions of what the child had known before, what they can do now, and what general plan there is for that child in the future.

The participants in this session involved themselves intensively with the school. Pat, a workshop participant, was impressed by sincere attempts to look at the classrooms fairly, and to ask critical questions. She was touched by some of the expressions of hope from people who tried to live according to the values embodied by the conference and which appeared to be evident in the school. We were concerned by the sense of failure that some participants expressed about communicating the value of progressive education and values to parents. Maxine Greene's discussion of the need to establish a common ground before communication can truly occur was a recurrent theme when we discussed making progressive education available in public schools.

Third Session
Back at Swarthmore College, Penny asked the participants to report on the ways each person's school communicates with parents about the progress of their children and general school activities. All of the schools used teacher reports or report cards, semi-annual parent-teacher conferences, special events such as grandparent days and fairs, field trips, classroom visits, and work that is sent home. The progressive schools tended to have more areas of contact between

school and home. This difference may have been a function of the progressive schools' smaller size. In the progressive schools, parents often had access to curricular materials and teachers' home phone numbers. These schools often published newsletters and held academic fairs. Parents sometimes contributed volunteer labor to the school, or helped raise funds.

The participants mentioned several ways that schools can allow parents to become involved in the education of their own children. Such efforts have the potential of building collaborative relationships that link the children to their neighborhoods and strengthen the entire community.

We concluded our working group by reviewing our activities, drawing out important themes, and making recommendations. We agreed that equal access to progressive education is a critical issue that has not been sufficiently addressed by progressive schools, especially in light of the tendency to be both private and expensive. We agreed that there is no one answer to the question of how to best educate children. Schools should give parents more substantial information about the education of their children.

Nurturing Teachers As Activists: The Power of Support Listening
A Workshop Presented by Marcy Morgan, The Shipley School,
Bryn Mawr, Pennsylvania, and Nancy Sleator, Lansdowne Friends School,
Lansdowne, Pennsylvania

Description by a scribe and the editors

The teaching profession often attracts people who are generous and caring, who work painstakingly to help schools and students solve their problems. The ills and inequalities of society are also reflected in schools and classrooms, making teaching stressful. Progressive education creates its own tensions as teachers forge new ways of teaching and structuring schools. Even in supportive settings with supportive colleagues, teachers often provide more nurturing and attention than they receive. Support listening is a technique which addresses these imbalances. It provides educators with the personal support needed to push through obstacles that get in the way of achieving their goals.

Support listening is a technique with which educators can assist one another to reduce stress and move towards positive change. It creates a space in which successes can be acknowledged, frustrations vented, issues clearly thought through, and strategies for problems developed. Using support listening, teachers can reflect on their own situations, organize their ideas, and overcome obstacles to action with the caring support and attention of other teachers.

Most people savor opportunities to share their personal stories. Typically, however, the sharing of a personal story results in discussion as others interrupt or add their own stories. Time for listening, therefore, needs to be structured. Marcy Morgan and Nancy Sleator have found attentive listening to cause profound changes in the lives of those who listen as well as those who speak.

Support listening is based on the assumption that all people are brilliant, creative, cooperative, and caring people. It also recognizes that all people have had hurtful experiences through criticism, rejection, humiliation, disappointment, and frustration. Unprocessed, the hurt from the experiences is stored within; the result is that we may not function as well or think as clearly. We feel less good about ourselves and become a little more mistrustful of others. The healing process takes place when we have a chance to share the experience with someone who is providing caring attention. Through support listening on a regular basis we feel better, function better, think more clearly, relate better to others, and are more willing to be flexible and to try new things.

A few guidelines are fundamental to the effectiveness of the technique: each person in a dyad or small group gets equal time to talk; confidentiality is maintained; and listeners do not interrupt, comment, analyze, or interject their own ideas or stories. Rather, listeners listen attentively and with care. Listeners maintain an attitude of relaxed confidence with regard to the persons speaking, thereby creating more space for the speakers to process their work on a deeper level without needing to worry about the effect upon the listeners. This is done even when there is a powerful urge to interject.

Support listening has the possibility of building community, creating change, and enabling teachers to rediscover their enthusiasm, determination, and creativity, while surmounting the inevitable discouragements from the limitations of our educational system.

One goal of support listening is to empower people to find their own solutions to the issues they face. The technique is based on the premise that within each of us is the ability to find solutions. Often emotions cloud our thinking, but having the chance to talk and to feel the feelings that get in the way of thinking well can allow us to figure out a solution that is better than anyone else could design. Therefore, support listening can be used for problem solving; however, it can also be used for goal setting, support on personal issues related to school, home, or past experiences, and support on multicultural issues related to one's identity, culture, heritage, or gender.

The workshop participants divided into pairs, allowing each person three minutes to share with their listener a success they have had in teaching. Discussion followed the activity, providing rich insight into the experience of the technique. Nancy, a participant, began. "Three minutes of uninterrupted time is long. I never experienced such a long time to finish a sentence." Martha said, "It is difficult for a listener when silent not to form judgments."

The persons talking are able to process thoughts as they speak. Andrea said, "When you know that someone is not going to interrupt you for a while you find yourself talking, you find a way to say something the right way, then say it again." The gifts that the technique provide both the listener and talker were recognized by Marcy and Nancy, "The listener benefits a lot from this process. It is an opportunity to build connections with people." And "For three minutes you need to be totally on the side of the person you are listening to. It is important to trust the other person is admiring rather than judging."

Pairs took five minutes each to talk about something difficult about teaching. Again, the discussion that followed captured the power of the experience. Mike commented,

"I cannot believe how freeing this experience has been. On paper it does not seem like much...I have a great difficulty speaking with other educators and I just did it twice. That felt very good."

For Dick, the workshop raised a potent question: how could this technique effect progressive education change on a large scale? Marcy said that support listening "is a subversive process." People will not change without a sense that they are cared about, and change can be assisted by making personal connections. "This is the most effective process I know to make change happen." Dick probed further, replying, "People have the right to be 'traditional teachers,' especially if that is how they teach best." Marcy recognized this as an interesting long-term question, and clarified that the issue at hand is rigidity, not traditionalism. "Rigidity is what we are trying to solve here. We can have rigid progressives as well as rigid traditionals. What we are after is flexible thinking," to which Andrea added that the listening process is important whether the listener agrees or disagrees with the person speaking.

Support listening has the possibility of building community, creating change, and enabling teachers to rediscover their enthusiasm, determination, and creativity, while surmounting the inevitable discouragements from the limitations of our educational system.

Creating Community for Teacher Research:
Philadelphia Writing Project
*A Workshop Presented by Judy Buchanan, Margo Ackerman,
Michele Jean Sims, and Shirley Brown, Philadelphia Writing Project, Philadelphia, Pennsylvania*

Description by Judy Buchanan, Margo Ackerman, Michele Jean Sims, Shirley Brown, presenters

The Philadelphia Writing Project is a school-university partnership serving K-12 teachers in the School District of Philadelphia. It is a site of the National Writing Project, located at the University of Pennsylvania. Central to the National Writing Project is the belief that "teachers are the best teachers for teachers." By interacting and sharing common experiences, as well as learning about research in the field, teachers gain insight from one another that offers fresh approaches to teaching and new solutions to classroom issues.

More broadly, the Philadelphia Writing Project is committed to teacher research as a form of knowledge generation for teachers. Rather than only contributing to traditional research methodologies, the Project seeks to open new areas and approaches of study. It also has a deliberate focus upon multicultural issues, including a search for ways in which a more multicultural community can develop in classrooms.

Three teachers from the School District of Philadelphia shared their experiences of working in a teacher-research group in the Philadelphia Writing Project. Each of them discussed a question or problem she had in her classroom, and described how she benefited from other teachers as a source of learning about her own teaching. Longer accounts of their projects can be found in *Inside/Outside: Teachers, Research and Knowledge.*[1]

Margo's Story
I teach a special education class for children who have been labeled Emotionally Disturbed and Learning Disabled. There are twelve students between the ages of eight and eleven, most of whom come from the predominantly white working class neighborhood that surrounds the school.

My principle concerns have been around the labeling of my students. By labeling the students and putting them into a special education class, I feel the focus becomes the child's disabilities rather than their abilities. I am also interested in my student's writing development. I began to ask myself questions such as: How does what we study and what we read in class influence a child's writing? How can I get better at recognizing change and development in student writing? When and what kinds of intervention methods are helpful?

Given the opportunity to work in a community of teachers doing teacher research, I decided to choose one student whose writing I would look at closely throughout the year. I hoped to gain a greater understanding of my student's writing development and effective techniques for helping the class as a whole.

I selected Michael. Michael was a nine year old boy who was thought of as being a quiet, cooperative, and somewhat shy child. His first piece of writing was a very short note, filled with mispellings, that he left for me in the class "mailbox." Despite this brave move, Michael was initially reluctant to write, claiming "I can't spell," and "I don't know what to write." After some initial encouragement, Michael would usually write a few sentences. Through the process of collecting Michael's writing, I noticed that he was using a lot of repetition and that he consistently began his sentences with particular phrases such as "I like...," "I love my..." This was totally opposite to the flowing and descriptive language Michael used when talking to me or to his friends.

Hoping to find ways to help Michael develop his writing, I brought my questions and Michael's work to the teacher research group. I presented Michael in what's called a Descriptive Review of a Child, developed by Pat Carini and her colleagues at the Prospect School in North Bennington, Vermont. This process includes a description of the child using the categories of physical presence and gesture, disposition, relationships with children and adults, activities and interests, and formal learning. The other teachers then ask the "presenting" teacher clarifying questions about such things as the classroom, the child, learning styles. Recommendations are made based on the collective thinking of the group. As a result of this process, I implemented many of the recommendations of the group in ways that expanded Michael's writing. I also became a more careful "looker"; by doing such a close study of Michael and his work, I was able to see more in all of the children's work. I also found that when I listened to others give a Descriptive Review, I was able to incorporate ideas, insights, and thoughts about children to enhance my teaching.

Although the answers to all of my questions have not been fully answered, through my work with Michael and the Philadelphia Writing Project, I have broadened my perspective and found different ways of documenting student growth with other teachers which I find invaluable.

Michele's Story
I am interested in the question of why children with average intelligence struggle with reading comprehension. It was working with adolescents who were designated as Chapter One eligible which prompted this concern. My question for

teacher research involved selection of a student and using a variety of diagnostic strategies which I hoped would provide insight into the question.

Surprisingly my first challenge was one of selection. Which student out of the sixty in my classes should I invite to become a co-investigator? I wished the selection process to be as non biased as possible. Eventually, Ricardo, a quiet, unassuming student about whom I knew little, became my choice.

The Descriptive Review Process facilitated a closer look at Ricardo. By sharing my observations of Ricardo and looking at his work in teacher research groups, I developed a more composite picture about Ricardo's learning style and personality.

During this process, many new questions emerged. One question led to a new focus of my inquiry; I realized that I needed to devote more specific attention to Ricardo. I questioned how I could meet the needs of the more demanding students in the class while providing quality time to Ricardo and other students. This resulted in experimentation with alternative forms of assessment that would serve as information sources to facilitate my awareness of all students I taught.

Although my research may not have directly given answers to my original concern about reading comprehension, the Descriptive Review Process helped me realize that looking closely at the needs of individual students was connected to a larger need for investigation of alternative methods of assessment in my classroom.

Shirley's Story
My personal interest in feminist scholarship occasioned my unease with the curriculum in the classroom, and dictated the need for complete change, particularly in the realm of the English curriculum.

I teach pregnant and parenting teens in a Graduate Equivalency Diploma class, and I couldn't separate the reciprocal needs of my students and my own intellectual interest. In both cases, I am dealing with the needs of women. I wondered how I could ignore the absence of women in the curriculum in light of teaching an all-female class.

Through a series of self-directed studies, I created a multicultural curriculum of women writers who captured the imagination and interest of the students in the classroom and kindled the fires of intellectual engagement. Dropping canonical writers such as Poe, Harte, and de Maupaussant, whose short stories had been a mainstay in the curriculum, I replaced them with the works of Alice Walker, Ann Petry, Dorothy Canfield Fisher, Audre Lorde, and Richard Rive.

While I felt that there was increased engagement with literature that related more directly to the students' lives, I also searched for more suitable methodology. The Philadelphia Writing Project provided the key to the merging of curriculum and methodology through its emphasis on valuing the personal voice of writers. It was in the Project that I found the theoretical justification for encouraging what Ursula LeGuin refers to as the "mother tongue" the "language stories are told in." What I previously thought of as a respite from real writing, for example impersonal expository writing, instead became the writing anchor in my classroom. Gone were the groans of, "I have nothing to say," and my own guilt over not providing proper writing assignments.

> I believe teachers have the power to transform a disempowering curriculum through their own research.

I believe teachers have the power to transform a disempowering curriculum through their own research. Being connected to a network of teachers in the Philadelphia Writing Project who see their classrooms as sites of inquiry, provides an intellectual climate that nourishes and sustains teachers' research.

As my own research continues in constructing a curriculum that addresses gender, race, and class, it is reassuring to know that there is a place where I can test ideas and receive constructive reactions.

Conclusion

The teachers in the teacher-research group are encouraged to keep a detailed journal and copies of student work, as well as developing their own approaches to documenting their classrooms. Many of the narratives and personal accounts written by teachers involved in the Project are published in *The Voice*, the Project's newsletter, so that they can be made accessible to a broad range of educators and researchers.

Endnote

1   Cochran-Smith, M. and Lytle, S.L. Inside/Outside: Teachers, Research and Knowledge. (New York: Teachers College Press, in press).

A Discussion Group for Men Who Teach Children in Grades K to 6

A Workshop Presented by Lee Quinby, State College Friends School, State College, Pennsylvania

Description by Jordan Saturen, scribe

Seven men, including me, reclined in soft black chairs comfortably arranged in a circle. We were all excited to have a group and a time in which to share our joys and frustrations, questions and beliefs — it was to be a unique opportunity to explore our similarities and differences as men who teach children in grades K-6. Discussions were already under way when Lee Quinby, the facilitator, began describing his intentions for the workshop. He asked us to share our expectations of the workshop, and describe our interests and backgrounds.

Lee talked about some of the joys and pressures of being a teacher, as well as the isolation he has sometimes felt being a male teacher. He described joys in working with children, often challenged by financial pressures and societal pressures to "do more with himself." Dan Klatz, a teacher at Abington Friends School, mentioned some issues that come about working with all women; namely, gender related differences in perspective. He also expressed his conviction that it is important to have opportunities to talk with other men. Then Bob, a teacher at Media-Providence Friends School, sarcastically but somewhat seriously, asked, "What is there to talk about?" David mentioned that it's "refreshing to be a minority for once," and he said that those differences he sees between men and women, he appreciates. Some of the men had mentioned nurturing qualities they discovered in themselves when teaching, and Greg added that he thought male elementary teachers tended to be more nurturing than most men. He also expressed a fear of losing his nurturing qualities in changing from a teacher to an administrator, because nurturing and interacting with children, he said, "feeds me spiritually." Next, I described some of the joys I'd had working with children, finding those interactions the most challenging and at times energizing experiences I'd had. I also expressed my excitement to be able to learn from the other men present. Then Dave, the final man in the circle, spoke of how he felt he is important as a male role model, but asked: "Is it enough to be a role model?" Lee, Dan, Bob, and Greg had mentioned that they were all working in administrative roles, and Dave followed his previous question, asking them: "Why did you end up as administrators?"

Lee summed up what he thought were some of the common thoughts folks had expressed, and he mentioned it was interesting that "many of us didn't think of this men teaching elementary school as an issue." In order to ground the discussion, he asked us what drew us to teaching and what were some experiences that had led us to teach. This time we didn't go around the circle, but we responded when we felt ready. From this point on, the workshop just flowed from one thought to another; anybody asking a question, anybody responding. We were eager to talk and listen to each other. As we talked about why we were teachers and what had led us to teach, we explored the joys and advantages of being elementary school teachers, the unique qualities we — as men — have to offer as teachers, and the challenges we — as men — face as teachers.

Greg began, saying he liked the opportunity to create a community; then he changed his wording to say "nurture" or "foster" (instead of "create") a community. He also said that teaching is a great way of learning, an exciting way to learn new subjects. Lee interjected, "What did you learn about yourself?" to which Greg replied he'd learned to be more loving and he'd learned skills for fostering communities. He also responded that he'd sorted out some of his own family's dysfunction, and then paused to say, "Hmm... I hadn't thought about that."

"I felt vital," Bob said, and he went on to describe teaching as "kind of like a liquor, you just want more of it." Dan expressed pleasure in the "unconventional aspect of teaching," and described being with children as "a good, safe place."

Some of the men had mentioned that some people questioned — and they themselves had questioned — the value of teaching, wondering whether they were doing something worthwhile, rising to their potential. I said that I personally had no question regarding the value of teaching, but I was curious as to whether those who had become administrators had done so in order to rise to their potential and really make a difference.

Lee described how he could never be a good administrator if he hadn't taught, and that he'd originally had no thoughts of ever being an administrator. He shared several reasons why he'd made the change, none of which intimated dissatisfaction with teaching. He had always had an interest in the entire functioning of systems, and administration seemed like a new, big, challenging way to be involved with the whole functioning of teaching. Lee also mentioned increased pay as an attraction to becoming an administrator. With conviction and enthusiasm, Lee encouraged me to teach, and teach as long as possible.

In response to another man's comment, Dave said that we do ourselves a disservice to use the phrase "just a teacher," and he said he couldn't imagine a more challenging job. He then went on to describe some of the tremendous skills teaching requires. Dave did, however, express that he had been concerned at times that teaching was a dead-end job.

Dan immediately leaped in, saying that teaching opens doors. He said that teaching is a great opportunity to further one's learning, and that good schools nurture further learning in teachers. Bob commented that changing jobs is accepted in many professions, but it is perceived as a bad choice when teachers do it, as though they "couldn't hack it." Most of the other men nodded; they had felt similar sentiments. Lee added that teaching skills — especially interpersonal skills — are useful in many other professions.

"Men who teach are going to be great fathers," Lee said. But Dan added that administrating and teaching are so time consuming that they don't leave much time for family. Thinking about his job — leaving early, coming home late — he exclaimed, "Geez, what am I doing?" We laughed at the irony, empathetically.

David described how he fell into teaching. He knew he couldn't make a living as a composer, but he didn't want to forsake his love of music for a career. He had done a little teaching, and realized that he really loved it. Of course, he thought, he could be a music teacher, and he felt he had found a "good marriage of his interests." Thinking of education as political, Dave chose elementary school, where there is less bureaucracy and you can "get 'em students while they're young." We laughed. I would venture to say that all the teachers who attended the conference on progressive education have an acute awareness and appreciation for the political nature of teaching.

Building on David's comments, Lee described another attraction of elementary school: the younger the children, the more professional autonomy. David noted that as a teacher, unlike many other professions, it is almost impossible to get bored. Lee described teaching and other jobs without career ladders as jobs that foster valuable measures of personal growth — measures other than money and fame.

David asked why more men don't become elementary school teachers, and offered one explanation that there are many fears of men as abusers. Dan said that he wouldn't go in the girls' bathroom to tell girls to get back to class, and that there are other situations when he is conscious of his maleness and thus a little more tentative in his actions. Other men described similar experiences.

At this point Lee expressed a need to have closure for the workshop, though it seemed discussion could flow for at least another hour. He said that it is important for men to meet in groups, and that there is no need for shame in making space for making groups. We laughed when he said that he was pleased no women had shown up. Then he gave some information about men's groups and encouraged us to find one or start one.

Even as we were walking out, Greg raised another question, and somebody suggested that we eat lunch as a group. The meeting ended as the beginning of a reflective and supportive process.

Encore: An Extended Day Program
A Workshop Presented by Teresa Alvarez, Pamela Good, and Jennifer Hill,
Taylor Elementary School, Philadelphia, Pennsylvania

Description by Sarah Keith, scribe, and the editors

Encore is an after-school program for academic enrichment at Taylor Elementary School. Its goal is to increase children's reading ability. Encore is taught in English and offered to the entire student population, both anglo and bilingual. Because instruction is in English, it increases the English language abilities of those students who are dominant in another language. Teresa Alvarez described the circumstances which led to the development of the program.

> I'm a bilingual teacher...I teach my children in Spanish. I teach reading, science, social studies, math, everything in Spanish including ESOL (English to Speakers of Other Languages)...and that's one of the reasons that Encore came about. About four years ago, I sort of complained about the fact that we were required to do a certain amount of reading minutes per week, and being a bilingual teacher, I was only allowed certain minutes to teach English and a certain allotted time went to the teaching of Spanish. Yet, the city-wide test was in English, and our bilingual children were supposed to take this English test. The test proved frustrating and upsetting to these students. The teachers emphasized the fact that we did not have enough time to teach English.

Three afternoons a week Teresa is joined at Encore by fourteen other teachers, about half the teaching staff at Taylor. They all believe that English and literature can be taught in a relaxed and unthreatening environment through a literature-based whole language program. After school, the teaching is entirely in English; if students do not yet know English, they still benefit from the environment and may begin to learn by "osmosis or memorization." Students are exposed to English through literature, stories, play acting, creative writing, choral speaking, and oral language development.

Encore does not use basal reader series, but instead uses trade books to initiate a multitude of related learning activities. The activities motivate students to learn English and develop an appreciation and love for reading. Encore teachers described some of the projects they have found successful, while other participants shared their favorites. Encore teacher Jennifer Hill emphasized before, during, and after reading activities, some of which were displayed on the wall. Mary Ann, of the School District of Philadelphia, related a project in which she took all the pages out of a book and asked the students to put it back together in chronological order. It was agreed that teachers set an example for the children by being enthusiastic and avid readers themselves.

Justifying Encore's funding is a priority. Teresa and other Encore teachers use an organized system of evaluation which includes quarterly reports, culminating activities for each book, and a seven point assessment. Without some form of evaluation, a program loses its credibility and the grants that keep it alive. Encore's seven points of program assessment are: Encore students' school attendance compared to that of non-Encore students, active participation from the students, parental feedback, advancement of ESOL levels, student portfolios, student drama performances, and student interest in the program.

Much of the evaluation of Encore on which Encore teachers pride themselves is quantitative analysis based on various reading and ESOL levels, and city-wide tests. Encore students often perform better than students who started at the same achievement level and did not attend Encore. In fact, Taylor School has made significant increases on the city-wide test.

Teresa and her fellow Encore teachers employ many progressive education methods in order to carry out their goal to improve their students' reading levels: invented spelling, cooperative learning, talking with the students about themselves and *their* ideas. Jennifer remarked that she likes to place high-level readers with low-level readers, as well as mixing boys and girls, and African-Americans and Hispanics in order to insure that everyone learns from each other. Even though Encore uses progressive techniques that the children and teachers enjoy, standardized tests are used to compare their favorable results with those of basal reader series.

Parent involvement and contact is a key element to any after-school program. Teresa, for example, lives in the neighborhood of Taylor Elementary School, and as a part of the community she visits the homes of her students and is a resource and a comfort for the families who do not speak English. Encore itself could not function without parent volunteers. Pamela Good's presence at the workshop as an Encore parent testifies to how respected and important parents are in the learning process at Encore. She described how her children, especially her daughter, have become very enthusiastic about reading since being in the Encore program. Her son, who was already an avid reader, appears to read even more. Lynne, a teacher in the School District of Philadelphia, shared one of her favorite reading/writing activities, "The Author's Tea." The tea is an afternoon when parents can visit the program and hear their children read their own stories and poems aloud, as well as share baked goods they brought with them.

Encore has found progressive methods, parental involvement, a creative and unthreatening environment, sound program assessment, and ties to the local community to be important components of the program. These characteristics, which have contributed to Encore's success, would strengthen any after-school program.

Cooperative Creativity: Exploring the Relationship Between Visual and Verbal Composition
A Workshop Presented By Sharon Parker, Strath Haven Middle School, Wallingford, Pennsylvania

Description by Sharon Parker, scribe, and the editors

After introductions, Sharon Parker described how she first became interested in the relationship between visual and verbal composition, and cooperative activities. She began using cooperative creativity after thirteen years of teaching language arts. Her son had a stroke shortly after birth. He did not speak until age seven. Sharon was deeply disturbed by the diagnosis that her son was retarded; she could see that he understood what was going on around him, and that he could compose with blocks and other materials. She "became fascinated by the connection between composition abilities and progress in communication."

Her teacher training did not prepare her for working with non-verbal children. However, through the observation of her son Sharon developed two theories: that composition begins on a non-verbal level and is an inherent part of learning in every child, and that creativity is enhanced by children working together.

A drawing activity demonstrated Sharon's theories of cooperation and composition. Working in groups of three or four, each person received a piece of paper and a colored marker, and was directed to "think like an inventor; to be as wild and as inventive as possible." As music was played, everybody began drawing part of an imagined machine. When the music stopped, participants passed their drawings to the person next to them, who then proceeded to continue inventing the machine just received. When the music stopped for the last time, participants had to defend the machine they were holding as being the best one within their small group, after which members of each group had to decide by consensus which machine they would stand behind. Once chosen, the machine received a name and advertising jingle. Laughter and playfulness filled the room as groups drew and made decisions together. A "Marvelous Multiple Flavoring Hydrating/ Dehydrating Polishing Freezon Masseuse" was advertised as being able to change the flavor of fruit, shine shoes while changing raisins taken from raisin bran into fresh grapes, and powder your face or give you a massage.

Sharon uses visual composition to assist students with their writing. Sharing examples of her students' work, she showed that realism, impressionism and cubism can be reflected in written composition: using facts for realistic portraits, using "facts softened with feelings" for an impressionist view, and using sharp, dramatic, "jutting" words for a cubist style. The student's work demonstrated how certain styles help students who are struggling with writing. For example, one of her students responded well to Cubism because, as Sharon said, she felt "free from the lines which make her crazy." Using a cubist writing style gave her the freedom to use words without the constraints of structured sentences. This student had once remarked to Sharon that "sometimes I think of myself as floating."

Sharon developed an activity called "Collide-A-Scope" to combine visual and verbal composition. Students make a simple "focusing tube" and select a spot in their environment which was previously unnoticed. Using their focusing tubes, students direct their full attention to their spot for five to ten minutes. Then they describe their focus areas in a way that gives "dignity, character and purpose to the 'overlookable' segments of our environment."

Together, the activities Sharon introduced promote visual and verbal composition as well as cooperation between students. A participant later reflected that the cooperative effort is the "common ground" where "children's individual approaches to learning, their creative instincts, and their strengths are best affirmed and most productive in the context of working together in community."

How to Support Our Students As Visual Thinkers:
Confronting the "I Can't Draw Syndrome"

Presenters: Francie Shaw and Amy Verstappen, Friends Select School, Philadelphia, Pennsylvania

Description by a scribe and the editors

What are the implications of the statement "I can't draw" and how can they be turned around? How can classroom teachers (who may themselves be saying "I can't draw") help? As teachers learn to help support students as writers, what can they do to help students in expressing the many different artists within them? Teachers need to be consciously aware of supporting students as artists and need to learn ways for doing it. These issues and questions were central to the workshop.

In a round-table format, participants shared their personal concerns and questions about supporting students as visual thinkers, which, in turn, reflected what they hoped to gain from the workshop. An analogy was made between art and math; just as in math, even young students develop perceptions that they are good or not good at art. Further, once they believe they are "not good" in either area, they "shut down and lose interest and enthusiasm," thus further stifling their development. Fran, of The School in Rose Valley, described how her three-year-old students "scribble-scrabble" frequently, but when a few students begin to do more representational art, such as stick figures, others begin to feel inadequate. She wondered how she could support these students as well as those who are ready to learn more, and how she could respond to a child who wants a drawing of a cat to look like a "real" cat.

She wondered how she could... respond to a child who wants a drawing of a cat to look like a "real" cat.

Questions about how to respond to and evaluate art, how to improve children's drawing without "shutting them down," how to turn the visual ability into a strength in other subjects, how teachers may color students' beliefs about themselves as artists, and how to develop confidence in students were potent questions raised. Teachers shared their concerns about how to preserve rather than devalue the visual life of children as they get older and how to understand visual thinking better. Relating the difficulty of recent behavior problems in her classroom, one participant expressed how she has become "stale" in this area and is seeking inspiration and fresh ideas for her classroom.

Francie Shaw and Amy Verstappen shared a list of reasons why art is important.
• Art is problem solving. It involves choices and discrimination.
• The ability to take risks with the materials and with sharing art with others is developed through the process of making art.
• Children gain self-confidence through art if they can begin learning expression without having to be literal.
• Observation and critical thinking skills are by-products of art experiences.
• Synthesizing is a skill learned by visually depicting an event or experience.
• Creating art is an emotionally gratifying experience.

Drawing on the experience of the participants, Francie asked the group to share ways they have already used art and visual experiences in their classrooms. The following ideas were included:
• Using no-line paper and colored pencils for journal writing
• Using mood colors in journals
• Observing bones in science class to see, and then draw or paint
• Using microscope slides and comparing differences
• Reading books and using illustrations as clues to understanding the books' meaning
• Sketching and building observational skills
• Filling the classroom with posters of Greek art in social studies
• Creating a mummy case, expressing patterns and colors of the time period
• Making clay pots and decorating them with images from current culture
• Using pattern blocks as a means to learn discrimination and visual observation skills
• Making quilt designs
• Illustrating stories and journals.

During this sharing period, animated and vigorous discussions occurred. When students use a form of art from a different culture and interpret it with their own vocabulary, what happens to the integrity of that form of art? For example, if Pueblo-style pots are decorated with Bart Simpson images, would it be offensive to that culture? Many people felt it is very important to be respectful of other cultures and aware that many cultural art forms have religious meaning. This sparked a discussion about individual perceptions and personal symbols. The media impacts the inner images of children, and thus their personal expression. Francie expressed that this impact colors, and perhaps perverts, the inner imagery of children, and suggested that their imagery needs to be enriched.

Another discussion emerged about student choice and developmentally appropriate activities. Should students choose what they want to draw, or is there reason to have everybody draw fruit, for example? Using the clay butter stick figures made by all of The School in Rose Valley students each year, Francie described how specific tasks can be developmentally appropriate for many ages. When she looked at a display of the students' figures, the progression of skill, technique, and expression over the years was evident. The repetition of a specific technique over multiple years provides a framework for children to expand skills, deepen their expressiveness and experience with the medium, and heighten their awareness of their own growth.

Attention turned to ways to make children more comfortable with art in the classroom. Again, participants offered their suggestions and ideas:
• Visit galleries and museums, providing opportunities for children to observe, and comment and respond to art.
• Use simple projects to demonstrate the diversity of styles and expressions found even when students receive the exact same directions. Communicate how fascinating and wonderful this is.
• Give students permission to draw rather than write in journals.
• Be comfortable with each student's personal expressive style.
• Engage in many science observation projects and encourage the expression of the observations.
• Hang "real art" in the classroom, discuss the artists and their work, emphasizing that different people make beautiful things in different ways.
• While telling stories, draw quick illustrations on the board, thereby supporting the students in "loosening up" and understanding that interpretation is personal expression.
• Fill the classroom with picture books. Give the message that they are for children of all ages as well as for adults.
• Have many and diverse art materials available in the classroom, and teach respect for the materials.
• Design drawing games that make drawing fun, less threatening, and not dependent on realistic style.
• Use the book *Powers of Ten*[1] to combine math and art.

Dita, of The School in Rose Valley, shared an activity the entire workshop was delighted by:
Day One: Pass around sea shells. Students observe them and select five shells each.
Day Two: Each child observes shells as a mathematician; sorting, counting, and creating patterns.
Day Three: Each child observes shells as a scientist, and then draws the shells as a scientist.
Day Four: Each child observes shells as an artist, and then draws the shells as an artist.
Day Five: Each child writes about shells as a writer.

Suchitra, a teacher at The School in Rose Valley, later described her experience in the workshop:

> There was a sense of awareness that we must inspire ourselves and be creative in our own lives in order to bring that quality into the classroom. There was also a sense of having compassion and deeper understanding for the child or adult who has creative blocks. The desire to help those and nurture artistic expression in all students was deepened in our hearts. We felt that we had much food for thought to take with us.... There was a sense that this short meeting would impact our lives. We had certainly found our common ground, and that sharing and connection had left us strengthened and renewed in spirit.

Endnote

1   Philip Morrison, <u>The Powers of Ten</u>. (Redding, Connecticut: Scientific American Library, 1982).

Chapter 3

Attending to Children

We value children's perspectives and interests. We choose to respect what our students know, how they learn and feel, and how they experience the world. Attending to children involves our best efforts to understand children, and our authentic caring. A teacher both knows and loves the students.

Much of what we learned as teachers we learned from our students. It is valuable to take the time to sit and talk with kids about what they're thinking, even in a busy schedule with lots of pressure to master discrete skills.

Teachers need to pay attention to the child. Too often, only the expected answers and expected interests are what the teachers are interested in.

We have to get into the kids' hearts.

Parents and Teachers: Describing Children and Their Works

A Working Group by Patricia Carini, Mary Hebron, and Peggy Richards, Mamaroneck School District, Bronxville, New York

Description by Carol Montag, Independent Consultant and, scribe

> There is a pattern in the things that catch a child's eye or ear, that matter to him or her, but the selections can't be predicted or explained in any simple way.[1]

The pattern in the things that matter to a child holds a central position in Patricia Carini's work. The processes developed at Prospect Center, of which she is a founder, give us a way of looking at children which allows a clearer understanding of these patterns: of children's abiding interests and pursuits; their purposes and standards; and their modes of thinking and learning. These processes, which include Reflective and Recollective Conversations, the Descriptive Review of the Child, and the Description of Children's Works, were at the heart of the conference sessions "Parents and Teachers: Describing Children and Their Works."

Carini's writing and public presentations pivot on the complexity of our humanness and the implications of that complexity for the education of the person. Those who have listened to her at conferences on progressive education or who have studied with her at summer institutes in North Bennington, Vermont, know that, addressed from that angle, the description of a child or the child's works is never complete. Rather, from this perspective, works and the persons who make them are characterized by a richness and ambiguity which compel us to return to them over and over again.

Her purpose is to allow us, as educators and parents, to see the children we are with each day as active agents in their own educations and lives. In particular, she shows us how to gain access to the differences among children so we have a better understanding of each child's strengths — strengths which are revealed in the patterns composed from description of a child's physical being and gesture, her or his learning and thinking, interests and choices, relationships with friends and family. She teaches us to celebrate those differences as expressions of human uniqueness. From "this way of looking," as Carini phrases it, new meaning is given to evaluation and fresh possibilities are envisioned for children at a time when there appears to be little hope even for compassion in a society that dwells on competition, excellence, and constant pressure.

By actively participating in the descriptive processes developed at Prospect, those of us who attended the sessions were privileged not only to discover the strengths and patterns of meaning for a particular child, but to capture the things that matter to us, too. In fact, the experience for us, as adults and educators, meant facing head on the value, or lack of it, that has been placed on our own work, both as children and as practitioners.

"Parents and Teachers: Describing Children and Their Works" required a commitment of all three of the conference's working sessions and for most of us the Friday morning and Saturday afternoon conversations as well. If you attended Pat's presentations at past conferences, you knew that even the time allocated on Friday and Saturday would be inadequate for the amount of questioning, looking, recalling, and reviewing that takes place as she weaves the group from one process to another.

As the title suggests, this series of sessions was focused on the partnership between parent and teacher in support of the child's education. Pat was joined in the sessions by co-presenters Mary Hebron and Peggy Richards. The child playing the feature role was Patrick, the son of Mary and George Hebron, and a student enrolled in the previous two years in Peggy Richards's K-1 classroom in Larchmont, New York. The sessions included the following activities and processes: recollection of an important learning or teaching experience; reflective conversation focused on the notions of "build" and "builder"; slide over-view of Patrick's works (ages two-six); description of work (a boat constructed from clay); Descriptive Review of Patrick, co-presented by his mother, Mary, and his former teacher, Peggy. The report of these sessions, which follows, is composed from excerpts that touch on each of the processes and activities in which we participated.

We began with a Recollection, co-chaired by Lynne Strieb, a teacher in the School District of Philadelphia, and Pat. In a Recollection, a word or theme is presented to the group to mull over for a few minutes. Following that interval for thought, each participant has the opportunity to talk about the thoughts and memories called to mind. On this day, the subject of the Recollection was "a significant teaching or learning experience." As we each took a turn recalling our thoughts before the group, the co-chairs took notes, looking and listening for patterns and themes to emerge. The common threads, and those divergent, served to make up a summary which was read to the group. As usually happens, the process as we experienced it gave focus to the group, allowed us to get to know each other, and set the atmosphere for our work together for the weekend.

A sampling from individual recollections will give the flavor of what we shared:

> My grandmother taught me how to make knishes. It was so significant for me that now when I make them I become her. I use her body movements. It holds great emotion for me...

> I remember a teacher who read *Thirty Seconds Over Tokyo* as daily reading. It brought science to the class in a way I had never experienced it. We built hot air balloons, we decorated them, we learned about heat and air, we discovered how far they could fly and how high they could go. We worked in groups. It brought everything together for me for the first time...

Lynne summarized the collection of memories such as these around these emergent themes:

Lynne heard repeated thoughts about comfort and safety, a willingness to take risks, to stretch and try new things. The vividness of childhood learning was discussed in terms of storytelling and stories that help children make connections, as well as how teachers learn from each other and from the children. This theme of childhood learning gave a sense of hope, clarity, and precision to individual goals.

The experience of Recollection is characterized by a range of complexities identified in the themes and threads that are a part of Lynne's summary. Each participant's contribution is pulled forward by the chair's keen sensitivity to rhythms in memories, thereby affirming each member of the group.

At the end of the Recollection, we were focused on what was to lie ahead in the description of one child's work. We were a working group now, something personal having passed among us, a mirroring of ourselves to others, with a better notion of those things which matter to each of us — when we were children, and now, as teachers.

The Description of Work is prefaced by a Reflection on a motif or larger idea embodied in the child's collected works.

Pat introduced The Description of Work. Just as in the Recollection, the group would continue to function as a collaborative body, each person contributing her perspectives to the whole, with Pat as the listener, pulling together the recurrent themes from the collective deliberations.

The Description of Work is prefaced by a Reflection on a motif or larger idea embodied in the child's collected works. In this instance, Patrick himself provided the word for reflection. Asked by his mother if there was anything in particular he would like said about him at the sessions, he responded, "Tell them I'm a builder." And so, we reflected on the word "build."

As we heard each other respond to the word, the range of its meanings grew, intersected, and as we made our way around the circle, reached its boundaries, played itself out. Each thought was important, yielding new images and possibilities. Our purpose was not to have the word define Patrick or his work but to call to our attention the richness of its meanings, the width of its boundaries, and so to look with more attuned lenses at this builder's constructions. Or to say that in slightly different words, we needed first to see the spectrum of our own understanding of "build" before we could hope to understand his.

In summary, the themes and images that came together from our Reflection included the following.

> Building happens from the bottom up, the foundation needs to be wide and strong...Build, rebuild, rework — the emphasis is on process...Building involves making things stick together — it matters how you assemble them and with what...Still, you can build with many kinds of materials, and in that sense, building is not defined by what you use: straw, sticks, bricks (as in *The Three Little Pigs*) or clay or blocks or stones...Building usually means a physical structure, requiring body, muscle, plan, and thought to construct, but you can also build with words and ideas or construct a castle in the air...People build alone, but often it is the kind of group endeavor emblemized by the quilting bee or the barn-raising...It is not only humans who build, there is also an animal architecture...Building implies stability and permanence but it can also be haphazard, ramshackle as in *The House That Jack Built*...Building suggests use, form, function, but it also suggests design, creation, aesthetic...Building starts with something, what is, and transforms it into something utterly other...

We turned from the Reflection to the Overview of Patrick's works in slides. His mother explained that these were pieces drawn or made when Patrick was between ages two and six-and-a-half; some were made in school, others at home. Mary said these pieces represented a larger collection from which they were selected. In order to become acquainted with Patrick as a maker and builder, we were invited to offer impressions of these works as they were shown; Pat and Mary also commented, sometimes calling our attention to a recurrent pattern or theme in the works. We were impressed with the range of materials employed including clay, paint, tape, lots of foil, markers, pencil, cardboard. We observed that there is less use of paint and in that medium the work is larger; pencil and marker work is much more detailed. Whatever the medium we felt that Patrick tends to fill up the space, often by layering or by giving both the outer and inner view. He tends to mix perspectives; for example, using a profile view for a driver and another for the truck itself. Line dominates the work from early on, often to show connections. The work tends to be energetic and at the same time purposeful, attentive to function.

We sat in the darkened room and commented, our responses ranging in many directions. We spoke of technology, circuitry, power, speed, a recurrence of large numbers as characterizing many of the pieces. We noted that Patrick tends to use everyday objects in his work — paper clips, stamps, labels, tape — and then to transform them. His name appears on virtually every piece of work. There are many machines and vehicles; in their construction, he is attentive to the whole, to important selected detail, to their inner workings. There are fewer pieces depicting animals or nature, but there are some. Many pieces imply a story or narrative line.

As a way to sum up these first impressions, Pat asked us each in turn to comment on something that stood out to us about Patrick as a maker and builder of things. Our responses to this request as we went around the circle included the following:

> Patrick seems to be attentive to the physical world, to construction and engineering...He understands what gives an object an identity and uses selective detail to convey that...He pays attention to the whole, to important elements, and also to the insides and the working parts...Patrick makes the map, the blueprint — what you need to understand how something works or goes...Number and speed seem to be interesting to Patrick...In Patrick's works, someone is always in charge — a driver or other powerful person...He tends to view an object from many angles, suggesting an interest in the three-dimensional...He uses his hands to mold, to twist foil, to wrap tape...Some work is very layered, conveying attention to safety and protection...His transformation of everyday objects suggests that he has an eye for possibilities, is inventive...In Patrick's work, point, line, and bold form are present very early...This work seems complex from the first — emblematic, symbolic, layered, attentive to how things are made and how they work...

The Description of Work focused us on one piece, a three-dimensional clay structure. However, as we turned to this work, Patrick's mother and teacher put before us a large array of other three-dimensional pieces. These, together with the slides we had viewed, provided the context for the close look at the work selected for description.

Before we started, Pat clarified the distinction between the impressions we had offered to the slides and a description by pointing out that an impression is just that, a general sort of response; description requires that the viewer ground her statements about the work in the work itself. For example, in the first round of our description of Patrick's clay construction, we began to identify the piece as a ship. Our evidence for that "naming" of the construction arose from the observation that the structure has portholes, it is boat-shaped, it appears to have a crow's nest. Still, we cautioned ourselves not to conclude too quickly that what we were viewing was a ship since that might block out other equally tenable possibilities. We tried not to be definitive in our descriptions, continuing to use qualifiers such as "seems," "might be," and so on.

We proceeded from one round of descriptions to another, noting that we were seeing more patterns and not only single elements. For example, there were many places in the construction characterizable in terms of symmetry, asymmetry. We noted that Patrick used a variety of techniques in its construction so that there are coils, slabs, rounds. Like other pieces we saw on the slides, this construction is layered and displays both inside "machinery" and the outer structure. The result is complicated, busy, with a lot going on. We also noted that the "ship" has a solid base and is very carefully put together. It is solid as well as energetic. We observed that the way Patrick twists the clay in this construction is similar to the tinfoil twists in other works. Looking further at the construction, we noted that the piece was fired but no color was added.

Further description called attention to how different the work looks up close and from a distance. Either way, though, the "ship" conveys largeness even though it is not a piece of large dimension. We could see evidence of experimentation and also of familiarity with clay as a medium and building as an activity. It was easily imaginable to us that the ship could also be made by Patrick in another medium familiar to him, such as foil.

As we proceeded, images also arose. Some of these were vivid for the entire group such as that of Rodin's "The Thinker." Others were of trees and the human body. Each image tended to capsulize some dimension of the work or some impression of the maker as that emerged from the work.

At the close of the description, Pat's summary confirmed many of our impressions from the overview of Patrick's work in slides, but this time with the weight of our close description of the "ship" to confirm them: this is work on the large scale, many-dimensioned, complex, attentive to the whole and to selected details and especially to the inner workings of things. The work, even the two-dimensional pieces, tends toward the sculptural, and involves considerable range of technique. The work is inventive, experimental and at the same time, careful, solidly constructed, displaying an eye for structure and form. And indeed, form, line, and number are dominant over color in most of Patrick's works.

Patrick is careful as a builder and maker, giving time and attention to his work. The piece we looked at closely and many others suggest that Patrick is a close observer of how things go, how they are constructed, where pieces connect. In a sense, the works replay or revisualize that knowledge of the world. At the same time, Patrick is experimental and inventive — especially in his use of materials and in his equally observant eye for the possibilities in a material. Although the works are solidly constructed, Patrick achieves an impressionistic, gestural "rightness" that makes each piece unique and memorable and identifiably what it is. Partly, too, this effect is achieved through his selection of just the right detail — again there is evidence of a closely observant and selective eye.

These works suggest that Patrick as a thinker and learner has particular strengths in conceptualizing wholes, in seeing and grasping three-dimensional events, and in perceiving events from several divergent perspectives. Equally, he is well able to see both form and function, stripping away from what he is looking at those details which are not essential to the structure. In keeping with these talents, he has an eye for the relational and for the connectedness of things. These mathematical inclinations are echoed in an interest in numbers. The linear and detail for its own sake would appear to hold Patrick's attention less. From Patrick's work, we also understood him to be an independent kind of thinker, in charge of his own work, and with a clear vision of what he wishes to accomplish.

Pat pointed out that from our description of the work, we would, as teachers, have some clear ideas of what we could do in guiding Patrick's education. We would, for example, be able to count on him to proceed on his own with any observational study such as science. In terms of approach to areas such as reading and math, it would seem advisable to start with the big picture so that Patrick could be in charge of making the connections and to avoid bogging him down in the sort of small details that don't appear to serve him well. Mathematics, sculpture, and art in general, science (especially physical observation), mapping, and information about the world would seem from what we have learned so far to be areas of strength.

Following the description, there were questions about the process; the length of time, the difficulty of withholding judgment in favor of description, the noncomparative approach with respect to external standards or to other children. Most of us were accustomed to evaluating work much more quickly and with much less attention to the depth and complexity of the work. We felt we learned a lot but at the same time wondered how this approach might fit into the expectations for efficiency that tend to dominate school life. We were struck with how clearly Patrick's standards of carefulness, "rightness," and good form were evidenced in the work. We also took note that these standards were very much his and not transferable to other children's works — or theirs to his. Again, in schools dominated by comparison, this approach to standards struck a novel note for nearly everyone.

What occurred in the Description of Work is what Margaret Himley, in her book *Shared Territory*, refers to as "Deep Talk."

> What I call deep talk is based on the reflective practice developed by Carini and her colleagues at Prospect, where they have enacted the belief that teaching practice and educational research should be grounded in phenomenological or descriptive understanding of each child as a particular thinker and learner.[2]

And continuing,

> I want to evoke here the child's unique and distinctive accent as a writer, in what Carini calls "the personal aesthetic." It is a way for readers to meet the child writing. This...is also a way to demonstrate in detail the process of description, or deep talk, as a way of knowing.[3]

We had, in fact, evoked the presence of this little boy, Patrick. As we described his work and looked at the many other three-dimensional pieces that were on display, it was as if he were in the room with us. We felt a rich and enlivening understanding of him, a child we had never seen. No photograph had been introduced, but each of us had a mental picture of him — not physically but as a maker of works, a thinker, a learner, a person. He had become for all of us a vivid character.

The third and final session of the working group taught us about the Descriptive Review of the Child. Pat referred to the process as correlative to the Description of Work, and also a process which can be used independently of it. In the materials available through Prospect Center, the purpose of the process is discussed as a means "to bring together varied perspectives...in order to describe a child's experience within the school setting."

Pat said that the Descriptive Review would add yet a further dimension to the picture of Patrick which emerged from his work. We would hear about him as a person at home with family and friends and in the midst of the classroom world from persons who know him well — his mother and the teacher who taught him for two years. Drawing on their perspectives would enable us to evaluate the understandings gleaned from the Description of Work and also expand on them.

Pat pointed out that the Descriptive Review is designed around five headings, with the intention of presenting as full and whole a picture of the child as possible. These headings are: physical presence and gesture; disposition; relationships with other children and with adults; interests, choices, and preferences; formal learning. She added that a major purpose of the review is to call attention to a child's strengths and the knowledge and capabilities a child brings to school. Pat suggested that in the context of strengths, any vulnerabilities are more easily supported and knots in the learning process are more readily untangled. She instructed us that in this review process, as in the Description of Work, the language used is descriptive and all jargon, labels and specialized language are set aside. For example, children are not referred to as hyperactive or learning disabled but are instead portrayed as aptly and vividly as possible in terms of how they move or learn. Usually a review is centered through a focusing issue or question around which parent or teacher or both are seeking recommendations from the group.

Patrick's mother, Mary, gave her description of him first. (The account which follows is paraphrased and condensed.)

Patrick is seven and now is in second grade. Peggy (the next presenter) was his kindergarten/first grade teacher. He has a sister who is eleven and grandparents who are very present in his life. The question we are focusing on is, how can school make room for Patrick's preferred modes of learning? More specifically, as he continues through the grades, can the materials, the time, and the space required for his way of thinking and working be made available?

Physical Presence and Gesture. Although he is short for this age, Patrick has a large and visible presence. His inclinations are also toward the large and real and he is interested in grown-up activities. In these respects, his hands serve him very well and mentally very little escapes him. When he handles materials, he understands their possibilities; tape and foil, for example, are used by him in an inventive fashion which goes beyond their typical functions. He is physically vigorous and, for example, sees himself as a hockey player, but he also has a built-in sense of his limitations. After expending a lot of physical and mental energy, he takes a break, curling up in a chair, relaxing by himself. As a very young child, he would ask for help with a new physical venture such as the stairs.

Patrick talks a lot and words are important to him. As a baby, he babbled unceasingly; as an older child, he questions constantly. As with materials, his use of words is often inventive — for example, skeletope. He never lets preciseness get in his way, but shows confidence in what he says and how he says it.

Disposition. Speaking generally, Patrick is confident, lively, energetic. Since his face and body are so expressive, his feelings are quite visible. If his feelings are hurt, or his sister teases him, he wells up and cries. For all the vigor of his personality, he is deeply sensitive, affectionate, and full of feeling. Books or movies that have moving themes or messages affect him very much. He loves animals and is attached to his stuffed animals, especially one named Wo-Wo, who has been his companion from infancy. For a long time Wo-Wo went everywhere Patrick went. Although that isn't true any longer, Patrick still takes his animals to bed with him at night.

Relationships. Patrick's sister is his best friend, his best critic, his model, his judge and his jury. She understands Patrick and appreciates him; he thinks she is wonderful. Patrick is an affectionate, loving child — a family person. His grandparents are extremely important to him. He has an uncle who is a builder whom he very much admires. That same uncle often encourages Patrick's liveliest, rowdiest side. Patrick's older cousins see him as one of the guys. Patrick's close friendships have been selective, but are deep, long-lasting relationships. Patrick's friends tend to see him as a leader and allow him to be in charge. He is usually the one to initiate an activity. He also tends to out-argue other children, sometimes becoming bossy. Whether family or friends are involved, Patrick is a loyal supporter, someone to be counted upon. Patrick also likes time alone and takes time out from social activities to do things on his own. He is very much a homebody and doesn't like to sleep over at other children's houses, but he will have friends over to spend the night at our house.

Interests, Choices, Preferences. You already have a good picture of Patrick's interests from his work. He likes things that move — machinery, vehicles. He observes them closely, makes them, invents them, using boxes, foil, and tape. The only purchased toys he really wants are usually trucks or other vehicles. In his play and the related building, the FBI, the police, detectives at work are frequent themes. In the play and in making things, he re-works, adds details to lend authenticity. In general, he is experimental, inventive — with food coloring, with recipes. He likes to help me cook. He loves movies and re-enacts them. Right now he has learned all the music for *Beauty and the Beast.* The *Back to the Future* series is another favorite. Books are an important resource to him for information and as a support to his own observations of the world. Patrick is an avid listener to stories. Books that appeal to him include Greek myths, books about how things work, the FBI, spies, and stories such as *The Firebird, My Father's Dragon.* Outdoors, he creates hideouts and collects rocks, "fossils," and other things.

Formal Learning. Primarily, Patrick learns by re-making the world around him. Doing this, it is as if he sees the whole, which he then sculpts or molds, using the malleable materials like foil which are his preference. Real parts and critical details are important to him, but he doesn't build up from them. The same is true for Patrick with respect to reading. Decoding didn't come early and wasn't learnable through a phonetic approach. When he was asked by his sister to try to sound out a word, he replied, "How can I sound out a word when it is already there?" For Patrick, learning to read has to start from the wholeness of story and from his own ability to use language fully and richly. In general, Patrick needs to be in charge of his own learning. As he sets about to know the world by re-inventing it, he needs adult support but not the kind of teacher-directed activities that take things out of his hands. The drama or story Patrick creates around his interests goes far in helping him explore the possibility of his own thought as well as provide a connection with others.

Immediately following Mary's presentation, Peggy, Patrick's kindergarten/first grade teacher, gave her description of him. Peggy prefaced her story of Patrick with a brief mapping out of her classroom, the activities available, and other important dimensions of the learning context. Drawing that map, she stressed the many materials available for the children, the flow of activities through the day, interrupted only by the schedule of special activities such as physical educa-tion and art, and the ease with which new children find their ways into activities through the familiarity of the children returning to this multi-age classroom for the second year. (The account which follows is paraphrased and condensed.)

Physical Presence and Gesture. Patrick is a small but well built boy, who is now seven. He has a big grin and even as he is entering the room, he's talking. He has large, strong, energetic hands which he uses to put things together and also to get things undone when they are stuck. As he works, he is typically in a kneeling position — a posture and manner of focusing which reminds me of Rodin's Thinker (Note: this is the same image that arose independently from the description of Patrick's work). He usually works on constructions and often invites other people to join him. Another typical stance is feet apart, hands on hips. It's "the look" that he likes. Patrick is verbally confident. The more he concentrates, the more he talks it out and ultimately solves it. Children listen to Patrick. He has a wonderful tone to his voice, a low, even register that is clear and precise. He captivates others' attention. He is playful and full of energy. He has both a great climbing ability and a built-in safety factor. His eyes especially show his sensitivity to people. He has a way of explaining himself with a look.

Disposition. Patrick is a watcher of things, but not merely as an observer. While it is not necessary for him to be the boss, he is the holder of the ideas and this is very important to him. We always know how Patrick is feeling. When he is upset, he will cry, but he accepts comforting and redirects his energy. He is very adept at arguing and explaining to others. Issues of fairness are important to him and repeatedly brought up. Patrick's ideas and his enthusiasm for them are magnetic for other children; they tend to be enticed into his story. He maintains a high energy level all through the day.

Relationships. His peers are important to Patrick. Other children tend to assume his leadership. It's usual for another child to ask, "What are we going to do today, Patrick?" Patrick is a loyal friend, but he is not dependent for his own well-being on the company of any particular person. He is not dependent on me either and there is no effort to win my approval.

Interests, Choices, Preferences. Patrick announces himself. He says, "I make things!" or "I'm a real scientist because I am an inventor and a builder!" The materials he uses are very important and he is remarkably adept in the way he handles them. He understands that tape is a fixative but also that it can be used to simulate a line or connector. Used for the latter purpose, he folds it in half to make it sturdy. What he does, he does with completeness. Sometimes there is a dramatic theme that appeals and appears in a series. Ghostbusters was one of these, at least in part because it provided a lot of room for invention and making things like slime packs, of which there were many versions. Often his play is a reenactment of some event or experience. For example, after the school pictures were taken, he returned to the room and made a camera, sat the children down, took a picture, and then presented them with the "photo" — a picture he had drawn of them. Patrick plays out his interests all over the classroom. He is filled to overflowing with spontaneous activity.

Formal Learning. Patrick interacts with all kinds of materials. Stoppers, beakers, tubes, wires, tape, batteries, bulbs are all familiar items in his repertoire. He gravitates toward information and has an abundance of it. He returns to the issues that are important to him like the fairness theme. He draws, recreates, makes, talks about what he is doing. He is a boy in charge of his own learning and full of questions. The questions verge on big ideas; for example, he asked, "Do numbers end?" He has confidence in his ability to "get" things. He found the library and quickly discovered its workings. He knows exactly where to go to find what he is looking for. He uses and recognizes all the words that are important to him like "spy," "police," "FBI." He knows the authors he prefers. He is interested in real books and big, important stories. He is not interested in little reading books. It is the large ideas that appeal to Patrick.

A sampling of the questions raised illustrates how caring the group had become of a child none of us had ever met.

After Peggy's presentation, Pat explained that in a school setting the chair would next ask for comment or descriptions from other faculty familiar with the child. The chair would provide any relevant medical information or pertinent material from the child's previous school experience.

Since there was no additional data to be provided on Patrick, Pat opened the discussion to participants, by requesting our questions and comments. As we raised our questions, photographs of Patrick, many of them depicting him at work on his constructions, were circulated. A sampling of the questions raised illustrates how caring the group had become of a child none of us had ever met.

Q: Does he write? A: He labels or dictates, but he isn't really interested in writing longer pieces for himself.

Q: Does he have any relationship with the girls in the class? A: He has four or five close friends of whom one is a girl. He certainly has conversation with many of the other girls.

Q: What will he read? A: While the small *One, Two, Three* books frustrate him, I'm confident he will be a powerful reader — he just hasn't decoded yet. His understanding of story is fully developed. In *My Boy*, the story of a puppy, he needed to know the whole story before he entered it on his own.

Q: Is the second grade teacher going to be as tolerant and facilitating of Patrick's interests as Peggy has been? A: The current second grade teacher allows him to bring in materials to make things. He will, though, start bumping up against things like spelling lists.

Q: Is there a downside to the focus on one's own child? A: Well, I suppose it is a little embarrassing, but it is such an important way for a parent to have a voice in the school and to be part of her child's education...

We ran out of time before we could make a full set of recommendations. It was clearly evident to most of us that Patrick needed to continue to have plentiful materials in the classroom and to initiate his own learning, with the teacher taking her cues from him. Pat pointed out that as suggested from the Description of Work, Patrick will come to reading and writing from his grasp of the big picture and the inner workings of the parts in relationship to that full context.

In her final summation, Pat called to our attention the way in which our focused look at Patrick had raised broad school issues affecting many children:

Patrick and many other children are active learners, requiring materials to make things and the time to do the satisfying work of inventing, re-enacting, internalizing knowledge. In schools, both materials, and the space and time to work with them, tend to disappear after kindergarten or first grade.

Patrick and many other children need to see the wholeness and complexity of a process such as reading or math in order to grasp the parts and details. In schools, the tendency to instruct in details and isolated parts persists as the definition of teaching and learning.

Patrick and many other children need to be in charge of their own learning. In many schools, the teacher continues to occupy center stage and to direct and control the learning environment.

She added that if we were a school staff, meeting regularly, the review of Patrick would create the context for us to enter into further dialogue on these important topics, using a process called The Review of an Issue.

There are any number of ways that the processes and ideas developed at Prospect Center can be translated into classroom practice (see Endnotes for examples). The way for me to use the Descriptive Review in my classroom was to introduce it to parents at the annual Parents' Night as the method we would use to structure each parent conference. In my presentation that evening, I emphasized the respect I hold for all the kinds of work that children produce. I suggested that we, the parents and I, could collaborate through the Descriptive Review process to identify areas of interest and strength from the work they had collected over the years and would bring with them from home to share with me. I said my effectiveness as a teacher for their children would therefore emerge from the common language we acquired about their child by looking at these works together.

The resulting work with this group of parents yielded the most informative, enjoyable, and rewarding conferences I have had in my 28 years of teaching. The focus allowed us to use our time together wisely. It directly pulled parents into the process as they searched for their children's work at home in preparation for the conference. Most parents allowed the children to take part in deciding which work would be brought to the conference to share. The children themselves, while not present at the actual conference, were not anxious about any "report" that their parents might receive because they knew the centerpiece of the conference was their work. We were all enriched by the process. Children who had stopped drawing, painting, and woodworking some years earlier in favor of more "grown up" work expectations began those works again. They contributed to my children's art collection and filled their school life with their many gifts. We all found common ground together.

Endnotes

1   Margaret Himley, Shared Territory: Understanding Children's Writing As Works. (New York: Oxford University Press, 1991), p. 28. Quoting Patricia Carini.

2   *Ibid*, p. 59.

3   *Ibid*, p. 149.

Developing a Child-Centered Program for Young Adolescents

A Working Group Facilitated by Cecelia Traugh and John Colgan-Davis, Friends Select School, Philadelphia, Pennsylvania

Description by David Philhower, scribe, and Simon Firestone, editorial assistant

Many people look to the youth of America for hope, but now they are worried by what they see: sexual promiscuity, drug use, senseless violence, and crime. It sometimes seems as if kids are growing up too fast. One conclusion that can be drawn from the increasing troubles of adolescents is that we, the adults, are failing them. As teachers, we must ask ourselves, Are schools meeting the observed and expressed needs of adolescents, or are they operating on the assumptions of adults? Ten of us met to consider how schools can better serve adolescents.

We decided to use our worries as our impetus and our personal experience as our guide. We began our query by silently reflecting upon what adolescence meant for us. Out of this meditation came a stream of memories and impressions, feelings, and observations. One of the first things we ran into was fear. We were afraid that the current generation of children is growing up too fast, but we also admitted a more universal fear of adolescence itself. One man said, "Who can walk through a hallway jam-packed with middle schoolers between classes and not feel uncomfortable?" Why are we unnerved? We all went through it, we responded, and it was uncomfortable at the time. There is so much turmoil and change implicit in adolescents that it is hard to know what to do with them. Their physical changes bring about a new set of questions and problems. Adults seem to have relegated adolescents to a marginal place in our culture. Set between the two known quantities, childhood and adulthood, adolescence is a mysterious unknown.

Our goal for the workshop was to develop a model for a child-centered adolescent program. In order to do this, we needed to get back in touch with the child's perspective through our own memories and experiences. We remembered all of the ways we changed — our relationship to family, authority, and even our own self-image. We either conformed or were radically, defiantly different, and in every case insecure. We struggled with too many questions and made up the answers as we went along, unaware of our own assumptions but extremely self-conscious.

From an adult perspective, adolescents seem out of control, full of emotional heights and depths. All agreed that adolescents were not too easy to live with. Adolescence is a time of parental fear, of worries about all of the powerfully negative ways a child can choose to express independence. Yet it is also a time of amazing imagination and energy, a time for discussions and brainstorms that could flood a school. All of our group's members worked with adolescents because of their vitality.

With all of these ideas out on the table, one of the facilitators raised a powerful and far-reaching question: considering the qualities that we just came up with, what would education be like if it were geared towards a typical adolescent? In order to free our minds to think in new ways about this problem, we were told to dream. We let our minds imagine a school that could respond to the needs of adolescence. We didn't think about the application of our ideas at all. We just dreamed, and from these dreams we hoped to find the inspiration to change the reality of middle schools.

The group came up with many different ideas. Adolescents need time to follow their individual interests. Let social issues drive the curriculum. Don't use the school as the sole center of their education. They should all do Ta'i Chi together. Adults who are connected to kids should set aside standardized expectations in order to create a personal space for the kids. Students should spend one day per week outside of school, in an internship. There should be real democracy in school.

After all of these ideas and others were expressed, the facilitators proposed general categories of changes, arranged according to the needs and issues that the changes address:
• Physical change
• Relationships among kids as a curricular issue
• Improving the interpersonal relationships between kids and adults
• Rites of passage and the roles of different people in the community
• Intimacy
• Personal changes and their effect on other's expectations.

The next exercise was to take one of the above issues, reflect upon our schools, and imagine a step we could take toward addressing it. Most of the ideas had to do with improving or changing the relationships between adolescents and adults, and more specifically between students and teachers. One man suggested that teachers should consider students to be their clients, rather than catering to the desires of parents. There are competing visions of what middle schools should provide, with government, parents, and students having some different interests. He pointed out that when conflicts between these competing interests occur, the needs of the students often come last. By thinking of students as clients, teachers will serve their needs, as in any other business relationship. While education is definitely not a business, his comparison pointed out a serious flaw in the curricula of middle schools — they don't truly answer certain needs of their students. We need a basic paradigm shift, away from the mandates of adults and government and towards the experience of students, in order to develop a child-centered program.

Autobiographies, curricula which develop out of student interest, and individualized programs were suggested as means of connecting teachers with student concerns. Dialogue journals, in which students are free to write what they wish and teachers can observe their students' thoughts privately, also came up as a way to help adolescents receive responses to their questions. Teachers can also anonymously share common issues among students, creating a space where issues that seemed too personal become a basis for unity. Eventually such a process could culminate in open class discussion of issues that are rarely discussed.

...in order for children to speak, teachers must be quiet.

Someone suggested that teachers must be empowered to have ideas and suggest changes through their own journals and discussions. Without allowing teachers' expression, there will be less willingness on the part of teachers to listen to kids, since they themselves feel ignored. Change must happen on all levels of a school if it is to occur at any level.

Another suggestion that involved the relationship between students and teachers was both simple and profound: in order for children to speak, teachers must be quiet. Teachers need to open up structured spaces that students can fill with their own ideas. Teachers need to stop being afraid of noise in the classroom, and instead focus on the tone of conversations. A room can be loud and full of disruptions, or it can be loud with ideas and excitement. Quiet can either mean concentration or the absence of interest. Noise is a less effective measure of what occurs in a classroom than tone.

Several teachers suggested that students should spend one day per week outside of school, and devote the time to a project of their own choice. Connecting the kids with experts in a field of interest, with older people who can share knowledge, and engaging them in family history projects were some of the possibilities of such a program.

The need to connect adolescents with adults was very present in our conversation, and was one of the goals of almost every suggestion. We cannot, however, hope to cure the dilemmas of growing up by providing kids with adult role-models. Middle schools should have the time and space to address the special needs of adolescents. There was a feeling that secondary schools need to lessen their academic expectations so that middle schools could provide an atmosphere in which other issues could be discussed as an integral part of the curriculum. In order for middle schools to become child-centered programs, there must be support from above, from the upper schools, high schools, colleges and universities. There is little time to value persons and their experiences when worries about college admissions drive our curriculum.

Much of our talk felt urgent as we discussed the needs of adolescents. All of us had needs which had never been addressed by adults when we were young, and we all felt a sincere commitment to helping young people. Each one of our ideas was a step closer to making a child-centered program in our own schools. Just being given the time to dream was very, very important.

Using The Big Questions Children Ask:
How Children's Interests and Teachers' Interests Can Intersect and Inform Curriculum and Assessment

A Working Group Facilitated by Rhoda Drucker Kanevsky, Philadelphia School District, Philadelphia Pennsylvania

A Description by Steve Smith, scribe, and Rhoda Drucker Kanevsky, presenter

Session One: Attending to Student Discussions and Student Work

We began by talking about children and how we can develop curriculum from closely observing the interests they reveal when engaged in classroom activity and, then, noting what they ask. We want to learn children's interests and ideas from examining their drawing, writing, and talk. Rhoda Kanevsky read from Eleanor Duckworth's article "Opening the World" in *Science Education, A Minds-On Approach.* "First we want to acquaint children with the world itself, with all of its fascination. Second, we must start and end with the student's knowledge rather than someone else's, no matter how authoritative."[1]

We discussed what the participants wanted to know about thematic curriculum, the meanings of terms like "child-centered" and "emergent curriculum," and their personal goals for this workshop. Although the group included teachers from many different situations — including independent, public, pre-school, and high school — we established some common ground for ourselves to consider curriculum. This included the value of observing and describing children and their work, and of providing opportunities for children to construct knowledge within the context of an educational program appropriate to their ages and needs.

As a way of gaining children's perspectives, we took turns reading aloud individual comments that first graders made about silkworm eggs developed in Rhoda's classroom. We discussed common forms of description used by the children, including reference to color and size, and the use of metaphors. We also noted how children listened to each other and developed each other's comments. One student constructed a theory that used another's statement. We observed that most of the children related what they saw to themselves; for example, one child talked about the "nose" of a caterpillar.

Large ideas and interdisciplinary activities could be developed from these discussions. Discussions could occur around other experiences and ideas in the classroom. We saw the importance of children's questions in curriculum planning. Teachers could find ways to reflect children's interests as they design educational programs. Rhoda emphasized the etymology of the word interest: *inter-* means between and *-est* means being. Taken together, our thought and the children's thought can create curriculum.

Student discussions can give us a way to evaluate the prior knowledge and ideas children bring and to make plans for provisioning learning activities. Discussions can help teachers evaluate understandings and chart the direction of children's thought. It is useful to look at the range of comments children make in order to provide activities and materials in the classroom that will interest all children.

We talked about how tensions in our own situations can make it difficult to connect with students. How can a pre-school teacher communicate effectively with young children? How can a special education teacher generate themes in her classroom when children are defensive and angry? How can older children who have not had exciting experiences in school begin to form a community and take ownership of their own learning? Teachers spoke about trying to interest all students and wondered how to provide entry points for all the children. How can we juggle the expectations of parents, administrators, school systems? It feels as if we can't do enough — we feel "overloaded," we need to establish priorities. We want to put excitement and wonder back into our classrooms at the same time as we give students what they need to succeed. Questions of risk-taking, trust, and time — time for students and time for teachers — came up again and again.

Rhoda suggested that ideally teachers should take the time to watch and listen to children, keeping notes for reflection. She encouraged teachers to save student work and whenever possible bring small groups of teachers together to talk about students. The descriptive processes developed by Patricia Carini, founder of the Prospect Center and her colleagues, are useful formats for conversations about teaching and learning. These formats make it possible for groups of teachers to have productive conversations about particular children. Rhoda described collaborative groups, like the Philadelphia Teachers' Learning Coop-erative, which regularly engage in these processes, emphasizing that the knowl-edge that emerges helps all the participants to become more thoughtful, responsive teachers.

Session Two: Describing a Natural Object

We described a plant, taking turns around the circle. There were many comments about how a plant grows, what it looks like at different times of year. There were questions about functions, purposes, uses, relationships of its parts, how it moves, feels, smells. Particular descriptive language included the aesthetic aspects as well as scientific ones. In general, teachers saw that the value of this kind of talk was that the more we know about how things grow in particular, the more it makes us think about other growing things. We realized that one needs time to see things. A teacher said, "I really wanted to know the name, but does the name add information?" "It made me think about the way things come together," another said.

We talked about the kinds of knowledge that we derive from description. Rhoda believes that we best know something by describing it. What large questions that relate to academic disciplines could be asked on the basis of a description? How could we go about designing projects and larger studies that would incorporate the questions and interests which emerged in discussion? Which ideas cut across academic disciplines?

Children and adults alike are always trying to make sense of the world, making relationships and connections. We pointed out the different ways each of us approached the task of making meaning. We closed by comparing our remarks to the ones children made when they were observing silkworms.

Session Three: Gaining and Sharing Teacher Knowledge

Examples of room arrangements, schedules, student journals, art work, and science diaries were shared. Participants discussed tensions and constraints in their work and the implications of this conference for their own classrooms and situations. We all agreed that teacher knowledge is rich. We are immersed in the classroom and need to have opportunities to articulate what we know about teaching and learning. It is important to provide opportunities — in classrooms at all levels — for student-initiated work in which students take charge of their own learning. Many teachers talked about how to develop a community within the classroom, where students feel like they belong and have a voice.

There was much discussion about the need for a long view. It was important to have time to share insights and discuss student work with colleagues. It is equally important for students to have long periods of time to stay with projects.

We then discussed learning as a process of making sense of the world. Connections are exciting for children — they create a sense of control. Seeing patterns creates safety. A teacher pointed out that it's important to let children know that you, the teacher, don't know all of the answers. Rhoda pointed out that when we look at the life cycle of a caterpillar, we pay attention to things that stay constant. At the same time as we are looking at growth and change, looking at the continuities themselves can be new and strange. She spoke of removing what Dewey called the "cotton wool of life," and seeing things from new perspectives.

Rhoda emphasized the importance of receiving continual input from the children. She insists that they write in their journals every day. One participant asked Rhoda how to create discussion when students are unenthusiastic and call themselves stupid. She said, tell them, "I'm interested in what you *think*."

Endnote

1   Eleanor Duckworth, Jack Easley, David Hawkins, Androula Henriques, Science Education: A Minds-On Approach for the Elementary Years. (Hillsdale, New Jersey: Lawrence Erlbaum Associate, 1990).

Progressive Education in Action: The School in Rose Valley
A Workshop Presented by Edith Klausner and her School in Rose Valley Students

Description by Richard Tchen, scribe

About a dozen teachers met with Edith Klausner, the principal of The School in Rose Valley (SRV), in the School's library for an informal talk. Edie began by stating that The School in Rose Valley teaches children from the preschool to sixth grade, and was founded by parents as an alternative to traditional schools. While many other progressive schools that were founded in the 1920s and 1930s have not held fast to their progressive ideas, SRV has. "Families," Edie affirmed, "continue to care for SRV," a comment which was later reinforced for me during a conversation with a faculty member. Between jump shots on the basketball court, he told me that he was also an alumnus of the School, his father attended SRV, and his father's father helped to found it. SRV has retained a tradition of family involvement, even to the point of their maintaining the School's grounds. The School tends to draw parents who like to work with their hands.

The School is organized in mixed age groups. The younger children look up to older ones as models. This grouping also discourages unhealthy kinds of competition because of the give-and-take dynamics among the different age groups. Edie said that one of the bonuses of her position as principal is getting intercom calls from excited teachers who want her to come and see what is happening in the classroom. The admission drew smiles from the audience.

SRV uses the National Council of Teachers of Mathematics (NCTM) Standards, which stress problem-solving and real life applications. In math kids do lots of surveys and survey results were posted on classroom walls everywhere. SRV also uses calculators as a "creative medium."

The school strives to educate the whole child's creative, emotional, social, physical, and intellectual capacities. SRV encourages children to make choices, as individuals and in groups, from how they spend their recess to how they will raise the money for their annual trip to the National Storytelling Festival in Tennessee.

A member of the audience asked Edie about faculty tenure at SRV. She replied that the teachers average between three and nine years of teaching experience, with a high of twelve years. Edie admitted some bewilderment at these figures because, she said, "The pay is not very good." Another member of the audience asked about class size. Edie said that there are between 12 and 20 children in any given class, and the average is about 18.

When the informal chat ended, we began a tour of the school. Edie asked that we notice how the classrooms allow for discussions, drama, and space for concrete materials. She noted that children are not "weaned" from concrete materials as they get older. Instead they are encouraged to continue constructing models as part of their learning experience. Once the student-guided tour began, we noticed an impressive construction made of wooden blocks and mountings of kernels of corn illustrating the magnitude of the number 100. Also, nearly every room housed a snake, rabbit, or other animal. Gail, a principal at an Upper Darby public school, was moved to comment, "Such a cozy place!"

We learned more about SRV from the student tour guides. The students and faculty are on a first-name basis; students remain with the same teachers for an average of two or three consecutive years; almost every class has an assistant teacher; science classes are usually held outside; the blackboards are most frequently used by the students as drawing boards. John, of the Devereaux Foundation, remarked that SRV appeared to him as a "combination of camp and school." Gail asked a student, "Is there anything about the School that you don't like?" to which the student guide responded, "No, not at all." "I bet nobody gets sick here," said Gail. "It looks like it's too much fun."

Everything found at SRV produces a youthfully-charged atmosphere. People spoke of children who are "ready to pounce" and "love to come to school." A student tour guide was likely right in claiming that The School in Rose Valley "will probably be my favorite school."

Saving Children's Work to Document Growth and Change

A Workshop Presented by Mary Daniels, Lisa Hantman, and Paula Paul, The Children's Collection Project, Philadelphia, Pennsylvania

Description by Paula Paul and Mary Daniels, presenters

> "Collecting children's work provides an extremely significant process whereby parents and teachers can work together to gain insight into a child's thinking and development." —Mary Daniels

> "For me the most valuable influence on my teaching is to ground myself in my children's creative work, which is done by collecting and reflecting on that work." —Lisa Hantman

> "The archive and our process for collecting and describing work became our statement of what we valued as educators. We were creating a place to document work otherwise passed over, preserving themes and concerns of young people that would have been lost." —Paula Paul

For the past eight years teachers in both public and private schools in the Philadelphia area have been collecting the art and writing of their students and meeting periodically to reflect upon and describe it. Presently this collection has grown to include over 160 files of work from students of diverse racial and ethnic backgrounds, K-12, and is housed in the Childlife Collection at Please Touch Museum.

The decision to collect and describe students' work, and to create a permanent archive for their writing and artwork was serendipitous. Many of the founding members of the Project were already familiar with the methods developed by Patricia Carini and others for looking at and describing children's work. We were also aware that she had founded an archive at the Prospect School in North Bennington, Vermont to preserve the work of students at that school. We drew inspiration from her work and began to imagine an archive in Philadelphia with works of students from many schools, both public and private, crossing racial and ethnic communities.

Simultaneously, many of our early participants were members of Philadelphia Educators for Social Responsibility (ESR). In 1984, ESR was exploring ways to empower teachers to develop more cooperative and participatory learning models through which teachers could respond appropriately to the needs and concerns of their students. ESR felt the Children's Collection Project was a unique way to do this. A steering committee comprised of teachers from the Collection Project planned meetings and provided direction for the Project while working with ESR on related logistics.

Finally, there was a passionate intensity with which many of the founding participants saved the work of students in their classrooms. They longed for a place to unload the cartons, folders, and even drawers full of stories, poetry, and pictures that were too valuable to discard.

The Children's Collection became a project with three key strands:
• Teachers saving individual students' work over the course of one or two school years
• Teachers meeting together periodically to describe that work. (At each meeting we might look at either a single piece of work, several pieces done by a single student, or the works of several students from a single age group.)
• Teachers placing the work they had collected during the year from a few students in The Children's Collection archive for preservation

The archive and our process for collecting and describing children's work became our statement of what we value as educators. We were creating a place to document work otherwise passed over, preserving themes and concerns of young people that would have been lost.

In 1989, we began to reflect on the project. What were we learning by collecting students' work, from coming together with other educators on Saturday mornings to describe that work, and returning to our classrooms with insights gained from the collaborative process? To discover the implications of what we were doing, we engaged in sixteen individual interviews over two years with teachers who had been collectors in our project. We asked them, "How has collecting and describing student work influenced your teaching?"

The following are a few salient themes and quotes which emerged from the interviews:
• We pay closer attention to the individual child buried in the large group, especially the less verbal child. We are better able to tune into the individual student's voice.

> One of the consequences of the teacher's recognition of the child's individuality is the growth of the child's self-esteem.

> Students from whom I have collected come back with work. They like knowing they have an audience. Collecting also supports those students who already like to write.

• Classroom curriculum changes as it grows out of the needs and interests of the students.
• We gain confidence making changes.

> I changed the way I talk with children about their work. It tunes you into what meaning a drawing or a story has for that child.

• We gain greater confidence in our students, even when
their skills are not up to par.

> The power and beauty of their work become accessible to us because we use a
> valuing rather than evaluating eye. We can describe the growth of a child through
> his or her writing and art over time. We gain respect for all students rather than
> honoring only the student who produces the "100," "A," or "excellent" paper.
> Evaluations and tests, by contrast, give information that is piecemeal or that
> merely records skill level.

• We have a better understanding of the impact the contemporary world
has on the child.
• We talk with our students differently.

> Focusing on the work becomes a way to talk to kids about what is important to
> them, their world, and their interests.

In addition to these changes in our teaching, the process of collaborating with
other teachers four or five times a year offers special rewards: the excitement of
shared thinking and the opportunity to compare themes which emerge across
ages (conflict, family, heroes, the future) as well as themes that appear within an
age despite diverse backgrounds.

> I've always loved thinking in groups. My own thinking is stimulated by others in
> this process. After every meeting I thought of lots of things in a different way...my
> work in the classroom had more of a feeling of aliveness.

> Working together feels energizing; our meetings feel like 'it is pleasurable to be
> smart together,' as one of us said. Our process relieves us of the burden of coming
> up with all the understanding alone. You come up with what you can, others do
> the same, and the end result is a fuller and deeper understanding of a work or a
> child than you had when you began thinking an hour before.

Thus, over the years, many of us who have been collecting the work of our students have come to rely on that collected work as a resource which helps us describe growth in our students independent of standardized measures, enables our
students and ourselves to view all of the work they do as work in progress rather
than as a series of isolated assignments or activities, informs us of the interests
and needs of an individual student in a large group, and enables parents and
teachers to view jointly a child's growth over time.

Mary Daniels described the valuable way that a collection of a child's creative
work may transform the usual pattern of the parent-teacher conference. A body
of work collected over time powerfully demonstrates the thematic and skill
changes which have occurred for the child. The presence of the child's work
rather than test scores distinctly alters the intensely evaluative framework of a
parent-teacher conference.

All too often the teacher's report to the parent of the child's "progress" as defined by standardized measures is heard by parents as a judgment of their own success or failure. The parent may react to the judgment of failure with anger, projecting blame on the teacher, or with guilt in the pattern of taking blame upon themselves. The third possibility which the dynamics of the parent-teacher-child triangle determines is that the parent and teacher may join in blaming the child. None of these afford the child the necessary space for her or his own learning task. Children's growth and development depend heavily upon the mutual respect and partnership of the parent and teacher: the parents appreciating the teacher's specialized knowledge and role; the teacher acknowledging the parent's intense and subjective commitment to the child's individuality and future.

The process of reviewing the child's work together is more than a casual look through. It needs to be a savoring, a puzzling over, a joint discovery of interests, themes explored, of problems posed and solved. The parent brings awareness of events and concerns that appear in the themes; the teacher adds her insights and the classroom context. This shared experience may then become a basis for their joint feelings of accomplishment and their joint consideration of what the next steps may be for the child.

No matter where the various members of the Children's Collection teach or how responsive or difficult the children we teach are, when we come together around the Children's Collection we find one striking factor that unites us: each time we approach a child's work we see that no matter where that child has come from, the child is struggling to make meaning out of the world he or she is experiencing.

Writing Mathematics: Math Journals and Mathematical Thinking
Susan Stein, Friends Select School, Philadelphia, Pennsylvania

Description by a scribe and the editors

> "I get angry at myself because I get answers but I just don't trust them...."
> — a participant

Six women and two men participated in Susan Stein's workshop; each explained in turn some of her or his own background and reasons for coming to the workshop. Several people expressed a lack of self-esteem in their mathematical ability. One woman recounted asking a grade school teacher why her answer was correct. He calmed her, "Don't worry. You don't need to know why. Girls don't do math." Another woman claimed that she had been a poor math student and was now a poor math teacher. The workshop focused on why many people lack confidence doing math and how student journals help to boost the students' confidence.

After we introduced ourselves, we broke into groups. Groups were given some non-routine problems to solve collaboratively. Then people wrote a journal entry describing their experience. The discussion which followed came out of the sharing of those entries. From the entries people identified learning styles and ways of thinking, raised issues about collaboration, and discussed the importance of self confidence. We also read the journal materials I gave out that students had written.

Susan mentioned that she assumes that everyone thinks mathematically and she views math journals as a way to expose those abilities both to her and to the students themselves. Someone else added that different people have different learning styles and think mathematically in different ways. Susan agreed and a working list of mathematical thinking was created.

• analytical thinking:
  describe how a procedure works
  explore why a procedure works
  break a skill down "into its parts"
  identify component parts
  find meaning in a concept or skill
  sort and classify

- synthetic thinking:
  put ideas together from different parts of mathematics
  make connections which deepen understanding
  draw ideas together
  recognize the "main point" of a concept
  see the whole

- numerical thinking:
  strong arithmetician
  good sense of number
  estimate accurately
  memorize number facts and arithmetic procedures
  sequential thinking
  play with numbers

- visual and spatial thinking:
  geometric, topologic
  see transformation
  see spatial relationship
  sense of shape, size, volume
  connect analytic/numeric/symbolic ideas with
  graphic/visual representations

- discovering patterns

- translating from verbal to mathematical thinking:
  make new math vocabulary part of one's own language
  decipher word problems using formal mathematics

- translating a solution back into verbal answer:
  bridge language of mathematics & real world, everyday language

- generalizing from observation of specific details

- specializing by trying an example:
  insight, intuition
  speculate, hypothesize, make a conjecture
  apply knowledge to new situation
  use common sense

Given such a range, a student is normally strong in at least some of these areas. When the criteria for evaluating mathematical thinking are limited, however, a student's strengths may not show, and she or he loses confidence in math.

Normally, a teacher will most value the most efficient and conventional answers. Susan considers various criteria beyond the most efficient answers, such as elegance and generativity. She values the solution that a student understands best and can explain best. The math journals help to reveal these strengths, which helps to boost the student's sense of assurance.

The group read a number of anonymous journal entries and math autobiographies photocopied by Sue. In the journals the students described a problem, described their methods of approaching the problem, named strategies for solving a problem, and explained their solutions if they arrived at one. One student wrote, "It has to do with factors of the numbers 1, 4, 9, 16, 25, and how they are different than all of the other numbers. Well, I know why. These are an odd number of factors of 1, 4, 9, 16, 25. Say for 16 — 1, 2, 4, 8, 16." They are also liable to write about a host of other topics; one eleventh grader wrote in the middle of a journal entry on inequalities, "Hopefully when we have our next test, I will do much better than before because I know I wasn't living up to my capability with the score I got. But the school year has just really begun to steady itself and I hope before our interims come out, I hope that my grade will be much better." Writing about the problems demands clear thinking and helps the students to understand and explain the problems. Instead of being unrewarded because they have not found an answer to a problem they are able to write what insights they do have, and thereby feel the process was worthwhile. One girl's eighth grade math autobiography showed that she had gained tremendously in poise and excitement when compared to her seventh grade autobiography, written before she had begun writing in a math journal. Such confidence was crucial in the eyes of the participants of the workshop.

Another benefit of the journals, which Susan did not expect, is that she learns a tremendous amount about expanding her students' repertoire of ways of mathematical thinking. She can identify their strengths and design appropriate teaching strategies.

Special Considerations in Advising Students With Learning Differences

A Workshop Presented by Lisa Barsky and Heidi Hammel, Delaware Valley Friends School, Bryn Mawr, Pennsylvania

Description by a scribe and the editors

Our opening task as participants was to select an item or condition which would act for us as a sensory deficit. Mirrors and blindfolds simulated visual impairments; radios and tape players created auditory distractions. We could also choose to write with our non-dominant hand or communicate by speaking only using words that included the letters "s" or "e." Using our selected device or condition, we then had to introduce ourselves and discuss our expectations of the workshop. In this way we simulated what it is like to function with a handicap.

The common goal expressed by the group was to learn specific strategies for working with children who have learning differences. Participants represented primary schools, high schools, medical schools, and prison education. Afterward, a discussion illustrated how a variety of subtle and not-so-subtle "disabilities" affected people. Most of the "visually impaired" said that they "didn't get the whole picture of what was going on," found it difficult to focus, couldn't rely on feedback from the group or the leaders because they couldn't see, and became irritable, nauseated, or headachy. Those with "auditory distractions" found it difficult to concentrate, felt their "head filling up with noise," and wanted "the whole thing to stop." One participant acknowledged she felt her personality change in the effort to adapt to her disability. We all clearly empathized with the severe blow to a child's self-esteem that any one of these deficits could generate.

John, a teacher at Miquon, raised the issue of educator bias in defining what constitutes a handicap or disability. Several participants noted that when educators discuss learning "differences" or lack of success in the classroom, they are really referring to lack of success in reading and writing. Others added that this is a result of pressure upon teachers to have children demonstrate success in these areas. The group agreed that this is a particular problem for progressive education, which is often misinterpreted by parents or outsiders as having too much "play" and not enough "work."

Strategies for helping children with learning differences in the classroom were identified by our group, including concrete ideas and concepts aimed at reducing the "cultural bias" of our present educational system against learning differences. Our suggestions included: change or alter the environment; ask children to identify their own learning styles and assist them in accepting their ways of doing things; partner strengths with weaknesses; use dyads; change seating; help students identify and practice new learning strategies; teach mapping and cognitive organization skills; differentiate between remediation and compensation; respond empathetically. The suggestions generated were then practiced in brief role plays.

The State of Pennsylvania's mandated definition of learning disabled applies to any child of average IQ or greater who is functioning below average academically. Heidi Hammel and Lisa Barsky suggested educators may find it more helpful and hopeful to focus on learning differences in the way children process information. These differences can then be translated into learning styles rather than the more pejorative label of learning disabilities. By the end of the workshop, our group had gained a renewed understanding of the challenge involved in being able to teach children with diverse educational styles and needs, and more deeply sensitized to the experiences of students in our classrooms.

Writing to Reflect On the Learning Process
Workshop Presented by Leonard Belasco, Northeast High School,
Philadelphia, Pennsylvania

Description by Amy McBride Barker, scribe, and the editors

Leonard Belasco opened the workshop saying that many times people do not
connect writing to practical concerns. Before we, as participants, introduced
ourselves, Leonard spoke to his goals and interests about writing. He said that he
was searching for ways to keep himself inspired to write, and also searching for a
kind of writing that leads to exciting discussion and new ideas. The group of five
women and one man besides Leonard was diverse: there was an administrator,
an art teacher, a word processing teacher, a humanities teacher, and a student of
teaching. One woman was from South Africa, where she teaches English as a
Second Language and teacher training.

Leonard began talking about students keeping journals to write about what they
are thinking. He used an example of a ninth grade communications class that he
was teaching, in which he used the journals as a way for the students to reflect
on themselves as learners and to find their own voice as writers. He noted that
this could be used in almost any classroom setting for students to document their
own progress and to understand something they are trying to learn. Reflective
journals can also be used to further enlighten a child's experience reading a
book. After every so many pages, the students can write how they feel and what
they are thinking about as they read. What is important is that they are looking
at what happened in an individual way.

Another powerful aspect of writing, according to Leonard, is to focus on questions. Students capture in writing the questions they generate as they read. Later
they write answers to their key questions and use this writing in the formulation
of original theses. They find they have a lot more to say when working from
these notes than starting cold.

One way to begin writing is to write about your past learning experiences. A
method that Leonard finds effective is to have students write an autobiography
of their learning, or to ask them guiding questions on a questionnaire about past
learning experiences. To give us an example, Leonard had each participant write
two short essays at this point in the workshop: one about specific experiences
where something had been easy to learn, and one about something that had been
difficult to learn. He further explained the exercise, saying that we should describe how we approached the subject and our feelings.

After we wrote, each of us described our essays, or at least their topics. They
ran the gamut, from learning Chinese tones to modern dance to making bread.

What we all had in common in our essays about something easy to learn was our personal investment and interest in the subject. Many people mentioned that the learning atmosphere felt tangibly different when they were learning something that was easy for them. There seemed to be a relevance that went beyond the classroom into a bigger world. When there is that kind of emotional and physical investment in the subject, a student just doesn't hold back and becomes more and more motivated to learn.

Having students write about their learning styles can be very useful — they can tell you what works for them and how you can work with them more effectively. Our essays about something difficult to learn all contained elements of intimidation, fear, and an unrequited need for support. Leonard talked about his own experience trying to learn French before he understood why it could possibly be of importance to learn a foreign language, and how he struggled with it for that reason. Breaking a difficult task into small pieces is a good way to alleviate frustration. Having students write about their learning styles can be very useful — they can tell you what works for them and how you can work with them more effectively.

Leonard summed up the exercise by saying that a past learning experience can inform future learning experiences, and that from our own essays we could learn the importance of the element of fun in learning.

Then, we started discussing writing as enhancing the learning process. Leonard read an essay that one of his twelfth grade students wrote recently about Kurt Vonnegut's novel, *Slaughterhouse Five.* In the essay, the student wrote explicitly of how she understood new concepts simply because she was not just thinking them, but describing them in writing. Other examples of the use of writing in other disciplines, such as home economics, were discussed. The main idea that came out of the discussion was that sometimes kids can "get stuck" or "get in a rut" in their learning, and writing can be a way to free them because of its explicit discussion of the learning process.

The next topic we discussed was specific ways to use writing in the curriculum. Leonard proposed to have students write an "advice column" to next year's students. By having the students pose the problem, discuss it, devise solutions, and then explain what they found out by solving it, the students are analyzing the way that they learn. Other teachers, he said, have the students do free writing at the beginning of every class. The writing may or may not have specific parameters or themes, but is mainly used to get the students to focus on the subject at hand. A Spanish teacher that Leonard knew had her students keep a journal of their reactions to learning about other cultures. They shared a range of feelings about bringing a new language and a new cultural point of view into their life. They wrote about how their sensitivity and understanding had changed since they had another culture to which to compare their own. The last example of writing that Leonard cited was about special education, and how one teacher had her students write short poems and explore the different levels of drama to enhance their understanding of the learning process.

We took five minutes to brainstorm ways to incorporate writing into our own classroom situations, and shared our ideas. Fiona, from South Africa, explained her idea of dialogue journals that she uses when she teaches ESL and teacher training classes. Dialogue journals are like letters from the teacher to the student, and then the student to the teacher, and so on. Dialogue journals can also be used to increase and improve communication between members of different racial and ethnic groups, and different age groups. For example, they can be used between high school and elementary school students. Dialogue journals hold the potential for helping people to know and understand others better. Fiona said that students can go back and see patterns of change as the dialogue journal grows. Jed, a teacher, noted that writing letters or some form of a dialogue journal could be used to increase and improve communication between parents and children.

The group also talked about students' resistance to writing. Many people had ideas that might help overcome this difficulty, such as the teacher transcribing the student's words, or the student speaking their assignment into a tape recorder.

The techniques and approaches to writing discussed in the workshop can be used singly or in conjunction with each other. They help both students and teachers see the value of writing as an aid to self-discovery and as a facilitator of understanding. Students can understand what their needs are and what strategies are most effective in accomplishing learning tasks. Teachers can find out what their students understand, and whether what they are teaching is what the students are learning. Then they can make appropriate adjustments. Used for these purposes, writing can be personally meaningful and give students mastery over their own learning process.

Writing to Learn Mathematics

Joan Countryman, Germantown Friends School, Philadelphia, Pennsylvania

Description by a scribe and the editors

Joan Countryman has been a math teacher for twenty-one years. She has taught mostly high school students, but now is becoming involved in projects for younger students. She introduced the workshop by explaining that mathematics provides a way for students to make sense of the world and that writing provides a way for students to make sense of mathematics.

Joan then asked participants to close their eyes and find a vision of themselves doing math — to think about a moment of triumph and a moment of disaster.

The workshop would explore writing in a mathematical context.

As people introduced themselves they explained their reasons for attending the workshop. They included interest in how students make meaning of math, interest in the power of language in math, a desire to find the links between math and other areas of the curriculum, and a wish to learn ways to work with troubled children. The majority of attendees were teachers; there were also a few interested parents and students.

Joan stated that when she initially explored the relationship between math and writing it was an innovative idea because there was an assumption that there was no common ground between math and writing. That assumption, she thinks, is starting to change. Joan then asked participants to close their eyes and find a vision of themselves doing math — to think about a moment of triumph and a moment of disaster. Then people divided into small groups to discuss these moments. In mine, each of the three members were teachers. There was an emphasis on the importance of a good teacher for math and also of a student making realizations on her or his own.

The group reassembled into a circle. Common themes about disasters were: freezing when someone did not understand something, expectations of others, arbitrariness — math being seen as someone else's rules. A common theme of triumphs was the difficulty of remembering the train of thought during a triumph. Triumphs were often framed in terms of one's own behavior while disasters often reflected someone else's behavior.

Joan discussed a method she uses in her classes — the math autobiography. She uses this in order to ascertain students' feelings and learning styles. Students write every week about what they have done. In small groups, we explored an open-ended math situation, the hundred square — which was distributed to everyone. The issue was what you can discover about the hundred square. This is an array of ten across and ten down with numbers from 1 to 100. When the group reconvened we discussed writing activities this problem could generate. The need to use precise language was brought up several times. The pleasure in communicating about math with other people was clear.

Joan reiterated the importance of using math as a way of looking at the world and not separating it from the world. By writing, students can explore what they know and what they don't know. Joan explained another exercise which asks students to write a mathematical explanation for the next year's students.

Writing in math is not an end but a means — a process of realization. Joan concluded,

> When students write to learn, we teachers learn from them. From first graders using calculators, from tenth graders thinking about ellipses, from precalculus students writing test questions, and from sixth graders writing word problems, we learn how students construct mathematics, make sense of mathematics, and come to appreciate their own ability to use it. When students write to learn, they discover their own interests, and come to see themselves as able — to learn, to act, to make sense of the world.

Resources

Countryman, Joan. Writing to Learn Mathematics: Strategies that Work. Portsmouth, New Hampshire: Heineman, 1992.

Edwards, Deirdre. Maths In Context: A Thematic Approach. Portsmouth, New Hampshire: Heinemann Books, 1990.

National Council of Teachers of Mathematics. First Grade Book, Addenda Series, Curriculum and Evaluation Standards. Reston, Virginia: NCTM, 1991.

Russell, Susan Jo, et. al. Used Numbers: Real Data in the Classroom. Palo Alto, California: Dale Seymour Publications, 1990.

Zinsser, William. Writing To Learn. New York: Harper and Row, 1988.

Progressive Education for the Significantly Different Learner
A Workshop Presented by Alexandra Bricklin, parent, The School in Rose Valley, Moylan, Pennsylvania

Description by a scribe and the editors

The history of education has been marked by separation of disabled children from non-disabled children. Only in recent decades has there been a movement toward inclusivity. In 1817 Thomas Gallaudet established the first education program for the deaf and dumb. The first compulsory education laws were passed in 1842, but excluded those with disabilities. In the 1950s and 1960s, there was a movement to have special education classes in public schools, although the profoundly impaired were still institutionalized. The Parent Advocacy Movement was initiated by parents who wanted an education for their handicapped children. Their efforts contributed to the enactment of Public Law 94-142 in 1975. This law requires free and appropriate education in the least restrictive environment for all handicapped children. Educational programs must provide "specially designed instruction and related services" and maximum opportunity for instruction with non-handicapped peers. The law also requires that programs be fit to the child, rather than the child being accommodated to pre-existing programs.

Recent decades have shown shifts in attitudes, awareness and approaches to teaching students with special needs. Terminology has changed from "retarded," and "handicapped" to, "students with special needs," and then to "significantly different learners." However, separate education leads to isolation, loneliness, and stigma, despite the change in label. A "circle of friends" diagram demonstrates the lack of inclusivity that people with special needs often experience. The diagram consists of four concentric and progressively larger circles. The small inner circle contains people who the student loves and with whom they are most intimate. The second circle contains people the student likes and with whom they are good friends. The third contains acquaintances and people with whom the student does other activities. The final circle is for people who are paid to be in the student's life. Most significantly different learners have few people in the intimate circle, nobody in the second and third circles, and the rest of the people in their lives are in the outer circle. Further, handicapped students are rarely included in any circles of most other students.

Merging special education and regular education is necessary to create inclusivity and provide learning environments which reflect the world. The participants reviewed a description of what inclusion means and does not mean, which was adapted from *Beyond Separate Education* by Lipsky and Garnter.

Inclusion Means:
• Children with disabilities are educated in regular school settings, regardless of the severity of their disability.
• Special services are provided in regular schools.
• Regular teachers and administrators are supportive of the student and parents.
• Students with disabilities follow the same schedules as non-disabled students.
• Students with disabilities are involved in as many academic classes and extracurricular activities as possible including art, music, gym, field trips, assemblies and graduation exercises.
• Students with disabilities use the school's cafeteria, library, playground and other facilities.
• Friendships and social relationships are encouraged between students with and without disabilities.
• Students with disabilities receive education and job training in regular community settings when appropriate.
• All children are taught to understand and accept human differences.
• Children with disabilities are placed in the same school that they would attend if non-disabled.
• Parents' concerns are taken seriously.
• An appropriate Individualized Education Program is provided.

Inclusion Does Not Mean:
• Students with disabilities are dumped into regular programs without preparation and support.
• Special education classes are located in separate wings within a regular school.
• Students with a wide range of disabilities are grouped into the same program.
• Children's individual needs are ignored.
• Children are exposed to unnecessary hazards or risks.
• Unreasonable demands are placed on teachers and administrators.
• Parents' concerns are ignored.
• Students with disabilities are isolated in regular schools.
• Older students with disabilities are placed in schools for younger children or in other inappropriate settings.
• Students in special education maintain separate schedules from those in regular education.

Alexandra Bricklin's daughter, Rebecca, is a special needs learner enrolled in The School in Rose Valley because it has an "attitude of a grand experiment and wants to find a way to include everyone." Inclusivity helps the whole school community grow and change. Students learn they might have to react differently to special needs learners than to others, and be sensitive to their needs. JoAnne said that having Rebecca at The School in Rose Valley "enhances our idea of what it is to be human to work with her." Another School in Rose Valley teacher said, "We are all different. It is our responsibility in a world divided to have difference everywhere. We can't shut children away. I'd prefer a whole world." The focus at The School in Rose Valley is not upon, "What is autism?" but upon, "Who is Rebecca and where is she going?"

The successful integration of Rebecca into The School in Rose Valley reflects the school's commitment to integration. The school's approach follows many of the suggestions made by the Pennsylvania Task Force for Inclusive Practices, which Alexandra shared with the workshop group.

What Makes Integration Work
• The existence of a clear philosophy and rationale for integration
• The presence of pro active, visible, and committed leadership from the principal
• A stable school environment
• Strong administrative support from the district
• Parental involvement
• Preparation and Planning:
   a) examine and assess the school and community
   b) staff training
   c) incentives and external encouragement
   d) networking with other schools who are integrating
   e) secure expertise through consultants or technical assistance
   f) develop action plans with realistic time lines
• Collaboration and communication between classroom teachers and special education teachers

Participants at the workshop realized the importance and value of inclusive practices, and the frustration that is "faced constantly with children who are taken out of class either for gifted programs or for problem learning." At the same time, participants recognized the resources and training necessary for successful inclusion. In particular, teachers are being pushed to their limits. The problem is not whether inclusive practices are a good idea, but that they ultimately put more burden upon the teachers. Many teachers say, "No, you can't give me more responsibilities. I'm already a hero." Support systems, including assistants and necessary classroom resources, are needed. Rebecca's successful integration into The

School in Rose Valley demonstrates the importance of a coordinated effort between teachers, administrators, and parents, and the attention given to the individual as a whole person, not just to her or his condition.

Resources

Lipsky, D. K., and Garnter, A. <u>Beyond Separate Education</u>. Baltimore, Maryland: Paul H. Brooks
Publishing Company, 1989.

Stainback, S. and Forest, Marsha. <u>Educating All Students in the Mainstream of Regular Education</u>.
Baltimore, Maryland: Paul H. Brooks Publishing Company, 1989.

Getting To Know Our Students Through the Descriptive Review
A Workshop Presented by Betsy Wice, Susan Shapiro, Kate Guerin, Patty Cruice, The Philadelphia Teachers Learning Cooperative, Philadelphia, Pennsylvania

Description by a scribe and the editors

The primary purpose of the Descriptive Review of a child is to bring together varied perspectives, in a collaborative process, to understand a child's experience within the school setting. By describing the child fully, and in a balanced way, one can gain access to the child's modes of thinking and learning and to see the world from the child's point of view. This understanding offers a guide to the education of the child's fullest potential.

The Teachers Descriptive Review process was developed at the Prospect School in North Bennington, Vermont. It has been used by the Philadelphia Teachers Learning Cooperative for over ten years. The group meets once a week for two hours.

At each meeting there is a chair, note taker, and presenter. The presenter is usually a teacher or parent who has a question she or he would like assistance thinking about with regard to a student or educational topic. The chair facilitates the session. One important role of the chair is to summarize the comments and insights made by the group at different stages of the Descriptive Review process. The chair's position is rotated from week to week.

There are four stages of the Descriptive Review process which are part of each meeting at the Teachers Learning Cooperative (TLC). The first stage is the description of the student or issue by the presenter. It is done according to physical presence and gesture, disposition, relationships with children and adults, activities and interests, and formal learning. Sometimes the presenter doesn't know the child well enough to respond fully to each aspect of the Descriptive Review. In this case, the review process allows for further exploration during the question period, the second stage of the process. Members of the group ask questions of the presenter in order to help understand the child or issues more comprehensively. The third step of the process is a period of recommendations; people offer their suggestions and insights to the presenter with regard to the child or topic. Lastly, the group critiques its own process.

Susan Shapiro, the chair for the workshop session, described her view of the Descriptive Review process:

> When a teacher presents a child, it's a child that is specific to her classroom. What is wonderful about this process is that the child becomes a universal child for us. The teacher's issue might be one that she also is dealing with in her own classroom. So, the kinds of things we find out about today and the recommendations that are made are recommendations that all teachers can take back to their own classrooms.

Betsy Wise described the Philadelphia Teachers Learning Cooperative as

> a loosely composed group. Anyone who wants to come is immediately part of the
> group. There is no head of the group; it is a collaborative cooperative. What we
> typically do is meet every two months to plan what we want to do. I think that is
> what has kept the group together all these years… we are putting energy back into
> people. One of the reasons it energizes people is that we are never doing this as an
> exercise. We're always doing this because it is a burning issue. It's a kid we really
> want to figure out, it's a topic in school district politics we really want to explore,
> it's a medium like Lego blocks, or magic markers, or a kid's picture that interests
> us. These are topics we really want to talk about.

The workshop itself was structured as a Descriptive Review. Kate Guerin, a
Philadelphia teacher, was invited to be the presenter for the meeting. Susan was
the chair of the session. Kate teaches in a split kindergarten. She has an assistant
in the morning and a severely handicapped child who has her own personal aid.
By law, she can take no more than sixty children. Due to the extra help she has
in the morning, she has thirty-one students in the morning and twenty-three in
the afternoon. Jennifer, the subject of the review process, is one of the twenty-
three. Kate and Susan met before the workshop to clarify the focusing question
for the meeting: How can I help guide Jennifer's singularity of purpose towards
academic success?

Kate began by describing Jennifer according to the Descriptive Review outline.
*(The workshop participants, all new to the Descriptive Review process, are re-
ferred to by their first names.)*

Kate: Jennifer is a chunky child with straight blond hair. She stands out in the
class not only because of her skin and hair but also because of her actions, which
are often in opposition to the group. When others move, she is still, thumb in
mouth, watching. When they are quiet and attentive, she is in motion clicking or
snapping her teeth to distract the other children. Failing to distract anyone, she
turns around and tries to distract someone else.

In circle time, Jennifer often sits by me, leaning on my right thigh — always the
right thigh. She is usually sitting in front of a gathered group. She doesn't sit
well. If she can't sit next to me, she often lies on her back. Jennifer's voice has a
hoarse quality like a smoker's cough and doesn't raise it to give answers, but uses
it only to communicate to an adult if necessary.

Jennifer has a kittenish quality about her. She is sort of curled up when she's
working; she hides her work or curls over it. There is something about the way
she rubs against me when she's curled up on me. Her movements are bounding
in a way. But mostly I think about her spirit of independence which is so preva-
lent in cats and kittens. Her disposition is one of cheerfulness or silence. When
she approaches other children, when she tries to get their attention, she acts

without malicious intent, but it has a teasing quality. That makes me think about kittens and how you sort of play with them, and they are sort of playful. She's a loner bobbing about the room on her own agenda.

When she first came I remember most significantly her mother scooping her or pushing her in the room, and leaving. She curled up in her seat and started to cry, but it was not a cry that was audible. Another mother picked her up and she stopped crying. That mother had to leave, so I picked her up. I picked her up the next day when she was crying. When I put her back down, she curled up again. Other actions seem to belie this shyness; she quickly puts herself in the front of a group or at the head of a line. I also caught Jennifer imitating people in a stage whisper kind of voice. In the beginning of class she imitates others rather than looks at her own book. I think she is either rehearsing for her own speech or reading. Or, perhaps she is teasing solely for her amusement as her mimicking goes unnoticed by others.

In gym, she doesn't participate, but sticks her thumb in her mouth and watches. I'm not sure whether she feels alienated by the male gym teacher, or if it is just her own personal disengagement time.

At choice time Jennifer's activities are varied. I name an activity and the children raise their hands if they want to participate in that activity. I then call on one person, who picks others to participate. Jennifer does not raise her hand, so she never becomes a chooser or one that is chosen. She also doesn't tell me what she wants to do, but after a while she gets up and does an activity. Her favored activities seem to be the doll corner and magnetic blocks. When the doll corner is empty, she often becomes very busy there. She does not seem to be aware of the blocks' magnetic properties. She engages in a number of activities that are unrelated to the blocks' magnetic properties such as sorting the blocks into piles.

I am a "book manic." I love books and want the children to love books as well. Jennifer, however, throws me into a panic when she takes the books and rolls them up. When she does this, I take them away from her and make her share with another person. When she shares with someone I have noticed recently that she has been particularly attentive to the other person reading.

Jennifer has no sense of number. She does not know the names of colors or letters of the alphabet. She even has trouble reading her name. I take attendance by putting the students' names on colored popsicle sticks. They have to pick up the stick with their name on it and put it in a can. Sometimes all the sticks are placed in the can by someone before all the children have entered the class. I suspect it might be Jennifer who does this.

Despite having a heavy touch, Jennifer has light handwriting. She does not hold her pencil well. Her hand curls awkwardly in, and she holds her pencil in her left hand at times even though she is right-handed.

Once I took both classes on a trip together in the morning. The parents had been notified beforehand that all students should be picked up by noon. Jennifer's mother was over two hours late. The other staff and I could not get hold of her for a while because she does not have a phone. We finally got in touch with her through a neighbor. When she finally arrived, she called for Jennifer, who was busy playing in the doll corner. Jennifer ignored her. When her mother moved to get her, Jennifer ran off. Her mother then said, "Come back here. I'm not playing with you." I realized I had heard that phrase from her mother before — "I'm not playing with you." I had a strong feeling that Jennifer does a lot of playing with her mother, and her mother does a lot of saying, "I'm not playing with you."

Kate shares two paintings done by Jennifer. She briefly describes Jennifer's brother as a "quiet, unassuming second grader." She also passes around multi-colored leaf rubbings and Jennifer's journal.

Kate: I take dictation to go with whatever the kids write or draw by saying, "Tell me about your picture." Twice Jennifer has said nothing. If I had not been looking forward to this descriptive review, I would not have allowed her to dictate nothing for a second time.

Jennifer's strength is her spirit of independence. Her weakness is lack of knowledge experience and academic confidence.

The chair summarizes Kate's presentation by illuminating particular characteristics. She brings our attention to the kitten metaphor and encourages us with humor regarding the nine lives of cats. She continues...

Chair: When Jennifer has her own paper to do she curls over it because she is not confident in her own work. The curling-in idea is also seen in how she holds her pencil or who she curls up on Kate's thigh.

With magnetic blocks she does not see that they make connections. She hasn't made connections with the blocks and with other people.

There is a contrast of overtness and covertness. She openly distracts, but at other times there are secret things done. Heavy touch and light handwriting.

Jennifer is a loner, watcher, or observer.

There is a period of questions, the second stage of the process. The first ones reveal that Jennifer has no friends. She is also in the minority in the class because she is the only white child. Her mother is known in the neighborhood, but we don't know if her relationships are more than acquaintances. The question period continues.

Fern: Would she respond more if you read to her?
Kate: Yes, but that is the tragedy of being the teacher of so many. If there is a fire in the corner, and there is a child on my lap I need to dump that child and put out the fire.

Fern: I sense a lack of connection in her life...that she so quickly on that first day...sitting on your lap was a comforting thing.
Kate: Well, if you've got nobody else...

Patty: Does she look at the other kids when doing her work?
Kate: I do not assign seats. Yes, she does check with other students, looking at what they are doing before writing. Her circles, however, are thought out. *Kate shows examples of different papers that have circles drawn on them.*

David: Do the other students ever talk about Jennifer?
Kate: No. They are not enough of a group to have discussion about other children. There are undertones of conversation, undercurrents of children making judgments about each other.
Patty: Have things been said about Jennifer?
Kate: I would say that Jennifer seems to be ignored.
Patti: Kind of like a ghost.

Betsy: Where do you think she will be in June?
Kate: That's my concern because I'm looking at her saying, 'You are not coming in with much. How much are you going to go out with?' Last year there were students I felt needed another year of kindergarten, but passed them on to first grade because they need a full day of school, not another year of half days. I'll do the same this year.

Chair: Does she imitate you when you are reading?
Kate: No. I haven't noticed. I've had them about twenty days and have only seen imitation twice.

The chair summarizes the question period to this point. A few of her comments are included below.

Chair: Sitting on Kate's lap is probably helpful for Jennifer. Since Kate has a class with twenty-two other students and only a half day, Kate just doesn't have the time to give her all that she needs. Coming in with little academic skill, another year of half days will not help her, unless there is great improvement. *The question period continued.*

Horace: Are there any relationships that seem stronger and more positive?
Kate: No, I don't notice that in her interactions.
Betsy: Have you seen her with her older brother?
Kate: No. I'm not sure but I may have seen him come pick her up. He was walking and she was skipping or bouncing. This could be really witnessed or it could be an account of how I imagine it would be
Betsy: Were they holding hands?
Kate: Definitely not.
Betsy: Were they carrying their own paraphernalia?
Kate: No. I don't let them out until coats are on. She doesn't have a bookbag.

Kate describes the homework she gives: read a book, write the title of it in a homework book, and copy one letter and one number.

Kate: He has not read her books. One week, however, she brought in her "Hs" that she had obviously done by herself and said, "Look, I did my homework!"

The chair summarizes the last part of the question period before introducing the third stage of the process, recommendations.

Chair: Jennifer takes responsibility for taking her homework book home and bringing it back. She was also responsible enough and proud enough to tell Kate that she brought her homework in even though she did not do the work herself. She is not read to at home. She has no relationships with other children; she is probing, but no solid relationships yet. The depth of the relationship with her brother is unknown. She is the only white student in her class, and one of only six in a school of 1000. The school is a microcosm of the neighborhood, which is also mostly black.

In preparation for the period of recommendations, the chair repeats Kate's focusing question: How can I help guide Jennifer's singularity of purpose towards academic success? Participants shared their suggestions and ideas.

Patty: I am concerned about Jennifer's elusiveness. How can you look at anyone to get a reading on how their academics are or aren't if this is a kid that is kind of elusive and catlike? So, I was thinking about something that helps her define who she is. Draw her hand. Outline her body. Get her to begin to define who she is.

Betsy: Offer her encouragement. Repetition will be helpful. Give her a buddy for reading and other assignments — even for choice time.

Fern: Look at her style of learning. She seems comfortable mimicking. Let her be with some kids that she can imitate, or with someone who has the kindergarten stuff down cold. Also, as I look at her drawings, I see she is striving for higher levels of development.

Chair: Give her responsibilities like putting her in charge of organizing books. Perhaps this activity will lead her to have respect for them.

Fern: I would be much more worried if this was a child that did not turn around and try to distract others or that didn't go to the front of the line. This is a strong little girl and she may have real deficits in terms of what her experiences have been. But she is actively working with her world by the fact that she sorts things by shapes or dumps and collects them. She's manipulating things. She is observing things. She is acting. There is real potential there. You have something to work with. There is potential for real success.

Horace: Have her mother be a chaperone on a trip.

Betsy: Have other children come in and work with your class.
David: Have older children work specifically on certain skills.

Betsy: Do group chanting so that she can experience her voice as part of the group.

Chair: Make a list of predictable books for her.

Horace: Get the older brother involved by helping her academically.

The chair introduces the final part of the descriptive process, the critique. The critique can be about any part of the process or anything that is related to the meeting. A selection of comments from the group's critique are included below.

David: There could have been more focused discussion of the artwork.
Kate: I noticed the lack of comment on the artwork, and thought I should just bring Jennifer's artwork to a review sometime in the future. Often looking at a piece of work in a careful way also brings a picture of the child. This workshop is my picture and the artwork would be her picture.

Patti: I feel that there is a limitation of what I can do. It's an impulse on my part to turn and look, because there are so many problems in so many homes. That's a given. But the processes we use stand on their own and their strengths on their own. Part of my understanding is that the personal stuff that comes to this process is minimal. I'm wondering if we didn't overstep our boundaries.

The chair reads about the inclusion of parental information. "Unless the parent is a co-presenter with the teacher, family data is used sparingly. If the parent is a co-presenter, the format for the review is adjusted."

Chair: The whole idea of the process is that we as teachers work with each child that crosses our threshold and this is the child that is presented to us. When we present a child, that is who we present without a lot of family history. We don't want to invade anybody's privacy. Usually we give an alias to the child so that if there are other people who may know this child, we keep that in confidence.

Betsy: I'm getting really interested in what Horace brought up about the teachers' job being more involved with parents than it once was. I used to be very strict about that threshold...Things have changed and I'm really glad there was room in the process for Horace to say what he said without feeling that he was invading the family's privacy. It helped me think about my own students and their mothers.

Chair: Out of the critique comes a very interesting issue: our role as teacher and where that role gets defined in terms of home. How much can we communicate with the family and in what terms? What are we talking about when we talk to the parents? There are some very fine lines. It's an issue that should be pursued at TLC at some point. When is it modeling? When is it intrusion? When are we just looking at the kid?

Horace: I didn't really think about this issue because I have a very small class. The issues of dealing with parents may be a bit easier for me because I have eleven students. When you are dealing with a larger class, maybe there are some other things that need to be thought of to facilitate that process if it's necessary.

Fern: I do recognize the struggle of dealing with sixty children. That means sixty families, sixty constellations. But I question what to do as a school entity to allow those parents who want to get involved to get involved. I feel that there are certain institutional barriers that frequently get put up. Because we respect privacy we may also send out a message of "don't enter." That's a problem for many parents who know that they don't know how to deal with their children in terms of school, and they want to. If we are so careful to respect privacy, we may do a disservice to those who are ready to ask when we don't have a way to let them in.

Kate notes that in a regular review, she would not be responding to any comments. Instead, all recommendations would be made before the presenter would respond.

Chair: I think your issue is a very valid one. What I think we are alluding to is that we don't want the process to get reduced to a gossip session. That is why we try to respect the privacy of the child's family.

This is a small group with people new to the process. It worked really well. Thank you.

Chapter 4

Philosophy of Experience

Learning best occurs when it is the outcome of interest and experience. Students construct knowledge most effectively when they encounter concrete problems through direct experiences. Learning should be fun, and can be messy. The process we use to solve problems is as important as the answers.

We need to learn not to provide the answers.

The wrong answers are so much more interesting!

Learning often takes time and means having the freedom to muddle through. There is a fermentation process that seems critical. This is where the depth of meaning grows — in the muddle.

We need to celebrate the confusion, reorganize what we're doing. We need to do again and again, like kids: to keep wondering, and looking.

Children and Teachers as Learners
A Keynote Address by Eleanor Duckworth, Graduate School of Education, Harvard University, Cambridge, Massachusetts

Description by Edie Klausner, scribe

My experience of listening to Eleanor Duckworth, like the experiences of other scribes at the conference, was uniquely personal. I encourage those who heard different messages to hold to their impressions; Eleanor's speech was many-layered. Indeed, I appeal to Eleanor herself to forgive my misunderstandings and outright mistakes. This is simply a small effort to collect some of what I heard and to represent that to the reader. My hope is that it might serve as a place-holder, perhaps, until Eleanor's next article or book appears to challenge and delight us.

Eleanor began her talk by placing herself in the context of the ideas of John Dewey. She told us he was her first intellectual hero, and that it was initially as philosophers that both Dewey and Piaget had attracted her attention.

Eleanor then went on to play at renaming her speech and she ended her talk by naming her "next article." Along the way, as she travelled that circle of renaming and naming, she dangled hypotheses before us, snatched them back to rephrase, and raised new questions for our consideration. For me, Eleanor's playfulness, among other things, reflected the mathematical elegance that informs all of her thinking and writing.

> My title, as you may have noticed, is, "Children and Teachers as Learners," and as I thought about it...I could reverse the "and" and the "as." I could say, "Children as Teachers and Learners."

And finally she suggested it could be "Children and Teachers and Learners." The title for her "next article," with which she teased us as she concluded her talk, was "Kids Are Very Different from Adults and Adults Are Just Like Kids." The mystery of that title reflects the labyrinth through which Eleanor escorted us as she revisited ideas from her early observations with children during the Elementary Science Study, considered the work of her colleague and co-author, Androula Henriques,[1] and described her own current work with adults and with graduate students at Harvard and the University of Ottawa.

We "messed about" with Eleanor — her phrase, borrowed from David Hawkins, for open-ended explorations of processes and stuff of science — thinking our own thoughts, catching glimpses of hers; she was a model for us, a moment at the end of the conference when it was okay *not* to understand it all, to let ideas float, catching some by the tail, some not at all, storing others, hanging in there, encouraged by her quote from Winnie the Pooh: "Poetry and hums aren't things that you get. They are things that get you."

In one example of "...and Adults Are Just Like Kids," Eleanor described Inhelder and Piaget's experiences of six-year-olds thinking about phenomena "What makes some things float and other things sink?"[2] The children "just wouldn't hold anything still." They had as many different reasons for each instance of the event as the number of events themselves... some things float because they're big...some things float because they're little...some things float because they're empty...Eleanor continued,

Is something an answer or isn't it? And if it is, is it useful? Is it really answers we seek? Or meanings, understandings, identities?

> I've since realized, that, in a lot of ways, children are not too different from me...perhaps you and me. An example that is very common in my life is, bread rises because there's yeast in it, and biscuits rise because there's baking powder in them, and cakes rise because there are eggs in them — and it doesn't seem to me very different.

Later Eleanor confounded us with drawings of Xs and Os, representing yellow and green one-inch cubes, which in turn represented lemon flavoring and lime flavoring. She asked us, as she has asked others recently, to consider various combinations of those Xs and Os. She began innocuously, placing them in clearly distinguishable sets, and simply wondering which combinations would taste more lemony and which more limey. Eventually she exclaimed delightedly when we were confused about a more complex combination and comparison, that this particular "wonderful dilemma" appeared to confound adults just as profoundly as it stumped children.

And there were questions about *answers*. Eleanor described circumstances when both children and adults pressed for answers, were excited to find them by happenstance, or angry when teachers wouldn't supply or confirm them. Eleanor wondered aloud if answers were satisfying. If indeed, they exist. What do they mean? Is something an answer or isn't it? And if it is, is it useful? Is it really answers we seek? Or meanings, understandings, identities?

Eleanor returned several times to her thoughts about language and her determination that her students "resist using technical terms we may not all know the meaning of." She included many common words in her examples of such technical terms, words such as angle and sonnet, north and south, syncopation and ragtime and Dixie. Her most compelling example for me was when she called for experiencing musical rhythms directly, for hearing and beating out "the relationship between the booms and the bas" and for many repetitions of hearing and feeling that same beat, those same relationships, until they were indelibly recognizable.

> ...the hard job, it seems to me is helping somebody else hear what you hear in the music. Then you can call it syncopation. But if the person doesn't hear it to begin with, it doesn't help to call it syncopation.

Another wonderful and lengthy language example had to do with understanding the meaning of *angle*, and with students' efforts to describe the turnings of strings and points and their bodies and clocks; examples of wedges of pie and camera close-ups and picture frames and The Three Bears...all in the hilarious service of understanding angle.

Eleanor challenged us to think about how we know what we know. Or if we do.

Endnotes

1   Eleanor Duckworth; Jack Easley; David Hawkins; Androula Henriques, <u>Science Education: A Minds-On Approach for the Elementary Years</u>. (Hillsday, New Jersey: Lawrence Erlbaum Associates, 1990).

2   Barbel Inhelder and Jean Piaget. <u>The Growth of Logical Thinking from Childhood to Adolescence</u>. (New York, New York: Basic Books, Inc., 1958).

Resource

Duckworth, Eleanor. "Twenty-four, Forty-two, and I Love You: Keeping It Complex," in <u>Progressive Education for the 1990s: Transforming Practice</u>. New York: Teachers College Press, 1991.

Search Projects: Helping Students Find Answers To Their Questions
A Workshop Presented by Bonnie Bishoff, Friends Select School, Philadelphia, Pennsylvania

Description by Bonnie Bishoff, presenter

> I just hadn't thought of my topic until I came into contact with a situation that dealt with radiation. What had happened was that in PE I hurt my fingers when I caught a soccer ball wrong. The next day, I went to the hospital to have it X-rayed. When I saw the "radioactive area" on the door of the X-ray room, I wondered about radiation. "How could it harm me?" I thought. What are they?...On the way home I realized that I could answer all of my questions on radiation by doing my "Humans and Nature" project on radiation.

Students' questions become the point of departure for personal searches at Friends Select School, where the search process is the center of the Middle School science program. The search process reflects real science, which consists of investigation, rather than memorization. Science is a process of looking for answers to questions one is passionate about and interested in; it is not a fixed body of knowledge found in science texts.

The students' search projects have several distinct elements: a search journal, the process of gathering information, a written narrative about the search, and a symposium presentation with a visual display. The process begins by helping students develop initial questions. Brainstorming possible areas of study gets the "juices" flowing. Sharing searches that others have conducted or continue to conduct helps students consider their own interests. Each year the search projects have a theme such as "math and science" or "humans and nature." Many ideas are generated for these themes when teachers ask key questions which allow students to make new connections between familiar ideas.

Classes read science journals, and the writing of people such as Jane Goodall. Students write about a time when they wanted to know something or became interested in something to which they wanted to find answers. Their stories are often amusing and help students see that they have already been scientists of a sort, and searchers and makers of knowledge.

> This idea came to me from seeing the first dolphins wash up on the beach in 1987. Every day I saw the numbers of dead or dying dolphins increase. Finally, enraged, I wanted to know why this was happening. Was it beyond our control? Or did we cause this catastrophe?

Once ideas are generated, journal writing begins. Journals are used by students to record the entire search process. Initial journal entries are more structured. Students write about the topic they have chosen, where the idea comes from, what interest it holds for them, and questions they have. This step is essential in enabling students to see their own connection to the work. Students also reflect upon their own strengths as a researcher and examine their assumptions. They are asked to describe in full what they know and believe to be true about their topic. This task helps them later when they look back upon what they learned.

> I noticed that the first thing I did was not even in the journal. This important step was brainstorming. In my head, just like in the beginning of the project, I brainstormed questions and ideas about dams. I started with the easiest, most obvious questions, "What does a dam do?" to the hardest question, "How is a dam built?"

Developing an action plan is the next step in the search process. Together, classes brainstorm resources they can use including museums, experts, and experiments. They are provided a calendar with a schedule and guidelines to help them with the long-term projects. In the beginning, students often give each other suggestions about helpful places to go and people with whom to talk. As the projects proceed, students share successes and also see that they are not alone in their struggle. Classmates are a source of inspiration and support.

Students are encouraged to use a variety of methods to learn about their topics. First-hand experience is an exciting and effective way to gain personal understanding of information. This is where the idea of "searching" versus re-searching comes into play. Observation and experimentation assist learning new ideas in a way which builds ownership of knowledge. Interviews, periodicals, and books are used to learn about ideas that other people have about their topics.

> To start my search project, I went to the zoo. I went four times in the course of my search. I observed the gorillas for many hours, mostly four hours per visit. I would bring a notebook and write down all of the things I saw.

As they conduct their investigations, students describe their work and their ideas in the search journal. Every time they do something, they record their activities. These entries include what they learned from each activity as well as new questions which emerge. The journal is not only a collection of notes and factual information, but also a place for students to begin analyzing the process of investigation. How am I getting information? How have my ideas and questions about my topic changed as I have learned more? The search journal also serves as the basis for writing the final narrative about the search project.

> Over the weekend I rode my brother's bike along what I thought was Cobbs Creek. What I found out was that the creek goes under a lot of streets. I saw that humans and nature come together because man made the streets.

Teachers regularly collect journals and correspond with each student. Because they are concerned not to influence or hurt the students' own thinking, teachers do not correct spelling and grammar in journal entries.

The search takes approximately seven weeks. In the first years of the search projects, students did much of the work at home and in local libraries and institutions. Class time was dedicated to library research and discussion of the steps of the process. Students practiced interviewing skills and shared progress reports together. Now, much of the search project is completed using class time. Students make phone calls, read, have conferences with teachers, go to the library, perform surveys, and visit museums during school.

At the end of the search time, students write a search narrative, submitting rough and final drafts and a traditional bibliography. They describe their entire search process including how they selected their topic, what they knew in the beginning, how they learned new things, what they learned, their answers to their original questions, how they might continue their work, and new questions they have developed over the course of their investigation.

The final stages of the search project involve a public sharing of all of the students' work. The Middle School holds a search symposium in which groups of students, grades five through eight, gather according to areas of interest, share the stories of their searches with each other, and ask questions of each other's work.

Then, in the most visible part of the process, the search fair displays are erected in the front halls of the school. For two days the corridors are transformed into a "museum" where each student shares a display explaining the search process and what they learned. The presentations are as varied as the projects; some are informational, others question the viewers' own assumptions, or involve the viewer in a part of the learning process. Students take great pride in their displays and much pleasure in seeing what others have learned.

Through the search process students gain a great deal. They learn to conduct interviews, use a word processor, and read articles for relevant pieces of information. Students develop a sense of themselves as learners and investigators. They learn about defining their question, pursuing something for which they have a personal interest, and documenting their work and ideas. By asking their own questions and writing about their work, students also learn that their ideas and experiences are central to the learning process. With the emphasis on the process of searching as well as what is learned, students gain a sense that it is relevant to think about where ideas come from, how they grow and change, and how ideas can continue to develop.

What becomes clear through their work is that knowledge is not static. Knowledge is not a stable, unchanging set of ideas. It is about working for answers, muddling through and trying out ideas, not always being right, and even making mistakes.

Hands-On in the Primary Classroom

A Workshop Presented by Wendy Towle, second grade teacher, and Robin Saunders, First Grade Teacher, Swarthmore-Rutledge K-5 School, Swarthmore, Pennsylvania

Description by a scribe and the editors

The excitement and vitality of fifteen first and second graders brought a special quality to this workshop. Participants gathered their chairs in a circle around the students, who were seated on the floor. They had come to help Wendy Towle and Robin Saunders demonstrate how manipulatives can enhance math learning in the elementary classroom.

Wendy produced a shopping bag which the children immediately and enthusiastically guessed was full of pumpkins. The anticipation of Halloween must have been on their minds! Robin divided the students into two groups, and distributed pumpkins to each of them. They were asked to sort the pumpkins in various ways, for example, by those which had stems and those which did not. Discussion about the different ways they could sort the pumpkins ensued, and they arranged them accordingly. Various ideas were generated: bumpy and not bumpy, short and long stems, dark and light, hard and soft, heavy and light, spin or no spin. All of the children were engaged and involved. Both groups cooperated and reached consensus quickly.

Each time a group found a new way to sort the pumpkins it was given one unifix cube. Automatically the students began assembling the cubes they received into color patterns, showing disappointment when they didn't receive a cube which had a color to fit their pattern. Interestingly, they had not been directed to make patterns; assembling patterns was second nature to them. Robin brought the two groups together to share the varied methods of sorting they applied. They noticed that each category consisted of exactly two groups. No zero subsets were included.

Wendy sat with the students clustered about her and placed a sneaker next to a big pumpkin, explaining that they would be comparing the pumpkin to a shoe. "Does it look like the shoe of a giant?" she asked. In reply, they said, "It looks like a giant pumpkin next to the shoe." Wendy then introduced and read *Pumpkin Pumpkin* by Jeanne Titherington.[1] As she read the story she asked for responses such as, "Show with your arms how big you think the pumpkin is now," to which they would shape their arms into the size they imagined it to be. Wendy pointed out throughout the book that the author uses objects to show how big the pumpkin is, making it easier to conceptualize the size of the pumpkin.

Each child worked with an adult. Together they measured their heads with string; estimated if the same length of string would be bigger, smaller, or just right to fit around their pumpkin; measured the pumpkin with string; and then taped the string to a chart which read "too small," "just right," and "too big." In this way, the children estimated how their head size compared to the size of the pumpkin, and then tested their hypotheses.

Shown a large pumpkin, the group was asked to estimate how many seeds were inside. Both adults and children estimated: thirty-five, one hundred, two hundred, sixty, one hundred eighty. The pumpkin was opened and the seeds taken out. "Count the seeds by putting ten in a cup." The students began counting and placing the seeds in small cups. "How many cups of ten would it take to make one hundred?" Two, five, and ten, they responded, at which point they were told that when they filled ten cups they could put the ten cups in a bowl to make a "hundreds bowl." The adults sat with the students, helping them count. In the end, there were three hundred ninety seeds — far above the estimates given by children and adults!

The language arts, math and science activities reflected a thematic and interdisciplinary approach to, in this case, a pumpkin theme. By actively involving students and participants, the lessons supported the understanding of concepts through direct experience. The measurement, sorting, and estimation activities were indicative of Math Their Way,[2] a mathematics program which is manipulatives-based and stresses the understanding of concepts through direct experience. Although Math Their Way was not the central focus of the workshop, it is an important resource for teachers integrating mathematics into thematic units, and exemplified Wendy and Robin's approach to hands-on teaching. For example, rather than focusing upon finding the right answer through computation, Math Their Way emphasizes developing strategy skills and tactics, and understanding the concepts and tasks. Strategy skills create understanding, which leads students to formulate answers themselves without a teacher, book, or math rules. The conceptual understanding developed makes the transition to computation and pencil and paper tasks easier and more meaningful. Further, direct experience with math manipulatives develops problem solving, reasoning, logic, patterning, predicting, measuring, and evaluating skills — skills considered by Wendy and Robin to be essential to critical thinking. These types of experiences are important to even very young students, whose early exposure and frequent contact with a hands-on approach strengthens their understanding and thinking skills.

Endnotes

1   Jeanne Titherington. <u>Pumpkin, Pumpkin</u>. (New York: Greenwillow Books, 1986).

2   Mary Baratta-Lorton. <u>Mathematics Their Way</u>. (Menlo Park, California: Addison-Wesley Publishing Co., 1976). The program outlined in this book is commonly nicknamed Math Their Way.

Thematic Unit Approach to Whole Language

A Workshop Presented by Parthenia Anita Moore, William Cramp Elementary School, Philadelphia, Pennsylvania

Description by a scribe and the editors

Literature can be the foundation for the total language program when used to integrate writing, reading, speaking, and listening through thematic units. Using this approach, students can learn across the curriculum in an authentic way while engaged in language skills. Lessons are active and interactive. They reinforce writing skills in context, and are made personally meaningful for students. Parthenia Anita Moore has found that she can use this approach and still meet the requirements of the standardized curriculum for the School District of Philadelphia School.

Recognizing the knowledge her students already have about a subject as well as their questions, Parthenia begins thematic units by asking, "What do you already know?" and, "What would you like to know?" In keeping with this practice, she asked these questions of workshop participants: What do you know about a whole language classroom and what would you like to know?

Parthenia responded to those who were interested in knowing how to incorporate whole language with children at home by suggesting reading aloud daily, obtaining or making tapes of children's books, and allowing children to make their own tapes of books as they read.

By far the biggest concerns expressed were how to use a thematic-whole language approach and still meet the requirements of the Philadelphia standardized curriculum and make sure students are prepared for standardized tests administered by school districts. Ongoing mini-lessons are an effective means for teaching specific skills. In large or small groups or individual meetings, five-to-ten minute mini-lessons teach grammar and punctuation skills in the context of students' current writing. In addition, Parthenia stressed that prior knowledge is the key to future learning. "Before," "during," and "after" activities are built into each unit to strengthen students' knowledge and experience. The "before" activities are designed to create awareness and knowledge upon which students build deeper understanding of the subject. A thematic unit on the *Titanic* demonstrated these three types of activities.

Centered around *The Titanic...Lost and Found*[1] by Judy Donnelly, the thematic unit began with a series of activities before the book was read. In order to better understand and appreciate the text and topic, students completed a mapping activity about boats; they pretended to be in a lifeboat and wrote about the

experience. Students also shared and discussed what they already knew about the Titanic and what they wanted to know.

Once the students began to read the book, they maintained journals of vocabulary words; analyzed the setting, characters, plot, theme, and tone of the story; pretended to be newspaper reporters writing about the sailing and sinking of the *Titanic*; wrote to the captain of the ship as if he were alive today; made up math word problems about the theme; did homework that they pretended was the homework of children on the *Titanic*; learned about the oceans that border the United States and the rivers that border Philadelphia; and made a scale model of the submarine that was used to find the *Titanic* years later. The activities went "across the entire curriculum." After students finished reading the book, they watched a movie about the Titanic and wrote in their journals about what they had learned.

Workshop participants applied the concept of "before," "during," and "after" activities to a thematic unit based on *Lin Po Po*,[2] a Chinese version of Little Red Riding Hood. Participants designed activities related to language arts, math, science, social studies, art, and music in each of the three categories: before, during, and after.

A range of methods is useful for the assessment of students' learning: teacher-and-student-made tests, reading fluency checks, conferences with students, and teacher observation. Helping children develop awareness of their own learning is especially important. Parthenia and her students use the following suggestions to nurture this awareness.

Student Entries in a Weekly Learning Log
• One thing I learned this week is...
• How I learned this:
• Something I didn't learn so well (for older students):
• Why I think I didn't learn this:
• A question I still have is:

Teacher Suggestions
While reading, encourage students to ask:
• Do I Give my full attention to the material?
• Do I Create mental pictures of what I read?
• Do I Stop and re-read what is not clear?

After reading, encourage students to ask:
• Do I Ask what I have learned?
• Do I Think about how this fits into what I already know?
• Do I Decide how I will use this information?

The notion of "before," "during," and "after" activities in thematic units is reflected in the way in which thematic units begin and end. Beginning with the question "What do you already know?" and moving to "What do you want to know?" Parthenia's units end with the question "What did you learn?" It was with this question and its subsequent sharing that the workshop closed.

Endnotes

1   Judy Donnelly. The Titanic, Lost...and Found. (New York: Random House, 1987).
2   Ed Young. Lin Po Po. (New York: Scholastic Inc., 1989).

Teaching for Inquiry: Using Primary Sources in History and Culture Studies

A Workshop Presented by Anna Roelofs and Anne S. Watt, Primary Source Center, Cambridge, Massachusetts

Description by Nora Walsh, scribe, and the editors

"Pottery," "needle threader," "clothing," "map," "toys." These were a few of many examples of artifacts or primary sources which could be used in classrooms in order to engage students in inquiry about other cultures. Anne Watt and Anna Roelofs stressed the value of having students work directly with historical objects in order to draw their own conclusions about what they are, their functions, and their value to a culture. In Anna's words:

> The whole notion of working with a primary source is so that the students can come fresh to the material and have their own reactions and generate their own ideas. They will obviously put it in context, but it is really helpful to have them think about things themselves. We give them real stuff, real materials, so what they are doing doesn't have to be filtered by other people's perceptions. They have a chance to engage first-hand.

Directing the participants to work with partners, Anne and Anna handed each pair a package with an artifact, wrapped up and undisclosed. Accompanying each artifact was an envelope containing written information about it, to be read only after observation of the artifact was completed. Partners scattered about the room to carefully examine their artifacts and work together to come to their own understandings and perceptions of the objects and the cultures from which they came. They examined a Southwestern Indian Kachina, arrowheads, metal skeleton keys, a hand-woven Guatemalan shirt called a huipil, a bronze ceremonial sculpture from China, a Mayan clay fish-shaped whistle, and a Japanese clasp for a sash.

A "Ways to Read an Artifact" worksheet asked participants to "study the object with your eyes and your hands...hold and examine the artifact. How was it made? What is it made from?" "How is or was it used? Can we understand anything else about the culture by answering these questions?" "What was the environment in which this artifact was used?" "Can you make any inferences or guesses about what value this artifact has or had to the culture which produced it?"

Through subsequent discussion it was apparent that each person brought his or her own experience and knowledge to understanding the object he or she was asked to describe. For example, one participant was familiar with various weaving techniques and was able to apply her knowledge when describing the Guatemalan shirt. Her description was rich in technical details, while an artist's or seamstress' description would have stressed different aspects of the same shirt.

One participant noted that artifacts allow us to make connections between the past and the present and to recognize the continuity in cultures. For example, the contemporary Mayan clay fish whistle is similar to the ancient whistles that have been unearthed by archaeologists. Here lies "the connection between the Mayans that were and the Mayans that are." Another participant related the exercise to Patricia Carini's work; just as the descriptive review of a child allows us to gain a more complete picture of the child's values, the descriptive process when applied to an artifact may give us insights into a culture's values.

Other participants described that "right away this process has them looking at details and making inferences — what children need to do a lot." "What is important is that children are making connections between artifacts and life experience. They share their own experience in the process." One participant exclaimed, "I would immediately know the object if I saw it again because I looked at it so closely!"

The Colonial Pocket is a collection of artifacts which shows students ways of thinking about the lives of seventeenth- and eighteenth-century women who wore these pockets in their daily lives. Anna put on an apron which was sewn to include a large pocket. After telling a personal story about how she learned about Colonial pockets, she began to pull objects out of it and asked the group to describe them, guess what they were used for, and list them. Participants called out, "wooden thimble," "wicking," "metal key," "container for needles," "packet of herbs," "diary of a young girl." Anna encouraged the group to think about how these objects would fit into a Colonial woman's life, adding that in a classroom there would be lengthy time for discussion on this topic. The lesson would end with the writing of a play or a story about the woman who could have worn the pocket. The challenge to the students: make the person as real as possible using the skills of inquiry developed.

Betsy, a teacher in the Philadelphia public schools, described her experience:

> This is a wonderful process. I think this is progressive education at its best. What I loved about it is that the kids that I teach, street kids, who are very observant, can get a whole lot out of the descriptive part... The descriptive process is a really nice process to get them motivated...What is more motivating than to look at this thing and wonder what it is?...They get attached to the natural objects we have studied. They want them, they wanted to know all about them, so they want to draw them, and read about them!

Resources

Anna suggested several places where one can locate artifacts for classroom use: replicas from museum gift shops, a person of the culture being studied or a person who has visited the culture, the International Classroom at the University of Pennsylvania Museum, or the Primary Resource Center in Cambridge, Massachusetts, flea markets, or your attic.

Published materials are available from the American Association for State and Local History, 172 Second Avenue West, Nashville, Tennessee 37201, Telephone (615) 255-2971.

A Progressive Approach to Teaching a Skill: Touch Typing on the Computer

A Workshop Presented by Kae Kalwaic, Wallingford-Swarthmore Community Education, Swarthmore, Pennsylvania

Description by a scribe and the editors

This workshop was intimate and informal in setting and delivery. In opening, Kae Kalwaic defined four goals she had for the workshop: to show the importance of teaching touch typing on a computer, to present an effective first touch typing lesson, to analyze a touch typing textbook, and to demonstrate how to use appropriate encouragement as a motivator.

Touch typing is the use of the correct fingers on every key on the computer keyboard, enabling the students not to look at their hands when typing. Learning touch typing is not dependent on the individual's reading or writing abilities. Kae said, "In today's world, we use computers in almost all fields. People must know how to type to operate computers efficiently."

Touch typing is no longer taught in many schools, and Kae feels that there are several reasons for this. First, students are now using computers starting in elementary school, but touch typing is typically not taught until high school. The skill is not being taught when the students need it the most. Many administrators believe that touch typing takes too much time to teach and are unwilling to hire business teachers to teach the course. Touch typing is not easy to evaluate; therefore, it doesn't fit in with preconceived grading methods.

Kae then introduced her own text for teaching touch typing, *Touch Down Typing: A Scientific, Energetic, Humorous, Encouraging Approach to Learn to Type on the Computer*. In this book Kae uses encouragement on every page. Even the cover page has a certificate that congratulates the student on having chosen to learn a valuable skill.

The book uses football imagery. "The football theme stresses the primary philosophy of the book — keeping fingers 'touched down' on the home keys. Basketball just doesn't have the terminology! The other reason I selected the football theme is that many young males associate typing with female occupations. Typing for some boys carries the 'stigma' of being feminine. The football theme helps to counterbalance this stereotype."

Kae believes the student cannot fail using this book. She uses small steps and guarantees to motivate students, "The problem with most texts is that they introduce too many keys at a time. The books don't give enough easy practice on each key. My text enables the students to experience success by introducing fewer keys at a time. Now students can focus more attention on each letter's location. As the students learn the key location, they color in each key, one at a time on a reproduction of the keyboard. The students can see and chart their own progress."

Kae presented a handout comparing encouragement and praise. "Praise can often be as much of a problem as criticism," she noted. "Not a single typing book uses encouragement as a major theme in helping students to learn. Yet in learning a skill, confidence in one's personal ability is of the utmost importance."

Kae introduced the necessity of teaching in context using the example of teaching the students to compose directly onto the computer. The students not only create original work, but editing their work becomes considerably easier for them, saving hours and hours of labor. Writing becomes enjoyable; and, of course, they will produce a very readable copy. Touch typing gives students a skill that will help them succeed in whatever they do.

In closing, Kae asked if there were suggestions or questions. She stated, "If it works, it works, I wouldn't change the model. Asking what kind of feedback you get from the kids two years after they've left your class, that's the question."

After Earth Day, What Now?
*A Workshop Presented by Greg Williams, The Miquon School,
Miquon, Pennsylvania*

Description by a scribe and the editors

The workshop was conceived as open-ended — an opportunity for participants
to share their work in environmental education in terms of successes and
constraints, to ask what progressive education principles have to offer environmental educators, and to share aspirations and dreams. The premise was that
Earth Day 1990 provided a spark for enhanced environmental education (EE)
in schools but left teachers with many questions as to how to best integrate it in
the curriculum.

Members of the group introduced themselves by describing their experiences
in environmental education. Greg started by taking his fifth and sixth grade
classes in San Francisco to an EE center at Point Reyes National Seashore. He
"found that the time I spent there with my class was the most substantive and
the most exciting and the most changing thing that happened all year." He
wanted to do this more, so eventually he became a freelance naturalist. He
started a program called Walk a Crooked Mile before returning to his former
school as a specialist.

He found it was possible to teach EE in an urban setting "with maybe three
trees in the whole complex. The kids encountered the natural world in a different
way than we do, I'm sure." He also learned that having access to diverse ecosys-
tems does help in teaching EE.

At The Miquon School, there are ten acres of land that the kids have abused by
playing on it. "The school is trying to figure out how to get kids to make some
decisions about their use of the land."

Jim, a teacher at Princeton Friends School, has successfully persuaded his administration of the need for EE, so has taught environmental science. They used the
proceeds of a community recycling program to purchase rainforest acreage.

He said, "Last year, I started teaching much younger kids because I could always
tell that those who arrived at my classes in high school already had made up
their minds on the subject of the environment." He was interested in "at what
age do those kinds of commitments form?"

Mike, a Swarthmore College student, said, "When I look back, those early years
in school were very formative, and had a large impact on who I am today. I've

had a lot of unusual experiences with EE, The Global Rivers Environmental Education Network, working as a camp counselor, and the Global Walk For A Livable World, a community of a hundred or so people walking from Los Angeles to New York educating people about the environment."

Mira is an art teacher at Princeton Friends and came to the United States from South Africa and Namibia last summer. "Coming to this country and finding different landscapes, different beauty and...seeing the amount of environmental awareness here," made her want to incorporate that into teaching art.

One of the things that I'm constantly facing is how to deal with environmental issues where people are already dealing with other issues of the immediate environment — violence, drugs...

Bart, also a Swarthmore College student, worked in an appropriate technology museum last summer. Now, he's working with a project called Create, in Chester. "One of the things that I'm constantly facing is how to deal with environmental issues where people are already dealing with other issues of the immediate environment — violence, drugs — and telling them what I think is important." This created concern that he find the balance between his values and what others might feel is most important in their situation.

Karen, a graduate student at the University of Pennsylvania, pointed out the importance of "choosing agenda items" — picking issues and making sure that what you discuss is important.

The discussion then centered upon questions of importance to the facilitator and the participants. Greg asked, "What ought we to be doing? What's the goal?...I hang out with kids in the natural world because I love it. It feeds my soul, and it's a great way for me to relate to kids, but I've got other agendas, and I think that kids ought to be learning how to become caretakers of the planet or else we've got a problem, ...but at the same time I'm coming from the place of 'why should I put the burden on these kids to solve the problems — does guilt do the trick?' What are realistic goals for doing EE for kids, from kids' viewpoint?...At the same time, what are the vicissitudes of the situation that we're in as a species, and as a planet, and what do you do with all that?"

Mike answered, "My immediate reaction to that is to emphasize the positive. What I mean is that you get kids going out and really loving the outdoors and really excited about all the neat things they're doing and exploring...and then gradually introduce to them the idea that the natural world is being destroyed, but come to it from the perspective of 'you care about it' so you want to do something about it, not from the guilt perspective of you've got to stop using plastic bags."

Karen said there's a lot of fear, "We're telling our kids that the world is very scary."

Jim uses the classic article "Tragedy of the Commons" by Garrett Hardin[1] to discuss what the nature of the problem is. He says not only is guilt not productive, but it will backfire. He suggests talking about the feeling of guilt — ask your class if guilt works or not. "If you just make kids feel guilty about it, nothing's going to get done."

Mike added, "Don't just tell kids the problems, tell them the solutions as well. Otherwise, they'll feel like it's hopeless."

"One success breeds the feeling that you can create other successes," according to Greg.

Jim said the recycling program his kids ran was one of the most empowering things he's ever done. Kids went home and said, "I know I did something; I know I made a difference."

It was felt that it is important to have kids be caretakers and decision-makers for a piece of land. Kids discuss their role in the environment, without adult intervention. It was felt this model would work in urban and nonurban environments.

In a closing discussion of what the goals and ideals for environmental education ought to be, several seminal questions raised by this kind of education emerged and were discussed:

How can EE change, redefine education in school, and widen communities?

How do we reconnect people with the natural world, especially in an urban setting?

What is the measure for environmental decision-making? Is it science? Is it God? Is it aesthetics? Is it morality? Is it economics? And how do we teach about these things?

Where does economy fit into the school curriculum?

The workshop, in closing, turned to questions of satisfying teaching settings and to staying alert to opportunities that would be useful for one's classroom.

Endnote

1   Garrett Hardin. "Tragedy of the Commons," Science, Vol. 162. December 13,1968. pp. 1243-1248.

Simulation and Role Playing Games in the Classroom

A Workshop Presented by David Millians, The Paideia School, Atlanta, Georgia, and Ellen Murphey, The School in Rose Valley, Moylan, Pennsylvania

Description by a scribe and the editors

David Millians and Ellen Murphey have used role playing games to augment learning for their fifth and sixth grade students. Last year, David's class was studying Greece, when he set up a Greek drama about a group of characters who were seeking a magic cup which would cure a King's afflicted daughter. David and Ellen involved the workshop group in a similar role play. Character sheets were handed out to each participant who then assumed the character. Each made contributions which would help the group find the magic cup while playing the role assigned. The role play was powerful and engaging; it involved the adults so intensely that the group, unable to stop, continued well past the workshop's ending time.

Role playing games combine elements of traditional classroom simulations with aspects of stage dramas and playground games of pretending. They can be written by the teacher or students, or can be based upon those found in published materials. Students can use the role plays during recesses, after school, or as an integrated activity within the curriculum. David often bases the role plays he develops on adventure stories in imaginary lands. One student player acts as a director or gamemaster, describing the setting for the action. The other student players contribute to the flow of events through their actions as they play their roles.

David has integrated role playing games into many subject areas including science, math, and social studies. He has also immersed his students in reading and writing related to the role plays. For example, when using published materials, students have enthusiastically read rules books, applied math skills and concepts, and worked with historical events. Students have also written voluminously, crafting characters and settings. They have created computer programs, made maps, written songs and poems, drawn illustrations of their characters, and learned to question patterns of history, culture, and human nature.

The games require students to organize and concentrate, question, explore, and create. Playing the games is a social exercise which develops cooperation and leadership skills, and nurtures friendships among students.

David's students did a year-long study of the Middle Ages. As one aspect of their study, David created an adventure in which the students played the roles of

Britons, Anglo-Saxons, and Picts fleeing the first Viking raids in the ninth century. As their characters travelled into unknown lands, students explored the cultural and physical landscape of the Dark Ages.

The potential of such role plays and simulations to inspire interest and motivation in students was aptly demonstrated by the workshop participants, who were enthralled with their own role play.

Back to the First Basic
A Workshop Presented by Pamela Vanderpoel Bishop, Abington Friends School, Jenkintown, Pennsylvania

Description by Karen Falcon, scribe, and the editors

Being told which colors to use to draw a fish, being asked to paint a Christmas tree with its branches pointing down in order to be consistent with everybody else, experiencing a sense of failure while painting a cat — these were childhood memories of participants in the workshop. The recollections powerfully demonstrated how such experiences have shaped our views as adults.

Art is a way to understand and experience other cultures. It fosters creativity and a deeper connection to other people and the natural world. Art is basic to our existence. The workshop title, "Back to the First Basic," reflected this belief and was also a response to the focus of the back-to- basics movement which emphasizes reading, writing, and math, while treating art as superfluous.

Participants experienced a variety of ways art could be integrated into the total educational experience while taking part in two art activities using imagination, observation, and drawing from experience and memory. While drawing and painting, participants shared activities they have used in their own classrooms, asked questions, and talked about the issues raised in the workshop.

Drawing was recognized as being the easiest but scariest way for teachers to introduce art. Nora, an assistant teacher at The School in Rose Valley, suggested that drawing in journals often feels safer than writing for children. Bonnie contributed an example of how she combines art and science: students draw and paint bones while studying anatomy. "How do you best comment on children's drawings?" asked a participant. Her daughter always draws a line at the top of her drawing for the sky. Should she point out the inaccuracy to her daughter? Pamela Vanderpoel Bishop noted that most young children draw sky at the top of a drawing. Therefore, she suggested that children could be asked to look outside to see if that is how it actually appears, or to consider whether to have the sky meet the horizon.

While working on observational drawings of shells, participants noticed that the objects which seem easiest to draw are often the most difficult because they lack obvious details. Bonnie pointed out that some of the best drawings come from observations done with microscopes, since students have no preconceived idea of what the objects look like. The value of collaboration between art teachers and classroom teachers was recognized by the entire group, alluding to the possibility that art is a powerful way to create community. Pamela noted that art is "individual but also community." Later, a participant reflected that "children flourish as individuals within the context of community."

Pamela students use self-portraits that they draw at the beginning, middle, and end of each year to see how their drawing skills and perceptions of themselves have changed over time. At the end of each year, she compiles the self-portraits and copies and distributes them to each student so that they have a portrait of their entire class. Workshop participants also drew self-portraits. While working on them, the group discussed talent, concluding that every child has talent, although exercises and practice help to develop drawing skills.

"How do you best comment on children's drawings?" asked a participant.

Exemplifying the attention in the workshop given to participant experience and ideas, closing suggestions were generated from the entire group.
• Use journals as a safe place for drawing.
• Ask students to finish drawing partially completed shapes already begun.
• Combine drawing and math for example, use shapes to create patterns around which to draw.

Much having been suggested and shared by participants, the workshop ended with their feeling empowered to introduce new methods in their art teaching.

Exploring Alternative Media: A Holistic Approach to Language Arts that Extends Literature to Include Newspapers and Television
A Workshop Presented by Susan J. Boal, School District of Philadelphia, Philadelphia, Pennsylvania

Description by a scribe and the editors

Whole language theory and practice are based on the use of "real literature" (tradebooks) rather than upon the use of basal readers series. Susan Boal has extended the definition of real literature to include the newspaper and television. She designed a project for her middle school students which used critical thinking skills, newspapers, and television to fulfill prescribed curriculum requirements regarding the teaching of fact versus opinion.

Students used newspapers to distinguish between fact and opinion. Working in groups of four or five, they prepared reading and writing portfolios which contained the results of the following tasks:
• First, gather six facts from each of two news articles. The articles must be on the same subject and come from two different newspapers.
• Second, compare and contrast the facts from the two articles.
• Third, read an article on the same subject one week later. Gather six facts. Evaluate and describe how the situation has changed.
• Fourth, summarize opinions from newspaper editorials in paragraphs.
• Fifth, compare and contrast editorial opinions from student opinions.
• Sixth, summarize all facts and opinions, including personal opinions.
• Seventh, write a letter to the editor about the subject.
• Eighth, complete a survey about the group's behavior.

Interested and enthusiastic about examining and evaluating media messages presented in newspapers, Susan and her students decided to extend the project to television. As one student remarked, "What about TV? It works on us, makes us do things." Students examined the use of advertising propaganda by watching television commercials, determining the facts and opinions about a chosen product, and discovering and employing propaganda techniques to create their own video-taped commercials. Again, they worked in groups at the following tasks.
• First, identify the product for the group project.
• Second, list the good and bad things about the product.
• Third, answer the following questions:
  What are the facts about the product?
  How does the advertiser avoid telling the consumer negative information?
  How does the advertiser create beliefs about the product?
  What is the importance of pricing?

• Fourth, convert the "negative" aspects of your product into potentially positive statements. (Use positive words; state opinions and/or make non-measurable claims.)
• Fifth, write a script for your commercial.
• Sixth, plan and prepare props.
• Seventh, practice the skit.
• Eighth, perform it.

The commercials were videotaped. Afterward, each student had to reflect upon and answer the following questions:
• What three products would you buy? Why?
• What one product would you not buy? Why? If you feel the commercial was poor, state your reasons.
• In what ways are you a better educated consumer?

The newspaper and television experiences gave the students an acute awareness of the media's deliberate persuasive powers and their impact on society. A survey of her students showed that the use of a visual medium affected deeper critical thinking abilities for some students who have difficulty comprehending print media.

Susan believes a multi-sensory and multi-media approach to the teaching of language arts can help students understand how their environment affects them and what control, if any, they have over their world. What is important is that students feel the power of knowing, and of knowing why. When they don't know why, they can feel the power of knowing how to find out. After viewing a video of commercials made by Susan's students, a participant wrote: "...the students experienced an impressive development of their critical thinking skills. The very nature of the project empowered the children to take responsibility for their own thinking and their independent formation of their opinions."

The Value of Service

A Workshop Presented by Robert Vitalo, John Scardina, Nancy Kersten, and their students Audrey and Amy-Margaret, Media-Providence Friends School, Media, Pennsylvania

Description by Heidi Lasher, scribe, and the editors

Involving students in service is one way that educators can promote citizenship. Service programs are varied, but generally three types of service programs are found:

• *Instrumental Programs* are service programs vital to the school's mission. The entire school community understands and supports service projects. Instrumental programs make up the smallest percentage of school service programs.

• *Strategic Programs* are fueled by small groups of people. The school community may understand the value of service, but other commitments take priority. There is not a commitment to a school-wide program.

• *Symbolic Programs* provide the option of service by default. Service projects are not supported by the school community. For example, students who don't want to take sports can do service instead.

Service programs vary in levels of exposure and engagement. Some programs focus upon exposing students to conditions in the real world, to the situations that some people live with. Other programs move beyond exposure to engagement, which involves students in working and interacting with people.

Kids know what we value by the time allotted in our schedules...

In order to make service programs both instrumental and engaging, the presenters made the following suggestions.

• Make service fundamental to the school's mission. For example, Quaker schools can connect service to Quaker tradition and beliefs.

• Create cultural dissonance by encouraging students to serve in situations where they confront different cultures and people in situations other than what they are accustomed to.

• Link service experiences to the classroom. Allow students to reflect, role play, share, and write about their experiences. Help them to question and understand issues of social justice and political process. Make it a priority to help students construct meaning from their experiences and consider ways they can help make change.

Service helps students to learn how to help others and is important to their development. Students should become care givers who enjoy lasting mutual giving relationships, as opposed to care takers who are not completely and/or intrinsically aware of people's real needs. There are three major ways service helps elementary aged students.

• It provides opportunity for exposure to adult models. "Kids know what we value by the time allotted in our schedules...If we participate and send clear messages giving the issue the importance it deserves, kids will, too." Adults should also be involved, thereby providing a message that service is important and creating a sense of joy in group response to service.

• Community service helps children understand parts of the world that they usually don't see. The realities of the lives of elderly, homeless, and handicapped people are important for students to understand. "These situations are very real and shouldn't be pushed under the rug." Preparation beforehand is essential. Students and teachers can share their concerns and anxieties.

• Service allows children to contribute on an equal basis with adults. Students and teachers (and parents wherever possible) can share their feelings beforehand, actively participate in the service project, reflect together about the experience, and share the satisfaction.

Students at Media-Providence Friends School have played bingo and had lunch with people at a nursing home, raised money to contribute to the purchase of a cow, a fish hatchery, and farming equipment for a small village, and made food for the homeless. Another Friends School in Philadelphia had students work with an inner city school on a production of "The Wiz." Parent support is exceedingly important to the success of service projects. Because they are concerned about taking time away from school and academics, parents need to be informed about the value and rationale of service.

Audrey and Amy-Margaret, students at Media-Providence Friends, described their service experiences. "Learning about cerebral palsy helped me to understand how it affects people. At first I felt sorry for people who had it, but a part of me also thought it was their fault. Studying about it and spending time with people who had it cleared this up." One student also watched domestic abuse trials in court. "It lets you compare your problems to other people's real problems." They like to pick projects themselves and especially enjoy programs where they can work and relate to other students, and physically visit other places.

Service projects promote self-esteem when students participate in projects in which they have an important role. That self-esteem can work for them when they face their own problems. If we can teach young people that they can be agents of change and that they impact people, they will not downgrade others, but help those that are less fortunate.

Adventures with Language through Literature and Art
A Workshop Presented by Betty Becton and Marcia Reed, Wallingford Elementary School, Wallingford, Pennsylvania

Description by a scribe and the editors

Betty Becton and Marcia Reed, librarian and art teacher respectively, have collaborated to develop and implement thematic curricula which bridge the domains of art, literature, and media. In the fall, Betty introduces a theme to her classes in the media center. Later in the year, Marcia integrates the theme into her art classes. They create information packets for other teachers which explain the theme, its objectives, activities Marcia plans to do in art, activity ideas for the classroom, and a bibliography of related books. Because Marcia and Betty recognize that teachers have full schedules, they provide information that facilitates the incorporation of the theme into teachers' regular classroom activities. At the end of each unit they plan some kind of culminating event for the entire school. Betty and Marcia send letters to parents informing them of the unit, how they can help, and inviting their participation. Over the years, both parents and teachers have become involved in the projects.

Some of the themes, objectives, activities, and culminating projects are listed below.

Celebration of the Future
Objectives:
• Create school spirit and cooperation (everyone loves a celebration!).
• Offer a subject that can be expanded in many directions — art, music, writing, math, social studies, science, etc.
• Use the art curriculum as a means to celebrate the future.

Possible activities:
• Study various artists and their impact on the future.
• Construct a future city.
• Discuss what we will be eating in 50 years.
• Dress-up in the clothes of your future profession.
• Read what newspapers say about the future.

All-School Culminating Activity:
• Design a giant sculpture of the future in the front hall using junk from home.

Heroes and Heroines

Objectives:
• Identify and study character traits of leaders, heroes, and heroines.
• Select a hero or heroine or leader and find interesting facts about him or her.
• Study the concept of courage.
• Identify individuals in our community and country who are working to bring about an improvement in people's lives.

Possible activities:
• Identify people in the local community who are "sticking their necks out" for others, making a difference. Invite them to tell their stories to the class.
• Adopt a hero or heroine and initiate correspondence.
• Select a hero/heroine of the week or month.
• Write about heroes and heroines. Read about them on the public address system in the school.

All-School Culminating Activities:
• Build a "Hall of Heroes." Each student makes a clay sculpture of his or her hero or heroine, designs a pictorial time line of the hero or heroine's life, makes a diorama of an important event in that person's life, and writes a detailed report about the person's life.
• Hold a "Pageant of Heroes" in which each class presents a short skit depicting a day in the life of their chosen hero or heroine.
• Film festival.

This unit was designed to promote the Wallingford Elementary School's goal: "To develop a positive self-image as a basis from which to approach the demands and challenges of responsible citizenship."

Participants at the conference workshop brainstormed their own ideas for thematic units:

weather	*insects*	*human body and masks*
exploration	*animals*	*dolls*
flight	*evolution*	*nature*
space	*Native Americans*	*habitat*
games	*television*	*dinosaurs*
food	*distant lands travel*	*endangered and extinct*

Many of the ideas generated had environmental themes, and caused the group to wonder whether this reflected a stronger need for environmental education. The participants also suggested that students be involved in exploring and deciding what the thematic unit will be. Betty and Marcia believed this would be empowering for their students and intend to introduce it for future units in their school.

Experiential Drama with Children
A Workshop Presented by Karlie Roth and Carol Woltering,
Montessori Country Day School, Marple-Newton, Pennsylvania

Description by Paul Blundin, scribe, and the editors

Experiential drama emerges from children's experiences and ideas. It maintains the spontaneity, enthusiasm, and playfulness of "backyard drama" that children improvise on their own. Artificiality often occurs when children act out plays written by adults or perform their own plays before an audience. Experiential drama preserves children's enthusiasm while minimizing the artificiality when acting in front of an audience.

Experiential drama begins with a theme. It can be an idea, an emotion, a story. *The Little Witch* books by Deborah Hautzig are the favorite inspiration of Carol Woltering's young students. She has used them as the basis of experiential drama. As a workshop group, we viewed a video tape of Carol 's students preparing a play based on one of the books. First, she read the story aloud. As she read, she asked questions which helped the children to break away from the story itself and extend the plot, or provide details not included in the book. For example, if a character in the story was sad, she asked "Why was she sad?" "She was sad because no one paid attention to her," Carol responded. The next questions extended the story into a new plot told by the students. "What do you think happened next?" "They brought her a present," the students answered. "Who brought her a present and why did they bring it to her?" The children's answers to these questions were recorded by Carol and later become the script for their drama. The main characters of the book remained in the drama, but a new plot and characters were created.

Experiential drama preserves children's enthusiasm while minimizing the artificiality when acting in front of an audience.

Who, what, "wear," when, and why are the elements of experiential drama. Developing characterization, selecting the actions they will do, and picking what they will wear are the elements most important to the children. What the children wear is sometimes more important to the children than the setting. Students make costumes and scenery. Many props are provided, helping students to develop physical actions for the drama. The development of physical action is key to experiential drama for children. For example, Carol's students culminated their witch drama by making a witches' stew.

A drama, scripted from earlier discussion, uses the students' own language. A student or teacher narrator prompts the children as they act. However, the drama maintains spontaneity and improvisation, changing each time it was done.

Students and teachers should have fun with it; it is not necessary for the drama to make sense.

Books about problems and issues that students face in their daily lives provide good material for experiential drama; students have an opportunity to help solve the problems in the story. Easy readers are effective with very young students. Carol and Karlie have found that many children go to libraries or book stores to get copies of the books upon which they have based their dramas. In addition, students who aren't successful in other areas of school-life are often very successful with experiential drama.

After watching the video, Karlie and Carol separated the adult participants into two groups to repeat the process viewed on the video, using the original props from the children's play. Karlie and Carol, acting as scribes, kept the process moving swiftly as an abundance of sterling contributions were made to the new script by the participants. One group produced a new drama entitled, "Little Witch and All Her Friends Meet and Befriend the Evil Skunkinhead on the Moon." Both groups brought the workshop to a close by performing their dramas for each other.

Our World Small to Big: Developing Friendship and Stewardship Programs through Earth Education

Tere Camerota, Oak Lane Day School, Blue Bell, Pennsylvania

Description by a scribe and the editors

Tere Camerota is a teacher of environmental education and science for children from pre-kindergarten to grade three at Oak Lane Day School, where her classroom is thirty acres of woods and streams. She explores the environment using science process approaches, hands-on discovery, and Native American folklore. She is involved in a number of unusual environmental education projects which she shared with the participants in this workshop.

As background for explaining an earth education conference Tere coordinated in Moscow with Penny Greenwell, another workshop participant, a comparison was provided of science, art, and general education in the U.S.S.R. and the U.S.A. They discussed Sharing Our Lives: A Children's Connection which is a Quaker U.S./U.S.S.R. Committee program linking partner schools. Participants also discussed many other partner projects at this point, ranging from children sharing Native American myths to trading fabric squares for quilt-making. Joint planting projects between companion schools in the two countries were explained, including studying common subjects, planting friendship forests which can be transplanted from country schools to urban communities, and exchanging bulbs with a companion school. The purpose of Sharing our Lives is for children to realize that

> as keepers of the Earth, we share our planet and breathe the same air, which is replenished by the trees and plants around us. By planting trees and growing gardens we foster our bonds of friendship and strengthen our commitment of stewardship to our common planet.

The All Species Project was explained by Penny Greenwell as

> an experiential education program working with schools and community organizations. Using an exploratory curriculum, it approaches serious environmental and cultural issues in creative ways exploring essential values and respect for the Earth and all living things. All Species Projects bring together people of diverse economic and cultural backgrounds in a creative expression of shared ecological and peace values. Through the arts of puppetry, masks, pageantry, theater, music, dance, and display, a magical process transforms children and adults from ambivalence and hopelessness to active awareness and positive participation.

Tere and Penny then talked about using myth to teach about culture and at the same time have the kids learn science. The example they used involved the Lanai myth of the Earth and the turtle. Tere described how her class looks at real turtles when they learn this myth, and look at how many squares there are on the backs of turtles, and how this relates to cycles on Earth.

With respect to science, Tere talked about some of the ideas she stresses in her classroom. The most important ones are sensory awareness — to observe, to manipulate, to measure, to record, and to have a sense of place. She also said that the circle is one of the most important concepts, because it signifies cycles, such as planetary, lunar, re-cycles and so on.

A question was asked as to how to deal with the fact that many kids in cities don't have basic ecologic ideas "such as that apples grow on trees." Tere responded by saying that we should "start at ground zero," and develop basic ideas. Penny added that such ignorance is not just in the city, it is found everywhere and she agreed that the focus should be on simple concepts. She reiterated that there need to be activities that depend on the use of the senses.

Some of the things that Tere and Penny thought were very effective in science and earth education were direct observation, recording in journals, and, especially, art. They said to keep asking of ones teaching, "Are you touching the future?" Tere closed by saying, "The only way we're going to make it is if kids fall back in love with nature."

Not for Math Teachers Only: Progressive Statistics Education
A Workshop Presented by Karen Rothschild, University of Pennsylvania, Philadelphia, Pennsylvania

Description by a scribe and the editors

After introducing herself as Coordinator of Teacher Education at Project Statistical Reasoning in Children (STARC) at the Literacy Research Center of the Graduate School of Education, Karen Rothschild introduced the topic question, "Should statistics education be a matter of concern to progressive educators, and if so, why?" The participants then introduced themselves and briefly stated their interests in the workshop. Karen distributed a questionnaire entitled "Progressive Statistics Education — What Could It Be?" which quickly became a stimulus for discussion.

The group discussed the questions one-by-one. It was determined that statistics are encountered in the media every day. Newspaper articles focus on giving numbers and percentages. In short, the media have a tendency to provide the citizen with many kinds of quantitative information. Statistics also play a prominent part in evaluating both education programs and children. Statistics dealing with learning problems amongst the minority children in a classroom were cited as an example.

A participant said, "The system of standardized testing of children relies upon quantitative data being used with a strictly impersonal and scientific method. The establishment of test scores and percentiles is a dehumanizing feature that nevertheless will affect the way a teacher will teach a class." Performance measured in statistics thus acts as a stimulus for selecting a method of teaching or for concentrating in areas of study that have been deemed problematic by the statistical information, and it also plays a role in classifying, labelling, and placing students.

Another participant said consumer reports and opinion polls also dictate many of the choices that we face in society. These choices range from buying goods based on information surveyed to assessing the climate of a decision-making situation through opinion polls. It was noted that political activity is heavily influenced by statistical analyses of survey data.

It was noted that statistics, by establishing norms, contribute to a centralization and homogenization of culture. Finally, many participants felt that statistics are used to simplify public debate, often in a way that masks important complexities and thus ultimately misleads.

A discussion followed on children's experiences with statistics in everyday life. It was agreed by all the participants that children not only encounter statistics with great frequency, but also tend to be influenced more than adults. An example cited was the popularity of the newspaper *USA Today* amongst children and young people. This newspaper not only gives a multitude of statistics, but also structures itself in a way that, through statistics, tends to simplify arguments and debates as a way of making this information more accessible to the readers. Children also are targeted by statistical onslaughts in a bid to persuade them to desire commercial products. In a broader context, children have difficulty critically analyzing the statistical method or purpose behind the quantitative information they receive. Instead, they take statistical information as given truth because it is presented in a seemingly scientific method, and they lack the training to question such "facts."

Critical thinking about quantitative information can combat a culture that dehumanizes important topics through the use of statistics.

Because of the above, the workshop determined that it is necessary to introduce children as early as possible to methods of collecting statistical information through inquiry techniques. It was argued that if students themselves learned about posing simple problems and investigating their solutions, that they would be able to establish a knowledge of statistical method and, hopefully, be more critical of the statistics they face outside of schools.

At this point Karen suggested the following as core questions for the design and/ or critique of a statistical study:
• What makes the question at hand relevant or important?
• What research design is appropriate to answer the question? What kind of data is important? What can/cannot be measured?
• How are sampling done? i.e., Who do you ask? How can you be sure your sample is "fair"?
• What techniques are involved in collecting the data?
• How are the data analyzed?
• What inferences, conclusions, or decisions can one make based on the information collected?

Karen stressed that the decisions about how questions are phrased, how samples are chosen, and how research is designed in general are crucial in determining the kinds of data you will get. She said that data analysis is the usual content of college statistics courses and that this ignores where the numbers come from and how they are used. The question that should be pursued with children is, "Once you get the numbers, what do they mean?"

At this point, Karen introduced the resources she had brought with her, most notably a booklet of examples from the *Quantitative Literacy Series*. Each participant was given a copy.

After the participants took some time to examine materials, the discussion once again shifted from a practical application of statistics learning in a progressive environment to a more philosophical concern over the role of statistics in society and modern culture. One woman, an environmentalist, questioned whether statistics should be an issue at all and saw no point in them as a topic. Karen responded by stating her opinion that statistics education is relevant in all disciplines and that environmental education is no exception, for example, statistics about the depletion of the ozone layer help to formulate attitudes and policy toward the topic. Karen also mentioned that learning to analyze and interpret statistical information could be a step towards becoming a more caring society. Critical thinking about quantitative information can combat a culture that dehumanizes important topics through the use of statistics.

In closing the group discussed the question, "What is the value system that underlies statistics and statistical methods?" Statistics are often used in a manipulative way by offering evidence as objective truth. It is important to be aware of the ease with which statistics can be biased. It is important to define goals clearly and constantly remind oneself of what is being measured when carrying out research.

The workshop set out to stimulate thoughts about the nature of statistics and their importance in modern society. Participants became aware of the multitude of ways in which statistics shape our lives and decision-making processes, both professionally and at home. It became clear that there are both appropriate and inappropriate uses of statistics. It was also seen how vulnerable children were to statistics and that by educating them about statistical methods and questions regarding the collection of data, children would over time become able to independently assess and analyze statistical information in their everyday lives. Participants engaged in debate about the philosophy and sociological implications of statistics. The discussion therefore served as a thorough introduction and definition of the issue.

Resource

Quantitative Literacy Series. Palo Alto, California: Dale Seymour Publisher, 1987.

Integrating Cooperative Games Into the Classroom
*A Workshop Presented by Heidi Hammel, Delaware Valley Friends School,
Bryn Mawr, Pennsylvania, and Ellen Murphey, The School in Rose Valley,
Moylan, Pennsylvania*

Description by a scribe and the presenters

Cooperative games offer many opportunities to learn while playing. Each game
contains a metaphor that can be experienced and then thought about and discussed. If a metaphor mirrors the dynamics occurring in your group and inspires
reflection, it will lead to learning. Choosing the best game for the moment is an
art which requires understanding of your group's dynamics and the metaphors
within each game, the ability to match the two, and the courage and insight to
watch and guide the unfolding learning.

Cooperative games address many different skills: listening, individual and group
problem solving, communication, idea generation, experimentation, evaluation of
experiments, cooperation, and leadership. Whenever a teacher sees a need for a
group or individual to practice these skills, she or he can use cooperative games.
If the teacher has identified an issue accurately and chosen an appropriate game,
she can then guide her students through the experience. The experience can speak
for itself, or the teacher can guide the group in thinking about how the game
relates to their lives and what is occurring in their group.

For example, if students in a group are having difficulty listening to each other,
the teacher may choose a game which requires students to communicate without
speaking. At the beginning of the game, she may introduce the game by stating a
goal. "We are going to play a game that requires each of you to send messages
carefully and to listen carefully to each other." At the conclusion of the game, she
or he may guide a discussion of what happened during the game, how it felt to be
unable to speak, how being mute affected or changed the ways the group commu-
nicated and 'listened,' what they learned about sending messages and listening to
messages, and how this learning relates to them. The teacher may also introduce a
few similar short games together before guiding discussion, although a short
check after each game often maximizes the group's awareness and learning.

A stronger sense of cooperation and group cohesiveness can be achieved by designing sessions so that they include a name game, warm-up activities, initiative
games, and a closing activity. A name game is a playful way to introduce people
to one another. Warm-up activities help groups to begin working together. Less
game-like than warm-up activities, group initiative games require planning, strategy, and cooperation. A closing activity brings focus to the group.

As a workshop group, we playfully engaged in activities of each type. For example, while standing in a circle the group learned the names of others by group juggling. The object of the game was to get as many objects aloft as possible while preserving a particular sequence. The sequence was established by throwing the object to a new person with each successive toss, and calling the person's name as the object was tossed. Once people became part of the sequence, they always threw to the same person and received from the same person.

A first round simply established the sequence, after which Heidi Hammel and Ellen Murphey checked to make sure everybody remembered to whom they were tossing to and from whom they were receiving. After every other sequence, the leaders introduced a new object. The more ridiculous objects evoked much laughter. Heidi and Ellen slowly pulled out the objects one at a time to gradually slow the game down.

As a warm-up activity, we played "Appliances, Feeling, and Food." We divided into groups of four and five people. Told that we would be playing a charades-type game, we established symbols of communication in our groups. When each group was ready, it lined up at the starting line, while Heidi and Ellen stood at the finish line holding cards.

At the word "go," the first person in each group ran and got a card from Heidi or Ellen. After returning to their group, those persons acted out the word until the group successfully guessed it. The next person in line then ran to get a new card, and so on until each group was done. The cards had words which described appliances, feelings, or food. Some of the words, such as "cucumber," left some of the groups far behind.

Later in the session, we were asked to form a straight line organized by our birthdays without speaking to one another. One end of the line was to begin with January and the other with December. We had to develop a form of communication other than speaking to determine where in the line to stand. Once we made a straight line, we called out our birthdays in order to see if we were able to successfully create the line in sequence by birthday. This game is a good way to examine group problem solving. If a group gets frustrated or is not working together well, they can stop and discuss what is occurring and what they can do to improve their efforts.

For a closing activity, we were asked to squat in a circular huddle with our hands on our neighbor's knees. The initiator tapped a person next to her, who then tapped the next person and tapped the leader back. This pattern proceeded around the circle until mass confusion and laughter broke out.

Full of new ideas for games and ways to use them, the group dispersed.

Share the Power: African and African-American Music

A Workshop Presented by Jane B. Miluski, The School in Rose Valley, Moylan, Pennsylvania

Description by a scribe and the editors

> If you can talk, you can sing.
> If you can walk, you can dance.
> — A Zimbabwean Proverb

Songs, games, and stories were learned from the African and African-American traditions in this totally participatory experience. It was the most popular workshop and the only one to be offered twice.

In the Georgia Sea Islands, music gave people in slavery the strength to endure, a community of belonging, and a way to talk about the power structure without fear of reprisal. The children's songs often have at least one other meaning; for example, Old Bill Rolling Pin is about the slaves' overseer. African-American music during the Civil Rights Movement also gave people power to endure violence and face the hoses. Songs drew people to march for the cause.

African music is music of power. Children of all backgrounds feel that power, and are quick to respond to it. On the African continent, music was traditionally central to all of the rituals of life, from birth through death. Music had a circular

nature, requiring no set beginning, middle, or ending. Musicians were free to build the music until it had the desired effect...until it worked! In this tradition, each person had an important role to play. While many pieces had a leader and a chorus, the leadership easily passed from person to person. It was understood that each participant was welcome and even expected to play a leadership role as well as to enhance the harmony of the whole. In instrumental play or in congregational singing, participants listened for the spaces and filled them. These same characteristics are central to African-American music. Jane said that this music of power is a strong metaphor for living. She quoted George Brandon: "...when everybody is playing their part correctly, when all the parts are linked up correctly, a single sound results which goes round and round and round."

African music is music of power. Children of all backgrounds feel that power, and are quick to respond to it.

We sang three spirituals at the same time, "Wade in the Water," "Sometimes I Feel Like a Motherless Child," and "I Want to Die Easy." We made African music including the Zulu call to meeting and an example of South African Isicathamiya from Joseph Shabalala, founder and leader of Ladysmith Black Mambazo. In addition, we played two games from Ghana, "Kye Kye Kule" and "Abwa Asi Mi Nsa," and we heard the story of the baby leopard and a canoeing song from Nigeria, "E Sum Buka Waya." Music of the Georgia Sea Islands, which remained in its pure state from the days of slavery until earlier in this century, included "Old Bill Rolling Pin," "Tom Tom Greedy Gut," "Juba," "Down on the Bingo Farm," "Josephine," and "Alabama-Mississippi." Background stories which accompany the Sea Islands songs were also told.

We particularly enjoyed one game and chant called "Abwa Asi Mi Nsa." Everyone sat in a circle crosslegged with a rock in front. Each person held the right
hand in the air. Each grabbed and passed the rock in front with the right hand.
Practicing grabbing and passing, everyone at the same time chants to the rhythm,
"Abwa Asi Mi Nsa Na-Na, Abwa Asi Mi Nsa." This is a challenging group
activity in which everyone had to work together in a coordinated fashion for it
to succeed.

The workshop was lively and engaging. As they performed songs, chants, and
games from South Africa, Ghana, Nigeria, the Georgia Sea Islands, and from
the American tradition of Black congregational singing, participants shared
the power.

Resources

Learning to Sing and Dance with Frankie and Doug Quimby; record and tape. Available from The Georgia
Sea Island Singers, Frankie Quimby, 2428 Cleburne Street, Brunswick, Georgia 31520. Telephone (912)
265-9545.

Let Your Voice Be Heard! Adzinyah, Maraire and Tucker; Book and tape. World Music Press, P.O. Box
2565, Danbury, Connecticut 06813.

Singing in the African American Tradition, taught by Ysaye Barnwell with George Brandon; Booklet plus
six teaching tapes. Homespun Tapes, Ltd.; Box 694, Woodstock, NY 12498.

Step It Down; Bessie Jones and Bess Lomax Hawes; Harper and Row, Publishers; 49 E. 33rd Street, New
York, New York 10016.

Judith Cook Tucker, World Music Press, P.O. Box 2565, Danbury, Connecticut 06813.

Chapter 5

Critical Reflection Upon Practice

We need to continuously struggle to become more aware of our teaching. Teaching occurs in a cultural context which demands critique. Taking time to reflect allows us to become conscious of who we are and why we teach. Reflection is a source of renewal and self-transformation.

I never stop sifting through my experiences. I ask myself, 'How would someone else have handled this?' I am constantly reprocessing.

We should feel aware of our weaknesses, and what we need to address.

We agreed upon the importance of continually questioning.

Conflicts Across the Curriculum

A Working Group Facilitated by Steve Weimar, Educators for Social Responsibility, Philadelphia, Pennsylvania

Description by Lisa Morse, Sue Edwards, Andrew Cummings, scribes, and the editors

Our working group gathered in a small meeting room. The furniture seemed to sigh as people sat in it, the cushion chairs molding to fit our bodies. This caused a lot of laughter, releasing the nervous tension in the room. And there was nervous tension; after all, we had come to talk about conflict.

Comfortable in our chairs, we read the summary description of the working group and contemplated what it meant to us and why we had chosen to attend. Our answers to the questions were richly varied. Each of us described our classrooms and what we were interested in achieving or learning as a result of participating in the working group. Many of us hoped to learn specific strategies for teaching conflict resolution and helping students to become mediators of their own conflicts. Each of us had specific situations in which this would be helpful: conflicts between five- and six-year-olds, social cliques in elementary school, students in learning disabled classes, and high school students in a remedial English class.

Our sharing raised questions among us: Do younger children need more adult mediation when solving conflicts than older children? If so, how do we shift to giving older students more responsibility? How do we make the process of conflict resolution more interesting? Are we expecting too much academically and socially from students (especially learning disabled students)?; Are their conflicts with one another a result of their lack of success in schools? How do teacher conflicts with the administration affect the students? How can teachers have different ideas or opinions about local and global issues than the students, without the students feeling put down or the whole neighborhood feeling confronted?

The sharing also initiated discussion. One participant noticed her own bias of labeling conflict as only physical conflict, which allowed everybody to recognize their own biases of labeling and handling conflict. Suchitra, a teacher at The School in Rose Valley, recognized that conflict, in her opinion, is a creative part of life, and that her interest is helping students be open and willing to experience it. Lisa, a student teacher at Strath Haven High School, acknowledged that her teacher training included wonderful books about theory, but had not prepared her to deal with the live conflicts between children in the classroom. Another participant recognized the frustration that teachers as well as the students feel, when conflict arises.

A discussion emerged around our varied experiences and perspectives of integrating the study of conflict in our classrooms. Sara, a teacher at the Springside School, said that she feels particularly uneasy about discussing world conflict in the classroom because she tends to teach her subject matter and avoid those issues. In contrast, Sue, a history teacher, feels that conflict enriches the study of her field. Lisa finds that theater revolves around conflict. While she knows how to deal with conflict in that context, she has had difficulty transferring the methods to her English class. Dru, a parent and substitute teacher at The School in Rose Valley, didn't agree that the conflict found in role-plays in theater class is the same as that found in other situations in life.

While what was occurring within the working group wasn't truly a conflict, Steve Weimar pointed out that "the basic structure of conflict is the basic structure of interaction in our world. So, what we're now saying about how we talk to each other is also a key element of conflict resolution in and of itself." Steve used the differences in opinion and experience emerging from our discussion to explore some of the common dynamics of conflicts.

Typically, one of the first occurrences is that people make assumptions and try to "fix" the opinions of others; they attempt to correct and make final other people's views. Attempting to fix somebody else's opinion doesn't help anybody move forward through a conflict. The more people are locked into their own ideas, the less likely they are to deal successfully with conflict.

Comparing people's responses to conflict to an iceberg, Steve also explained that we often make assumptions based on the tip of the iceberg rather than first making an effort to uncover more of it. Rather than making assumptions based on incomplete understanding, and fixing the opinions of others, Steve suggested that

> points of view need to be understood in terms of biography. When someone makes a statement about what their question is or what their problem is, we will serve that best by first getting the biography, or assuming that what this person is saying makes sense, or, if it's a question, that it's a deep and profound question. And our task is to figure out what it is.

Thus, it is the way we look at fixing others' ideas and the attachment we have to doing that which determines how a conflict will proceed. The goal is not to eliminate the conflicting thought, but to give voice to it in a productive way. It is important to formulate the idea clearly, but what gets dropped is the need for the idea to be in opposition to the other person's. Both the speaker and the listener hold responsibility; it is the work of the speaker to articulate the idea but it is also the work of the listener to hear the statement, not as a challenge, but as an opportunity.

We reflected upon our conversation and the comments that Steve made. Anna, a teacher at Lansdowne Friends, commented that young students need things fixed for them or chaos would break out. Sara

...how do we help young people see alternative resolutions to conflicts and how do we make those options more appealing?

began to tell Anna that she "was absolutely right," but somewhere in the middle of pronouncing the word "right," she stopped, looked at our group, and announced in laughter, "I was about to fix that!" This was the first time we noticed Steve's words beginning to enter our own conflict resolution methods, and we laughed with acknowledgment and approval.

Anna went on to say that she thought the feeling of helplessness that many young students feel is lessened through set rules and organization. Sue, again modeling our newly learned conflict strategy, responded, "I'm just trying to figure out how their feeling of helplessness is addressed if we set rules that also don't empower them." Anna and Sarah both responded to Sue's confusion by saying that fixedness allows them a space in which to be creative. Suchitra added her observation that people attach to things that work in the moment, but as teachers we must constantly be willing to change and notice that what students need one week to create order might not be what is needed the next week. We must be willing to alter what is "fixed"; this is, to use Grace Rotzel's term, "freedom with a fence around it." The group began to recognize it was applying the framework for responding to conflict that Steve was providing. Exclaimed Dru, "You fixed us, Steve!"

The first session's discussion came to a close with two concerns raised by the group. The first was the frustration the group felt about the mixed messages young people receive about conflict from schools, parents, and the media. The other was the options that young people have when dealing with physical conflicts commonly found on school playgrounds. Dru told the story of her son who felt he had only two options besides fighting: being a tattletale or being a "wimp." Since he found neither appealing, he chose to fight. Faced with this logic, Dru didn't know how to proceed. This raised important questions that the entire group held: how do we help young people see alternative resolutions to conflicts and how do we make those options more appealing? Steve suggested that we each come back to the second session with one question to pull together the threads of discussion we had started.

We returned to session two with many questions:
• What options can we help kids with other than walking away, fighting, or tattling?
• How can we create a culture in schools in which students will be able to think of alternatives?
• How can we understand the nature of a problem and peel it away to expose its roots?
• How can we use conflicts as constructive rather than destructive?
• How can we help ourselves and children be more awake in each moment in order to choose our responses rather than be reactive?
• Violence is seen as a positive thing in many children's lives. How can we show them the other side of it?
• How does working on conflicts intertwine with a democratic, experiential classroom, so that we are drawing upon students' ideas as opposed to teachers providing the methods and answers?

Steve proposed that we hold all of our questions in mind as we moved forward in our work together. The questions would help us to reflect upon the qualities and habits we are trying to cultivate in our personal lives, and to consider our responses to specific situations in which we find ourselves in our classrooms.

With the group's assent, he asked us to imagine a person who does well in the world, a person whom we greatly admire. What is it about those persons — their strengths, culture, habits — that enables them to do well? How did they become that person? And can we *name* what it is about the persons that we would like to cultivate in children? Individually we reflected upon these questions and then shared our thoughts about what we would like to cultivate in children.

Lisa mentioned that awareness about conflict and a desire to avoid negative conflict are important attributes. Steve asked her to hypothesize from where these qualities come. She responded that one must have confidence that different points of view can be right at the same time. Probing further, Steve asked what might provide that confidence, inviting others to contribute ideas.

Another participant suggested that having one's feelings recognized is essential to confidence. Questions and discussion ensued which Steve summarized: feelings have a legitimate place in a conflict curriculum; learning to identify one's own and others' feelings is an important component of conflict resolution; and understanding feelings helps in problem solving. People have confidence in handling conflict when they feel they "know the territory." This comes from practice, success with handling conflicts, and from students learning that they can do something they've never done before.

The ability to predict consequences and to understand cause and effect are also qualities the group would like to cultivate in children. There are "linear" and "emergent" notions of cause and effect. We want children to understand and experience the interdependence that exists between every action that individuals choose and the impacts those actions have on other members and elements of a community.

Sharon, a teacher at Ridley Middle School, raised the issue of control; children should learn what is within their control and what is not. Steve reflected that there is a lot to "unpack" in the word "control." What do we mean by control and what kind of control do we want as teachers? Our discussion led us to other related terms such as "choice," which was the springboard for another group direction: the distinction between "choice" and "control." Steve observed that as adults we tend to talk about control over what *kids* do, but choices about what *we* can do. Bill Kreidler, a conflict resolution educator and author of *Creative Conflict Resolution*,[1] stresses the value of young people coming to understand that they have authentic choices about what to do. In moments of conflict, adults and children need to learn that they can choose to hear something as a threat or as an opportunity, and that it is powerful to make that choice.

Whatever the choice may be in a given situation, it is important that there be room for people to express their feelings safely. Beyond the awareness of individuals that they have choices, people need to understand that others also have choices, and that those around them appreciate their struggles because of the shared context of the classroom.

The practice of believing was also acknowledged as a piece of conflict resolution, and as an attribute to be fostered within ourselves and others. In order to understand where believing in another person comes from, it is worthwhile to consider how we learned to doubt and be skeptical. What caused us to be doubtful? Can we also view the same person or incident in a believing mode? The practice of believing helps to create environments of care and compassion, and develops greater understanding between people.

A number of physical activities were identified which can be used to help students practice their conflict resolution skills or to convey metaphors related to conflict. Role-playing games can be used to give students an opportunity to try on and rehearse new roles so that in the heat of conflict, they will be more comfortable with them. The martial art form of Aikido also provides physical metaphors for handling conflict.

The second session of the working group came to a close with our awareness that Steve's facilitation style was speaking to us loudly. His method of "teasing it out" describes a certain kind of discovery process with which we were involved.

It suggests a gentle discovery with a certain amount of playfulness, and is a rich metaphor for the style of conflict resolution we were discussing and the quality of dialogue we were having.

After contemplating a plate of options Steve presented for our last meeting together, we decided to focus session three upon several techniques and concepts Steve has found helpful in conflict resolution.

Steve contrasted qualities we want to cultivate in ourselves and others, such as awareness and strength, with strategies for conflict resolution. Qualities often help in many situations, whereas a particular strategy may be useful in only some circumstances. Comparing them to karate, strategies are like hand movements, while a quality, such as awareness, is the centeredness that is the foundation for all karate movements. Both are necessary.

One strategy for conceptualizing conflicts is the "escalator model." Pictorially, it looks like a set of steps, and it is used to help map or "unpack" conflicts. As teachers, we might ask young people what happened in a particular conflict. Each thing that occurred would be entered on one of the steps. During the process of unpacking the conflict, we would make it clear to students that they could intervene at any stage, and that different consequences occur depending upon when they intervene. At each step or point in the conflict, there are different opportunities which exist and actions that can be taken.

Steve provided a concrete example of the mapping process. A child wears a hat to school. Another child wants it and grabs it. When asked what happened, the students might place the grabbing of the hat on the first step. However, there may have been less obvious occurrences before that step — for example, why the student wore the hat or why the other child wanted it — requiring earlier steps to be added to the diagram. An analogy which many young people can relate to is the notion of "Don't Feed the Bears!" There are things we do before a conflict begins which contribute to the conflict occurring. We might think the conflict started when the bears attacked, but we need to look at what we were doing that led to the conflict. It is the feeding of the bears which is the first step on the escalator model.

The feelings and interests of the people in the conflict can also be added to the escalator model by writing feelings on the top of each step, and interests beneath them. Interests are defined as what people are carrying around in the world that underlies their external struggle. Finally, the thoughts, analyses, and decisions of the participants in the conflict can be added; what they actually decided to do. The process of conflict mapping helps people to slow the world down and "tease apart" events that may have happened very quickly, allowing them to understand situations more comprehensively. By practicing, people will become more able to map conflicts for themselves.

A second conceptual model is the "cycle of conflict," attributed to Gail Sadalla at Community Boards, an organization in San Francisco dedicated to conflict resolution. The cycle begins with beliefs and attitudes. Conflict then occurs, and responses are made. Finally, there are consequences of the responses.

Steve noted that most young people recognize that one characteristic of conflict in their lives is that it recurs. By asking them questions about this, their choices about when to intervene in conflicts can be enriched. For example, we might ask: Why do conflicts recur? What is happening if they don't recur? Where in the cycle described above can changes take place?

Most commonly, people intervene at the point of consequences. For example, teachers ask students to sit out for recess if they break playground rules. The other common point of intervention is at the stage where conflict occurs. For example, adults take measures to prevent conflict by cutting down on children's sugar intake or keeping young people away from each other. The most difficult parts of the cycle to work on are beliefs and responses. They are challenging because they are aspects of the cycle people need to do for themselves, and they take long-term work. We can let young people (or other adults) know that it's possible for them to alter their beliefs and responses. We can even model it. However, we cannot do the work for them.

...young people recognize that one characteristic of conflict in their lives is that it recurs.

Understanding that we can intervene in conflicts at all stages of the conflict cycle is a systems approach to understanding conflict. Increasing our responsiveness to feedback we receive when conflict arises is key. If we are aware of the entire cycle of conflict, understand that every response has a consequence, and have a method of analyzing conflicts, we can do our best to change our patterns of intervening.

In our first session, we discussed the simple "fight or flight" options that many children experience in conflicts. The escalator model, or conflict mapping, introduces the notion of temporal choices, or when to intervene. The conflict cycle model offers a more comprehensive set of intervention options.

Throughout Steve's description of the two models, our groups diverged into discussions about related topics or questions that were raised in earlier sessions. In response to Dru's earlier question about how teachers can help students see that violent conflict is a dead end, Steve mentioned the work of Maxine Greene and Denise Levertov, who stress the importance of cultivating imagination. Imagination is not a flight from reality but a way to make experiences real. A poem, for example, can help us experience the pain of a conflict such as the Vietnam War. Art is both compelling and redemptive in a way that more graphic realism is unable to be. We feel not only despair but also hope through art. Imagination also helps us to cultivate new visions and alternatives for what can be.

Teaching conflict resolution, we discussed, will enrich children's lives only if we bring their own issues into the classroom. Thus, if fighting is part of their lives, we need to bring in fighting experts to see what we can learn from them. We might find that they talk about the qualities of centering, and becoming relaxed.

Finally, Steve referred to Maxine Greene's statement in her keynote address that she didn't think she could dialogue with George Bush because he wouldn't understand her. True dialogue, he explained, is not about changing the other person, but one's own willingness to enter into a conversation in which one might change or grow. Dialogue is about opinion, not biography. It is not about agreeing with others' opinions but about understanding why one has the opinions one does.

Our group had a sense that the dialogue we had begun in our three sessions to-gether was important and vital, and it was one that we wished to continue. We closed our last meeting by discussing our interest in meeting on a regular basis as a group to continue the dialogue we had started.

Endnote

1   William J. Kreidler, Creative Conflict Resolution. (Glenville, Illinois: Scott, Foresman and Company, 1984).

Classroom Talk: Who Talks? Who Listens?
A Workshop Presented by Sara Allen, Springside School,
Philadelphia, Pennsylvania

Description by Susan Ruff, scribe, and the editors

Once, Sara Allen began her story, she used to think that her role as a teacher was to develop good questions for the students. Starting with factual and progressing to inferential questions, she would stand before the class asking questions to which the students would respond. Through Socratic dialogue, Sara believed, students would gradually make connections and move to a greater understanding of the material, an understanding that Sara had already preconceived.

In this type of interaction, the teacher controls both the questions and the responses. Courtney Cazden in her book *Classroom Discourse*[1] refers to this approach as teacher *I*nitiation, student *R*esponse, teacher *E*valuation (IRE), the most common pattern of classroom discourse at all levels. A teacher initiates by asking a question, the students respond, and the teacher evaluates the response through body language (nodding, smiling, looking skeptical or unsatisfied) or by responding "yes," "good answer," "uh huh," "wow," or, if unsatisfied with the student response: "Has anyone else thought about this one?" "Any other ideas?" or, "How did you get to that point?"

Teachers who use the IRE approach have complete control of the discussion. Usually they have an end goal in mind and the students are aware of this. Frequently Sara's students ask, "Is this what you wanted us to get, Mrs. Allen?"

Not only do teachers control the discussion, they also control who talks. If teachers do not directly control who talks by requiring raised hands, they may still control by responding to the first student to answer. For example, when teachers ask a question the more confident students, usually male, respond quickly. Frequently, teachers have evaluated the initial responses and moved on to the next question before the less confident students or students who require more thinking time can formulate their own answers. Therefore, the voices of these students are not heard. Sara acknowledged that even in the best discussions when all of the students contribute, the "talk" is still teacher controlled; the students are talking to the teacher, not each other.

Sara told the story of a class of second semester seniors who would not talk. She described how she would ask a question to which they simply would not respond. They knew she "counted" writing more than talking; therefore, they did not *need* to talk. Embarrassed by the silence, she would answer questions herself. As time passed, she became frustrated and angry, and found herself muttering, "Second semester seniors are impossible to teach! Let's send them all away." One day she was making a similar remark in the teachers' room when a colleague suggested that she turn the discussion over to the students since they had the experience to discuss literature together. Although unclear how it would work, she made changes the next day.

As her colleague had mentioned, Sara pointed out to her students that they had twelve years of English experience to discuss the material on their own. While directing their own discussion, she suggested that those who talk a lot in class restrain themselves, and others who don't talk as much to speak up. She would become an observer. Once she explained the process, Sara went to the side of the room, sat down, and started writing. A long, uncomfortable silence ensued, followed by giggling. Then, a girl, who rarely spoke in class, shared thoughtful comments about the reading. Nobody responded, and another long silence followed before a discussion began. Near the end of the class Sara stood up, described to the students what she had observed about the interactions they had with one another, and made suggestions for how they could improve the group interaction. Sara continued this process with her class for the remainder of the semester. The classroom dynamic changed dramatically; classes became very "alive and chaotic."

Sara's position now, rather than dispenser of information and controller of discussion, was as a coach of discussion; she did not play on the field, but supported the players from the sidelines. At the end of each class Sara mirrored to her students what they said and especially how they interacted. It took three years of teaching in this new way before Sara was able to get her students to effectively talk about talking. Now, she talks with them about what makes a good discussion, what is frustrating, whether all voices in the class are being heard, and the effect of arguments upon discussion.

Sara related a story from her third year with this approach. The students were having considerable difficulty with group discussions; the boys were particularly aggressive and argued loudly. The girls, in turn, became angry with the boys. To assist them, Sara videotaped the class. In small sections she showed the tape and asked the class to describe non-judgmentally what they saw. Although being non-judgmental was difficult for them initially, they eventually become aware of their talking habits. Once they were able to describe their behavior, they could discuss why they behaved as they did and how they could change it.

By using a new approach to teaching and examining her previous methods, Sara's fundamental beliefs about learning changed. She discovered that students can make their own knowledge and create their own understanding of literature. Her question, she noted, has shifted from, "What are the answers I want students to get out of a text" to, "What is happening in my classroom?" "Observation and reflection" are the "daily tools in the constant revising of my teaching." Sara described her delight when students' understandings disagreed with her own and they challenged her ideas. When she was in control of discussion, students never questioned her about the literature or her opinions. To deal with differences of opinions on tests, Sara explained to her students that they should argue their own understanding; what was most important was that they back it up.

Sara used the term Student Sustained Discussion (SSD) to describe her new approach. She acknowledged both the benefits and the challenges it provides, asserting that its success depends largely on the students and the material. Her students use it to discuss relatively straightforward poetry; she questions whether the method would be as successful with material that is unfamiliar to the students, such as Dostoevsky's *Crime and Punishment*. Sara also recognized the uncertainty, unpredictability, and risk which occur when using SSD. The teacher no longer knows what issues will be discussed or for how long, and more of class time is spent on process than content. Consequently, less material is covered.

However, Sara believes SSD is very powerful in the long run because "as learners we create what we know through talking and we discover what we think through talking. Talking is essential to learning." The idea that talking is essential to learning led Sara to ask, "What about those students who don't talk?" Typically in her classes the girls are quieter than the boys. "How can the girls be encouraged to talk so that they can become involved in learning, too, and so their voices can be heard as well?"

The poem "A Filling Station" by Elizabeth Bishop[2] inspired a discussion applying the SSD approach. Sara asked for volunteers to discuss the poem and others to be observers. Five participants volunteered to read and discuss the poem while Sara and the four other participants observed. Following the discussion of the poem, the "observers" and the "observed" shared their observations and reflections. Without the teacher leading, the discussion experience shifted for participants. For example, one person felt more responsible for her learning and free to ask, "Could you repeat that? Could you clarify that?" Participants discovered that they understood better what others in their group thought, and realized that they could interpret the poem similarly or differently than others. Lana, a teacher in Philadelphia, commented that for her there was power in the enemy teacher being located outside the circle.

Important questions were raised. "What do we do as teacher-observer when the students never catch on to something we see as important in the poem?" Phil, a student at Swarthmore College, felt uncomfortable being observed, which raised the question: "How does being observed by the teacher affect how students discuss?"

Filling Station
Elizabeth Bishop

Oh, but it is dirty!
— this little filling station,
oil-soaked, oil-permeated
to a disturbing, over-all
black translucency
Be careful with that match!

Father wears a dirty,
oil-soaked monkey suit
that cuts him under the arms,
and several quick and saucy
and greasy sons assist him
(it's a family filling station),
all quite thoroughly dirty.

Do they live in the station?
It has a cement porch
behind the pumps, and on it
a set of crushed and grease-
impregnated wickerwork;
on the wicker sofa
a dirty dog, quite comfy.

Some comic books provide
the only note of color —
of certain color. They lie
upon a big dim doily
draping a taboret
(part of the set), beside
a big hirsute begonia.

Why the extraneous plant?
Why the taboret? Why, oh why, the doily?
(Embroidered in daisy stitch
with marguerites, I think,
and heavy with gray crochet.)

Somebody embroidered the doily.
Somebody waters the plant,
or oils it, maybe. Somebody
arranges the rows of cans
so that they softly say:
ESSO — SO — SO — SO
to high-strung automobiles.
Somebody loves us all.

Another question followed: "How can we turn classroom talk over to younger students?" Sara believed her seniors were more likely to be polite to one another than younger students, who lack the same maturity and need more structure, in her opinion. Frank, of Friends Select School, suggested having the discussion in written form. The students could pass around a piece of paper upon which they would respond to what the students before them had written. Lana explained how she has her students lead "connections," a brief sharing time at the start of the class. This helps students get used to the teacher not having complete control.

At the middle school level the problem may be that students will want to talk *too* much. Phil suggested playing the "shoe game." All of the students throw one of their shoes into the center of the circle when they talk. After they have thrown in both shoes, they cannot talk anymore. This requires that students carefully consider how important their comments are. "Is it worth a shoe?"

Tselane and Sara each suggested ways to involve students in discussion without turning complete control over to them. Tselane asks her lower level English class to "teach me English." They tell her what they know and give her assignments. Sara asks her 6th and 8th grade students to choose their favorite passages from the book the class is reading and explain why they made that choice. In this way she can get them to do higher level thinking about the book and at the same time test their understanding without boring them with questions like "Who is the main character?" and "What did she or he do?"

Sara reminded the group that students are interested in their own valid questions. When teachers impose questions upon them, they will not be engaged unless the teachers' questions happen to coincide with theirs. To make learning relevant to the students, "Let them ask their own questions. Let *them* lead discussion."

Endnotes

1   Courtney Cazden, Classroom Discourse: The Language of Teaching and Learing. (Portsmouth, New Hampshire: Heinemann Educational Books, Inc. 1988).
2   Elizabeth Bishop, The Complete Poems, 1927-1979. (New York: Farrar, Straus & Giroux, Inc., 1983).

Using Principles to Effect Change
A Workshop Presented by Holly H. Perry, Academy for the Middle Years, Philadelphia, Pennsylvania

Description by a scribe and the presenters

Academy for the Middle Years is a public middle school located in northwest Philadelphia. In 1988, it became a member of the Coalition of Essential Schools, which was established by Ted Sizer of Brown University. Since then, the faculty and parent representatives have been consciously exploring what it means to make school decisions based on a set of Nine Common Principles to which Coalition schools adhere. The Nine Common Principles are:

1. *Intellectual focus.* The school should focus on helping students learn to use their minds well.

2. *Simple goals.* The school's goals should be simple — that each student master a limited number of essential skills and areas of knowledge.

3. *Universal goals.* The school's goals should apply to all students, although the means to the goals will vary as those students themselves vary.

4. *Personalization.* Teaching and learning should be personalized to the maximum extent feasible.

5. *Student-as-worker.* The governing metaphor of the school should be student-as-worker, rather than the more traditional teacher-as-deliverer of the instructional services.

6. *Diploma by "exhibition."* The diploma should be awarded upon a successful final demonstration of mastery — an exhibition — of the central skills and knowledge of the school's program.

7. *Tone.* The tone of the school should explicitly and self-consciously stress values of unanxious expectations, trust, and decency. Parents should be treated as collaborators.

8. *Staff.* The principal and teachers should see themselves as generalists first and specialists second.

9. *Budget.* Ultimate administrative and budget targets should include a total student load of 80 or fewer per teacher, substantial time for collective planning, competitive staff salaries, and a per-pupil cost no more than 10% above that of traditional schools.

Holly Perry is the principal of the Academy for the Middle Years, a school of two hundred and forty students from all parts of Philadelphia. Students are accepted on a lottery system; however, the school maintains a racial balance within the population. Mildly handicapped children are integrated into the programs. There are three teaching teams grouped by grade, each with a special education teacher. The Academy for the Middle Years is the only public school in Philadelphia that is a member of the Coalition.

Fundamental change is rarely simple or painless. The members of the Academy for the Middle Years community have struggled to institute practices and attitudes consistent with the Nine Common Principles of Essential Schools. They have come to realize that this is a way of life if genuine learning and teaching is to occur. Holly commented, "The school is the messiest it's ever been...I also think it makes the most sense."

There are no class periods at the Academy for the Middle Years. Each teaching team determines how time will be structured, thereby making the use of time flexible. The curriculum is designed after deciding what skills are essential for the students to learn. Lana, a teacher at the Academy, discussed her switch from being a Spanish and English teacher to being a humanities teacher because that was what was needed. Grades are not used; they are viewed as being punitive and as an inappropriate source of motivation. Instead, alternative forms of assessment, such as interviews with students, are used so that students have an authentic opportunity to demonstrate their knowledge and understanding.

Lana fully supports the changes occurring at the Academy for the Middle Years, and feels that as a model of change, it is making a contribution to education. A participant commented that, "We give kids more opportunity to use their minds in kindergarten. Later on, we tell them what to do. That bothers me."

Change within schools is difficult, and the Academy for the Middle Years has had its own set of challenges. Teachers who are trying to change their methods of teaching and instructional areas require a strong support system; even when they see the changes that are important to make, they do not always know how to accomplish the changes. The school also suffers from the effect of being part of a larger bureaucratic system. Teachers can be assigned to teach at the school, causing disagreement about the philosophy and purpose of the school. If an assigned teacher fails to support the mission of the school, there is often no respectable way to dismiss that teacher. The school also suffers from marginalization within the larger Philadelphia School District. Many of the workshop participants shared the difficulties they have had incorporating such principles into their institutions. Change is often time consuming and slow. As Holly exclaimed, "I feel like I'm running as fast as I can to stay ahead."

Changing from the Inside Out: Whole School Renewal in An Urban Context

A Workshop Presented by Andrew Gelber, PATHS/PRISM: The Philadelphia Partnership for Education, and Susan Hirsh, Earl Jefferson, Susan Linder, Nancy Morgan, and Arleen Swidler, Frances E. Willard Elementary School, Philadelphia, Pennsylvania

Description by a scribe and the editors

In early 1990, several Philadelphia elementary and middle schools commenced an intensive process of whole school renewal, focused on educational innovation and improvement. Each school has pursued a range of educationally focused objectives, while also drawing on shared decision making and school-based management as supportive structures for involving entire staffs. Andrew Gelber is the Director of School Programs for PATHS/PRISM, which serves as the support and technical assistance agency for elementary and middle school renewal in the School District of Philadelphia through programs, instructional assistance, and grants.

The workshop began with focus questions related to creating whole school change.

> If, when you return on Monday morning, you could change one thing in your school for maximum positive impact on the school's program and mission, what would you change? Why? How would you try to go about it? What support would you want or need? What obstacles would you anticipate?

Drawing upon the focus questions, the workshop participants developed a "wish list" of changes in the politics of education that could be made in order to improve education.

Wish List
• Increase teacher flexibility
• Decrease curricular restraints
• Redesign schools to meet students' needs
• Incorporate community service projects
• Have smaller class sizes
• Involve students in current issues and give students credit for their involvement in them
• Strive for more heterogeneous groupings
• Use multiple methods of assessment
• Make students more active participants in the school community
• Have public schools address the human needs of people in the local area

• Put less emphasis on city-wide standardized test scores, and explore alternative means of assessment
• Give professionals more trust in judgments based on teaching
• Move away from IQ testing
• Treat teachers professionally in all aspects of their responsibilities

The Frances E. Willard Elementary School is one of the Philadelphia schools involved in whole school renewal. The teachers in the school were involved in a "Dream Weekend" through which they identified the changes they wanted, and developed overarching goals for Willard School.
• Developing a language-centered focus for *all* curriculum and instruction
• Involving the whole School in interdisciplinary and thematic curriculum and instruction
• Restructuring the school day, the school year, and the K-4 sequence to enhance and support the above goals
• Focusing explicitly on ways in which assessment can help Willard faculty to accomplish and succeed with all the goals described above

Related to each overarching goal are a number of projects or ideas through which the goals can be met.

PATHS/PRISM has offered funding to the Willard School, but has also been an important source of inspiration to the teachers at Willard. PATHS/PRISM acts as a magnifying glass through which the teachers at Willard have been able to see and achieve their goals.

Resources

David, Jane L. "What It Takes to Restructure Education," Educational Leadership. May, 1991. pp. 11-15.
Glickman, Carl. "Pretending Not to Know What We Know," Educational Leadership. May, 1991. pp. 4-10.

Current Issues in Evaluation and Assessment
A Workshop Presented by Lynne Strieb, Greenfield School,
Philadelphia, Pennsylvania

Description by Susan Thibideau, scribe, and the editors

Lynne Strieb is currently examining forms of evaluation and assessment used in schools. She invited workshop participants to share the methods and forms they have developed for themselves or that their schools or districts require. This sharing was the basis of the workshop.

Lynne is interested in the periodical *The Primary Language Record*, developed at the Center for Language in Primary Education in London, England, by Myra Barre and colleagues. One of the influences on the Center's work was *Inquiry Into Meaning* by Ann Bussis, Edward Chittenden, Marianne Amarel, and Edith Klausner.[1] Lynne described the Record which requires, among other things, teachers to write descriptions of children's reading at regular intervals; to interview parents about children's reading at home; and to interview children themselves about their reading.

Lynne herself maintains two types of written records on the children in addition to samples of their work. The first is a chart for each child on which she writes what the child does in reading, math, writing, and project/choice time, and the child's behavior (including social interactions). She attempts to record something each day. At the end of two weeks, this information is rewritten in narrative form for anecdotal records. She writes anecdotal records on three children each night, rather than trying to cover the whole class at one time. Both the daily record and the anecdotal record are used for report card comments and to prepare for parent conferences. She does not give the unedited records to the parents to read.

Lisa, a high school teacher, struggles with writing evaluation for her students. She wonders who the audience for these records is: parents, students, or colleges? Although her principal has encouraged her to write narrative evaluations for the students, she is concerned that they may be too informal for college admissions. When and how are the evaluations public documents?

Vivian of Central Park East School in New York City writes narratives, and maintains records of class discussions and contributions students make to them. She observes students as they work within groups and notes how they choose to use their time. She sends records of class discussions home to parents to show the group effort. Her student teachers learn shorthand so they can record class discussions. Students save their drawings in folders and they keep a record of their choices in class. They prepare class work to show to their families at conferences which parents, children, and teachers attend. Preparation for the conferences is extremely time consuming, though valuable.

Gail tapes her students as they talk with her about their progress, and as she shares with them what progress she sees. The tapes are replayed during parent conferences.

At Taylor School, Teresa has curriculum standards which require that each skill be evaluated quantitatively. Forms are filled out for every aspect of the curriculum, and her class must meet the schedule of progress dictated by the standardized curriculum. Because of special funding, some of the forms are very detailed and specific, but necessary in order to comply with the requirements of the funding.

Marcia, of the Pennsylvania School for the Deaf, raises the special documentation problems associated with special education students. The school is required to write a narrative description of the students' education and growth when they enter the school. Although done for legal purposes for the parents, it is used procedurally for the district. The dual purpose of the document causes problems for parents who have difficulty with the language of official documents. She feels that the documents for parents and the school district should be separate.

Questions were raised. Should student work be taken home or kept at school? Alex shared her frustration that students' writing books are sent home for parents to see, but sometimes never come back to school. Gail uses a Friday folder to send home selected works by students. Parents return the folder Monday. Lynne suggested the possibility of working out an agreement with the child to send home every third drawing or writing. She tells both parents and children at the beginning of the year that she will save all writing and drawing and will return it at the end of the year. Children and parents may look at the folders at any time, and time is set aside at parent conferences to do so in a more formal way.

What is the purpose of evaluation? How do grades assist students in learning? What is the purpose of portfolios? What are new ways of evaluating student progress which can further learning? This group sharing raised issues of audience and language, of privacy, of the purpose of all levels and types of evaluations, and the influence evaluation systems have upon teaching methods, styles, and planning.

Endnote

1   Anne Bussis, Edward Chittenden, Marianne Amarel, and Edith Klausner, Inquiry Into Meaning: An Illustration of Learning to Read. (Hillsdale, New Jersey, Laurence Erlbaum Associates. 1985.)

Appendix A: Participants

Conference registration and the formation of working groups was done in alphabetical order by the first letter of the first name. This list is organized similarly.

Aileen Gardner
The Miquon School
Harts Lane
Miquon, PA 19452

Alex Kendrick
Goshen Friends School
814 North Chester Road
West Chester, PA 19380

Alexandra Bricklin
836 East 15th Street
Chester, PA 19013
The School in Rose Valley

Alison Davis
2717 Parrish Street
Philadelphia, PA 19130
Alison's House

Amy Verstappen
Friends Select School
17th and the Parkway
Philadelphia, PA 19103

Andrea Wormley
302 Cardinal Road
Edgewater Park, NJ 08010
Friends Child Care Center

Andrew Gelber
1100 Spruce Street
Apartment #3C
Philadelphia, PA 1910
Philadelphia School District, PATHS/PRISM

Andy Doan
Friends Select School
17th and the Parkway
Philadelphia, PA 19103

Angie Feltman
Friends Select School
17th and the Parkway
Philadelphia, PA 19103

Ann D. Hazard
403 Cedar Lane
Swarthmore, PA 19081
Delaware County Community College

Ann Renninger
Program in Education
Swarthmore College
Swarthmore, PA 19081

Anna Kennedy
4100 Garrett Road
Drexel Hill, PA 19026
Lansdowne Friends School

Anna Roelofs
P.O. Box 1711
Cambridge, MA 02238
Primary Source Center

Anna Rosa Kohn
Princeton Friends School
470 Quaker Road
Princeton, NJ 08540

Anne Fretz
Green Acres School
1170 Danville Drive
Rockville, MD 20852

Anne Javsicas
1316 Church Road
Oreland, PA 19075
Plymouth Meeting Friends School

Anne M. Brady
6620 N. 7th Street
Philadelphia, PA 19126
The Miquon School

Anne S. Watt
P.O. Box 1711
Cambridge, MA 02238
Primary Source Center

Anne Thomas
Friends Select School
17th and the Parkway
Philadelphia, PA 19103

Arabella Pope
The Miquon School
Harts Lane
Miquon, PA 19452

Arleen Swidler
c/o Andrew Gelber
1100 Spruce Street, #3C
Philadelphia, PA 19107
Philadelphia School District

Barbara Weaver
6330 Farmer Lane
Flourtown, PA 19031
Abington Friends School

Beth Gross-Eskin
3345 Bowman Street
Philadelphia, PA 19129
The Miquon School

Betsy Elliott
225 Washington Avenue
Sellersviller, PA 18960
The Miquon School

Betsy Wice
2410 Spruce Street
Philadelphia, PA 19103
Philadelphia School District, Teacher Learning Cooperative

Betty Becker
980 North Orange Street
Media, PA 19063
The School in Rose Valley

Betty Becton
912 Truepenny Lane
Media, PA 19063
Wallingford-Swarthmore School District

Betty Ratay
Unknown
Montgomery School

Betty Tilley
3311 Baring Street
Philadelphia, PA 19104
The Miquon School

Bill Northcutt
112 East 6th Avenue
Conshohocken, PA 19428-1717
The Miquon School

Bob Gross
Swarthmore College
Swarthmore, PA 19081

Bob Vitalo
16 North Olive Street
Media, PA 19063
Media Providence Friends School

Bonnie Bishoff
420 West Schoolhouse Lane
Philadelphia, PA 19144
Friends Select School

C. Michael Pfoutz
1 Old Mill Road
Apartment #1
New Hope, PA 18938
Graduate School of Education, University of Pennsylvania

Carol Leckey
509 Enfield Road
Oreland, PA 19075
Abington Friends School

Carol Montag
Cornerstone School
2313 Southeast Lake Weir Road
Ocala, FL 32671

Carol Ouimette
P.O. Box 6028
Evanston, IL 60204
The Network of Progressive Educators

Carol Woltering
Marple-Newtown Montessori School
79 Spring Avenue
Broomall, PA 19008

Cassandra Hyacinthe
29 Fairway
Mt. Vernon, NY 10552
Sarah Lawrence College

Catherine S. Fisher
5 Pendleton Drive
Cherry Hill, NJ 08003
Swarthmore College

Cecelia Traugh
2112 Spruce Street
Philadelphia, PA 19103
Friends Select School

Cecily Selling
514 East Durham Street
Philadelphia, PA 19119
Stratford Friends School

Celester McLaughlin
Swarthmore-Rutledge K-8
Wallingford-Swarthmore School
District
100 College Avenue
Swarthmore, PA 19081

Charlotte Hartley
623 South Avenue
Media, PA 19063
Penn-Delco School District

Cynthia Adams
The Miquon School
Harts Lane
Miquon, PA 19452

Cynthia Potter
State College Friends
State College, PA 16801

Daisy Newbold
Radnor Township School
District
135 South Wayne Avenue
Wayne, PA 19087

Dan Klatz
1009 South 2nd Street
Philadelphia, PA 19147
Abington Friends School

Dan Schaffer
Unknown
*Wallingford-Swarthmore School
District*

Daryl Polansky
1606 Rodman Street
Philadelphia, PA 19146
Philadelphia School District

David Heitler-Klevans
Friends School, Haverford
Haverford, PA 19041

David Millians
1696 Dyson Drive
Atlanta, GA 30307
Paideia School

David Nagel
918 South 49th Street
Philadelphia, PA 19143
*Project START, University of
Pennsylvania*

David Philhower
1511-B Wallingford Road
Springfield, PA 19064
The School in Rose Valley

Debbie Bakan
108 West Phil-Ellena Street
Philadelphia, PA 19119
*Plymouth Meeting Friends
School*

Debbie Wile
Wallingford Elementary School
Wallingford-Swarthmore School
District
20 South Providence Road
Wallingford, PA 19086

Deborah Sax
14 Broad Street
West Chester, PA 19380
Independent

Deborah Twombly
23 Bridgewood Court.
Belle Mead, NJ 08502
Princeton Friends School

Diana Undercuffler
8113 Washington Lane
Wyncote, PA 19095
Abington Friends School

Diane Anderson
210 Yale Avenue
Swarthmore, PA 19081
Swarthmore College

Dick Gibboney
Box 91
Birchrunville, PA 19421
*Graduate School of Education,
University of Pennsylvania*

Dita Small
605 South Avenue
Media, PA 19063
The School in Rose Valley

Dolores L. Gmitter
258 South 44th Street
Philadelphia, PA 19104
Philadelphia School District

Doris Outerbridge
Germantown Friends School
31 West Coulter Street
Philadelphia, PA 19144

Dorothy Flanagan
Darby & Llandillo Roads
Havertown, PA 19083
Stratford Friends School

Dru Finkbeiner
222 Woodward Road
Moylan, PA 19065
The School in Rose Valley

Earl Jefferson
c/o Andrew Gelber
1100 Spruce Street, #3C
Philadelphia, PA 19103
Philadelphia School District

Edie Klausner
16 Locust Lane
Norristown, PA 19401
The School in Rose Valley

Eileen Gruenwald
State College Friends School
State College, PA 16801

Eleanor Duckworth
Graduate School of Education,
Harvard University
Longfellow Hall
Appian Way
Cambridge, MA 02138

Elizabeth Useem
352 Woodley Road
Merion, PA 19066
*Bryn Mawr College, Haverford
College*

Ellen Ayres
1 Crum Ledge
Swarthmore, PA 19081
The School in Rose Valley

Ellen Murphey
3551 Providence Road
Newtown Square, PA 19073
The School in Rose Valley

Ellen Stevenson
1210 Thorndale Road
Downingtown, PA 19335
*Delaware County Intermediate
Unit*

Emily Richardson
868 North 23rd Street
Philadelphia, PA 19130
The School in Rose Valley

Emily Wolf
Chestnut Hill Academy
500 West Willow Grove Avenue
Philadelphia, PA 19118-4198

Emma J. Lapansky
46 Pennock Terrace
Lansdowne, PA 19050
Haverford College

Eric Sievers
Post Office Box 1083
Wellfleet, MA 02193
Independent

Estelle Goldsmith
312 Old Forest
Wynnewood, PA 19096
Pennsylvania School for the Deaf

Eva Travers
Swarthmore College
Swarthmore, PA 19081

Fern Culhane
438 West School House Lane
Philadelphia, PA 19144
The Miquon School

Fiona M. Jackson
306 International House
3701 Chestnut Street
Philadelphia, PA 19104
*Graduate School of Education,
University of Pennsylvania*

Fran Catania
11 Twin Pine Way
Glen Mills, PA 19342
*The School in Rose Valley,
Widener Law School*

Fran Felter
37 Longpoint Lane
Media, PA 19063
The School in Rose Valley

Francesca Vassalluzzo
552 Churchville Lane
Holland, PA 18966
Friends Child Care Center

Francine Shaw
7145 Crittenden
Philadelphia, PA 19119
Friends Select School

Frank Fisher
Friends Select School
17th and the Parkway
Philadelphia, PA 19103

Gail Apfel
Stonehurst Hills School
Upper Darby School District
Upper Darby, PA 19082

Gail J. Sklar
2931 Berkley Road
Ardmore, PA 19003
Philadelphia School District

Gerry Seymour
22 Slitting Mill Road
Glen Mills, PA 19342
The School in Rose Valley

Gloria Hoffner
Unknown
The Philadelphia Inquirer

Greg Williams
The Miquon School
The School in Rose Valley
Harts Lane
Miquon, PA 19452

Hattie Stroman
c/o Pam Gibson
1335 S. Chadwick Street
Philadelphia, PA 19146
Philadelphia School District

Heide Lasher
State College Friends School
State College, PA 16801

Heidi Hammel
P.O. Box 71
Bryn Mawr, PA 19010
Delaware Valley Friends School

Helen Manglesdorf
371 Lyceum Avenue
Philadelphia, PA 19128
*Tyler School of Art, Temple
University*

Hollis A. Koljian
#1 Old Mill Road
Apartment #1
New Hope, PA 18938
Pennsbury School District

Holly H. Perry
1847 Guernsey Avenue
Abington, PA 19001
Philadelphia School District

Holly Terry
313 Port Royal Avenue
Philadelphia, PA 19462
*Plymouth Meeting Friends
School*

Horace Means
Jubilee School
4211 Chestnut Street
Philadelphia, PA 19104

Iddo Gal
Graduate School of Education
University of Pennsylvania
3700 Walnut Street/LRC
Philadelphia, PA 19104

Jacquelyn Allen-Bailey
5816 Washington Avenue
Philadelphia, PA 19143
Philadelphia School District

Jane Bassman
626 West Upsal Street
Philadelphia, PA 19119
*Community College of
Philadelphia*

Jane Freman
Princeton Friends School
470 Quaker Road
Princeton, NJ 08540

Jane McVeigh-Schultz
15 Waverly Road
Wyncote, PA 10095
Abington Friends School

Jane Miluski
18 Brookside Road
Wallingford, PA 19086
The School in Rose Valley

Jeanne Murtha
205 North Swarthmore Avenue
Apartment #5
Swarthmore, PA 19081
*Trinity Co-operative Day
Nursery*

Jed Kee
Green Acres School
11701 Danville Drive
Rockville, MD 20852

Jennifer Hill
Taylor Elementary
Philadelphia School District
Randolph Street & Erie Avenue
Philadelphia, PA 19140

Jennifer Moser
61 Maine Avenue
Apartment E-25
Rockville Centre, NY 11570
Great Neck Public Schools

Jenny King
Princeton Friends School
470 Quaker Road
Princeton, NJ 08540

Jenny Taylor
Germantown Friends School
31 West Coulter Street
Philadelphia, PA 19144

Jerry Nowell
99 Briarcliff Court
Glen Mills, PA 19342
The School in Rose Valley

Jim Comey
105 Treaty Road
Drexel Hill, PA 19036
*Wallingford-Swarthmore School
District*

Jim Larkin
Graduate School of Education
University of Pennsylvania
37th & Walnut Streets
Philadelphia, PA 19104

Jim Strick
Princeton Friends School
470 Quaker Road
Princeton, NJ 08540

Joan Countryman
433 West Stafford Street
Philadelphia, PA 19144
Germantown Friends School

Joan Harrington
Germantown Academy
Fort Washington, PA 19034

Joan O. Sloane
6 Tulip Lane
Rose Valley, PA 19065
The School in Rose Valley

Joan Ranere
17th and the Parkway
Philadelphia, PA 19103
Friends Select School

JoAnn Miller
501 Moylan Avenue
Media, PA 19063
The School in Rose Valley

Joe Ramsey
The Miquon School
Harts Lane
Miquon, PA 19452

John Colgan-Davis
Friends Select School
17th and the Parkway
Philadelphia, PA 19103

John F. Pepe
Stonehurst Elementary School
Upper Darby School District
Timberlake Road
Upper Darby, PA 19082

John Krumm
421 Kingwood Road
King of Prussia, PA 19406
The Miquon School

John Scardina
Media Providence Friends
School
125 West Third Street
Media, PA 19063

John Shaifer
22 Cedar Avenue
West Conshohocken, PA 19428
Chestnut Hill Academy

John V. McNealis
Brandywine Learning Center
Devereux Foundation
Devereux Road, R.D. 1
Glenmoore, PA 19343

Judy Buchanan
3726 Spring Garden Street
Philadelphia, PA 19104
Philadelphia School District,
Philadelphia Writing Project

Julie Gould Marothy
4648 Silverwood Street
Philadelphia, PA 19128
Pennsylvania School for the
Deaf

Justine P. DeVan
707 North Third Street
Philadelphia, PA
Philadelphia School District

Kae Kalwaic
447 Briarhill Road
Springfield, PA 19064
Wallingford-Swarthmore School
District

Kara Howard
89 Orchard Court
Royersford, PA 19468
Philadelphia School District

Karen Falcon
15 South 43rd Street
Philadelphia, PA 19104
Jubilee School

Karen M. Glaser
371 East Gowen Avenue
Philadelphia, PA 19119
Independent

Karen Rothschild
21 East McPherson Street
Graduate School of Education,
University of Pennsylvania

Karen Scholnick
6825 Milton Street
Philadelphia, PA 19119
Office of Assessment,
Philadelphia School District

Karla Read
323 Mount Alverno Road
Media, PA 19063
The School in Rose Valley

Karlie Roth
79 Spring Avenue
Broomall, PA 19008
Marple-Newtown Montessori
School

Kate Guerin
7901 Henry Avenue
Apartment B-309
Philadelphia, PA
Philadelphia School District

Kathe Jervis
1170 5th Avenue
New York, NY 10029
Network of Progressive
Educators

Kathleen Dalton
714A Wolcott Drive
Philadelphia, PA 19118
Upper Darby School District

Kathy Wiley
Swarthmore-Rutledge K-8
Wallingford-Swarthmore
School District
Swarthmore, PA 19081

Kendall Landis
450 Osage Lane
Media, PA 19063
Swarthmore College

Kit Wallace
The Miquon School
Harts Lane
Miquon, PA 19452

Lallie O'Brien
The Pew Charitable Trusts
Three Parkway, Suite 501
Philadelphia, PA 19103

Lana Gold
11974 Dumont Road
Philadelphia, PA 19116
Philadelphia School District

Laura Wood
Germantown Friends School
31 West Coulter Street
Philadelphia, PA 19144

Lauren deMoll
848 Upton Road
Aston, PA 19104
The School in Rose Valley

Lee Quinby
611 East Prospect Avenue
State College, PA 16801
State College Friends School

Leigh Pezzano
The Miquon School
Harts Lane
Miquon, PA 19452

Leni Jacksen
14702 Sylvan Street
Van Nuys, CA 91401
Children's Community School

Leonard Belasco
5917 Pulaski Avenue
Philadelphia, PA 19144
Philadelphia School District

Linda Ehrlich
2233 West Chester Pike
Broomall, PA 19008
Philadelphia School District

Linda Glovack
Swarthmore-Rutledge K-8
Wallingford-Swarthmore School
District
Swarthmore, PA 19081

Linda Kuffler
1774 Cloverly Lane
Rydal, PA 19046
Abington Friends School

Lisa Barsky
Delaware Valley Friends School
P.O. Box 71
Bryn Mawr, PA 19010

Lisa Hantman
9442 Kirkwood Street
Philadelphia, PA 19114
Philadelphia School District

Lisa Richardson
Parkmont School
4842 16th Street N.W.
Washington, DC 20011

Lisa Smulyan
Program in Education
Swarthmore College
Swarthmore, PA 19081

Lois Ann Rose
430 Wellesley Road
Philadelphia, PA 19119
Haverford Friends School

Loretta Zaklad
600 Parrish Road
Swarthmore, PA 19081
The School in Rose Valley

Louisa Walsh
1151 West Sterigere Street
AC-26
Norristown, PA 19401
*Plymouth Meeting Friends
School*

Lynne Strieb
232 West School House Lane
Philadelphia, PA 19144
Philadelphia School District

Maggie Ellis
Friends Select School
17th and the Parkway
Philadelphia, PA 19103

Marcia Reed
412 Scott Lane
Wallingford, PA 19086
*Wallingford-Swarthmore School
District*

Marcia Volpe
176 Benezet Street
Philadelphia, PA 19118
*Pennsylvania School for the
Deaf*

Marcy Morgan
4712 Windsor Avenue
Philadelphia, PA 19143
Shipley School

Margaret B. Rawson
7924 Rocky Springs Road
Frederick, MD 21702
Orton Society

Margaret Guerra
Friends Child Care Center
1501 Cherry Street
Philadelphia, PA 19102

Margaret Pennock
P.O. Box 354
South Freeport, ME 04078
Soule School

Margo Ackerman
7143 Lincoln Drive
Philadelphia, PA 19119
*Philadelphia School District,
Philadelphia Writing Project*

Marguerite Goff
Unknown

Marilyn Cochran-Smith
Graduate School of Education,
University of Pennsylvania
3700 Walnut Street
Philadelphia, PA 19104

Marilyn L. Boston
654 Arbor Road
Yeadon, PA 19050
Philadelphia School District

Maris Cutting
Princeton Friends School
470 Quaker Road
Princeton, NJ 08540

Marna Matthews
320 South Lincoln Avenue
Newtown, PA 18940
Newtown Friends

Martha Wolf
Friends Select School
17th and the Parkway
Philadelphia, PA 19103

Mary Alice Hoffman
Swarthmore-Rutledge K-8
Wallingford-Swarthmore School
District
Swarthmore, PA 19081

Mary Ann B. McBridge
2008 State Road
Bensalem, PA 19020
Philadelphia School District

Mary D. Shaw
1017 Houserville Road
State College, PA 16801
State College Friends School

Mary Daniels
512 Woodland Terrace
Philadelphia, PA 19104
Beaver College

Mary Hebron
c/o Renee Coscia
1376 Midland Avendue
Apartment #707
Bronxville, NY 10708
Mamaroneck School District

Maxine Bailey
Community Housing Resource
Board
23 South Olive Street
Media, PA 19063

Maxine Greene
Division of Philosophy, The
Social Sciences and Education
Teachers College, Columbia
University
New York, NY 10027

Meg deMoll
424 Gayley Street
Media, PA 19063
Lansdowne Friends School

Mercedes Villamil
215 Overlook Road
Philadelphia, PA 19128
Germantown Academy

Mia Genif
Princeton Friends School
470 Quaker Road
Princeton, NJ 08540

Michael Carbone
Muhlenberg College
Education Department
Allentown, PA 18104

Michael L. Nowell
848 Upton Avenue
Aston, PA 19014
The School in Rose Valley

Michael Rothbart
Swarthmore College
Swarthmore, PA 19081

Michael Smith
7 Benjamin Franklin Parkway
Suite 700
Philadelphia, PA 19103
*PATHS/PRISM,
Philadelphia School District*

Michele Jean Sims
502 East Gorgas Lane
Philadelphia, PA 19119
*PATHS/PRISM,
Philadelphia School District*

Mona Bergman Dewane
1500 Locust Street
Apartment #3801
Philadelphia, PA 19102
*Pennsylvania School for the
Deaf*

Nancy Kersten
125 West 3rd Street
Media, PA 19063
*Media-Providence Friends
School*

Nancy Morgan
c/o Andrew Gelber
1100 Spruce Street, #3C
Philadelphia, PA 19107
Philadelphia School District

Nancy Sleator
4 The Knoll
Lansdowne, PA 19050
Lansdowne Friends School

Nancy Wilson
Princeton Friends School
470 Quaker Road
Princeton, NJ 08540

Nancy Wolff
Unknown
Philadelphia School District

Nickie Miller
8206 Ardmore Avenue
Philadelphia, PA 19118
*Springfield Montgomery County
School District*

Nora Walsh
302 South Gayley Street
Media, PA 19063
The School in Rose Valley

Pam Gibson
1335 South Chadwick Street
Philadelphia, PA 19146
Philadelphia School District

Pamela Good
c/o Parthenia Moore
Philadelphia School District
Howard & Ontario Streets
Philadelphia, PA 19140

Pamela V. Bishop
245 Woodlyn Avenue
Glenside, PA 19038
Abington Friends School

Parthenia Anita Moore
William Cramp Elementary
Philadelphia School District
Howard & Ontario Streets
Philadelphia, PA 19140

Patridcia A. Suyemoto
521 South 46th Street
Apartment #3
Philadelphia, PA 19143
*Graduate School of Education,
University of Pennsylvania*

Patricia Baxter
Unionville-Chadds Ford School
District
Administration Office, Route 82
Unionville, PA 19375

Patricia Bradley
7904 Flourtown Avenue
Wyndmoor, PA 19118
Chestnut Hill Academy

Patricia Carini
RD #1, Box 166
Eagle Bridge, NY 12057
Independent

Patricia F. Hamden
48 North Sproul Road
Apartment 1
Broomall, PA 19008
University of Pennsylvania

Patty Cruice
4644 Hazel Street
Philadelphia, PA 19143
Philadelphia School District

Paul Blundin
12 East Road Valley Road
Wallingford, PA 19086
The School in Rose Valley

Paula Paul
5917 Pulaski Avenue
Philadelphia, PA 19144
Philadelphia School District

Peg Perlmutter
6618 North 7th Street
Philadelphia, PA 19126
Philadelphia School District

Peggy Richards
c/o Renee Coscia
1376 Midland Avenue
Apartment #707
Bronxville, NY 10708
Mamaroneck School District

Penny Colgan-Davis
101 West Mount Airy Avenue
Philadelphia, PA 19119
Friends Select School

Penny Greenwell
139 Meetinghouse Road
Jenkintown, PA 19046
Independent

Penny Starr
359 Owen Avenue
Lansdowne, PA 19050
Pennsylvania School for the Deaf

Peter Blaze Corcoran
Department of Education
Bates College
Lewiston, ME 04240

Renata Ritzman
Hurricane Hollow
Wawa, PA 19063
The School in Rose Valley

Renee Coscia
1376 Midland Avenue
Apartment #707
Bronxville, NY 10708
Mamaroneck School District

Rhoda Drucker Kanevsky
418 West Price Street
Philadelphia, PA
Philadelphia School District

Richard Fisher
Princeton Friends School
470 Quaker Road
Princeton, NJ 08540

Robert J. Templeton
13 West Jefferson Street
Media, PA 19063
*Wallingford-Swarthmore School
District*

Robert Kay
P.O. Box C
Paoli, PA 19301
The School in Rose Valley

Robin Ann Ingram
136 West Upsal Street
Philadelphia, PA 19119
Project Learn School

Robin Saunders
19 Letitia Lane
Media, PA 19063
*Wallingford-Swarthmore School
District*

Robin Smart
Friends Select School
17th and the Parkway
Philadelphia, PA 19103

Rosemarie Gulla
13062 Kelvin Avenue
Philadelphia, PA 19116
Abington Friends School

Ruth G. Goodenough
204 Fox Lane
Wallingford, PA 19086
The School in Rose Valley

Sandy Caesar
324 Darlington Road
Wawa, PA 19063
The School in Rose Valley

Sandy Gruber
125 West 3rd Street
Media, PA 19063
Media-Providence Friends

Sara Allen
7120 Cresheim Road
Philadelphia, PA 19119
Springside School

Sharon Parker
1207 Manor Road
Havertown, PA 19083
Strath Haven Middle School

Sharon Silver
Ridley Middle School
Free & Dupont Streets
Ridley Park, PA 19078

Sheila Marcy
Swarthmore-Rutledge K-8
Wallingford-Swarthmore School
District
Swarthmore, PA 19081

Shirley P. Brown
6905 Wayne Avenue
Philadelphia, PA 19119
Philadelphia School District

Simon Firestone
539 West 112th Street
Apartment 2A
New York, NY 10025
Swarthmore College

Steve Smith
605 South Avenue
Media, PA 19063
The School in Rose Valley

Steve Weimar
20 Prospect Avenue
Rutledge, PA 19070
*Educators for Social
Responsibility*

Suchitra Davenport
133 Ogden Avenue
Swarthmore, PA 19081
The School in Rose Valley

Sue Edwards
32 College Avenue
Swarthmore, PA 19081
The School in Rose Valley

Sue Gold
125 West 3rd Street
Media, PA 19063
*Media-Providence Friends
School*

Sue Graf
The Miquon School
Harts Lane
Miquon, PA 19452

Susan Bartolini
Unknown
Montgomery School

Susan Bartow
Unknown

Susan Dean
508 Harvard Avenue
Swarthmore, PA 19081
Bryn Mawr College

Susan Hirsh
c/o Andrew Gelber
1100 Spruce Street
Apartment #3C
Philadelphia, PA 19107
Philadelphia School District

Susan J. Boal
3215 Earle Street
Harrisburg, PA 17109
Philadelphia School District

Susan Linder
c/o Andrew Gelber
1100 Spruce Street
Apartment #3C
Philadelphia, PA 19107
Philadelphia School District

Susan Proctor
11 Twin Pine Way
Glen Mills, PA 19342
The School in Rose Valley

Susan Shapiro
7834 Old York Road
Elkins Park, PA 19117
Philadelphia School District

Susan Stein
7128 Crittendon Avenue
Philadelphia, PA 19119
Friends Select School

Susan Thibedeau
237 South 44th Street
Apartment #2R
Philadelphia, PA 19104
*Graduate School of Education,
University of Pennsylvania*

Susie Robillard
State College Friends School
State College, PA 16801

Suzanne B. Perot
Germantown Academy
Fort Washington, PA 19034

Suzanne Blank
320 South Lincoln Avenue
Newtown, PA 18940
Newtown Friends School

Suzie Laborda
2441 North Feathering Road
Media, PA 19063
The School in Rose Valley

T. Sheppard-Williams
Parkmont School
4842 16th Street N.W.
Washington, DC 20011

Tere Camerota
1112 Church Road
Wyncote, PA 19095
Oak Lane County Day School

Teresa Alvarez
3906 North 7th Street
Philadelphia, PA 19140
Philadelphia School District

Thresa Edler
841 Yeadon Avenue
Yeadon, PA 19050
Philadelphia School District

Toni McDonnell
8509 Glen Campbell Road
Philadelphia, PA 19128
The Miquon School

Val Sandberg
200 South Providence Road
Wallingford, PA 19086
*Wallingford-Swarthmore School
District*

Viviane P. Tallman
P.O. Box 63J
Arch Cape, OR 97102
Fire Mountain School

Viviane Wallace
3515 Henry Hudson Parkway
Bronx, NY 10463
Central Park East 1

Wendy Towle
203 Larchwood Road
West Chester, PA 19380
*Wallingford-Swarthmore School
District*

Zara Joffe
236 Dickinson Avenue
Swarthmore, PA 19081
*Community Housing Resource
Board*

Zelda Davis-Jones
405 Edison-Furlong Road
Doylestown, PA 18901
Philadelphia School District

The following Swarthmore
College students were
participants, also.

Alexander Cooley
Amy McBride Barker
Andrew Cummings
Bart Smith
Brendan Kelly
Chris Verdecchia
Christina Richards
Daniel Keleher
Daniel Long
Dina Sieden
Eric Sievers
Gloria Lee
John Bulavage
Jordan Saturen
Kate Ehrenfeld
Lani Seidel
Lisa Morse
Michael Rothbart
Mimi Keller
Miriam Marx
Nicole Hollings
Phaedra Swift
Phil Costa
Rajesh Kumar
Richard Tchen
Sarah Keith
Sheila Fitzpatrick
Simon Firestone
Susan Ruff
Vladimir Sheftelyevich
Zaine Khan

Appendix B: Participating Schools and Organizations

Representatives of the following schools and organizations attended the conference. The school districts, schools, and organizations participating in Common Ground are, except where noted, located in the Delaware Valley.

Public Schools and Districts
Central Park East School 1 (New York)
Delaware County Intermediate Unit
Great Neck School District (New York)
Mamaroneck School District (New York)
Penn-Delco School District
Pennsbury School District
Radnor Township School District
Ridley School District
Rose Tree-Media School district
School District of Philadelphia
Soule School (Maine)
Springfield Montgomery County School District
Unionville-Chadds Ford School District
Upper Darby School District
Wallingford-Swarthmore School District

Colleges and Universities
Bates College (Maine)
Beaver College
Bennington College (Vermont)
Bryn Mawr College
Columbia University (New York)
Community College of Philadelphia
Delaware County Community College
Harvard University (Massachusetts)
Haverford College
Medical College of Philadelphia
Muhlenburg College (Pennsylvania)
Pennsylvania State University (Pennsylvania)
Sarah Lawrence College (New York)
Swarthmore College
Temple University
Tyler School of Art
University of Pennsylvania
West Chester University
Widener University

Non-Profit Organizations and Foundations
Community Housing Resource Board
Devereaux Foundation
Educators for Social Responsibility
The Network of Progressive Educators (Illinois)
Orton Society
The Pew Charitable Trusts
The Philadelphia Foundation
Philadelphia Teachers' Learning Cooperative
Philadelphia Writing Project
Primary Sources (Massachusetts)
Project START
PATHS/PRISM
Prospect Center (Vermont)

Independent Schools
Abington Friends School
Alison's House
Chestnut Hill Academy
Children's Community School (California)
Cornerstone School (Florida)
Delaware Valley Friends School
Fire Mountain School (Oregon)
Friends Child Care Center
Friends School, Haverford
Friends Select School
Germantown Academy
Germantown Friends School
Goshen Friends School
Green Acres School
Jubilee School
Lansdowne Friends School
Lehigh Valley Friends School
Marple-Newtown Montessori Country Day
Media-Providence Friends School
Miquon School
Montgomery School
Newtown Friends School
Oak Lane County Day School
Paideia School (Georgia)
Parkmont School (Washington, D.C.)
Pennsylvania School for the Deaf
Plymouth Meeting Friends School
Princeton Friends School (New Jersey)
Project Learn School
The School in Rose Valley
Shipley School
Springside School
State College Friends School (Pennsylvania)
Stratford Friends School
Trinity Cooperative Day Care Nursery

Appendix C: Supporting Organizations

The School in Rose Valley
The conference was sponsored by The School in
Rose Valley. The School is also co-publisher of
these proceedings.

It is an elementary and preschool located in
suburban Philadelphia which was founded in
1929 by a group of parents who wished to create
a learning environment for their children that
embodied their personal values and philosophy.
They felt that all children should be treated as
individuals with unique strengths and interests, as
whole people whose bodies and souls should be
nourished as well as their minds. They believed
that children should be allowed to ask their own
questions, follow their own cues and instincts in
the pursuit of constructing knowledge for themselves; that the knowledge and understanding
gained for its own sake would be most meaningful
and valued; and that learning would be fun. In
such a supportive and enriching environment,
children would grow into whole, healthy, self-
confident, moral, and happy human beings.

After over sixty years of operation, The School in
Rose Valley's basic philosophy and program have
remained as they were envisioned and established
by its founders. The approximately 120 children
currently enrolled are placed in one of seven
multi-aged classes based on their social and
emotional development. Their academic needs are
met through individual and small-group instruction designed to suit their personal learning paces
and styles. Much of the curriculum is developed
by the children themselves as they pursue their
own interests, such as by choosing reading books
they like, solving real mathematical problems,
learning about other cultures through first-hand
experiences, and genuinely discovering, experi-
menting, and practicing scientific concepts as they
explore their world.

Recent surveys of graduates of The School in Rose
Valley have confirmed that the program works
and the goals of its founders and current staff and
families are continuing to be met. Many alumni
have expressed that it was the most important and
enjoyable school they attended. Specific activities
that they cited as most memorable often included
science and social studies projects such as making
time-lines and models of the universe; real responsibilities they were given such as maintaining
school facilities and caring for class pets; and
creative endeavors such as producing plays,
books, and art and wood work. A large number
of the graduates of The School in Rose Valley
have continued their education into graduate and
post-graduate studies; many have entered into
service careers such as teaching, social work, and
medicine; many others have become successful
writers and artists. Above all, the school's alumni
have atested to the fact that it gave them the
values, self-confidence, skills, and love of learning
that have made their lives full, rich, and satisfying.

For further information, write:
Principal, The School in Rose Valley, School Lane,
Moylan, Pennsylvania 19065.

The Network of Progressive Educators
The Network of Progressive Educators is co-
publisher of the proceedings.

The purpose of the Network is to support progressive principles; to connect educators and organizations, both public and private; to encourage
progressive classrooms practices and democrati-
cally organized schools; and to pursue diversity,
equity, and inclusion for all children.

The following statement of principles was adopted
in 1991 by The Network of Progressive Educators
• Students learn best through direct experience,
primary sources, personal relationships, and
cooperative exploration.
• The blending of students' interests and teachers'
knowledge is the starting point for all work.
• Schools pay equal attention to all facets of
students' development.
• Assessment is accomplished through multiple
perspectives.
• The school and the home are active partners in
meeting the needs of students.
• Parents, students, and staff cooperate in school
decision-making.
• Schools encourage young people to fulfill their
responsibilities as world citizens by teaching critical
inquiry and the complexities of global issues.
• Schools help students develop their social con-
science and help them learn to recognize and
confront issues of race, class, and gender.

The editors encourage you to join the Network of
Progressive Educators and help promote:
• Regional and national conferences
• Local networking and opportunities for exchange
and inquiry
• Broader communication about progressive ideas
and practices
• Teacher Action Research.

For further information, write:
The Network of Progressive Educators, Post Office
Box 6028, Evanston, Illinois 60204.

Swarthmore College
Swarthmore College, in addition to being the site of
Common Ground, provided considerable support
for the conference and the proceedings. Swarthmore College students also gave generously of time
and energy. Their enthusiasm and sincerity of
purpose greatly enriched the quality of the experience of *Common Ground* for all present.

Swarthmore was founded in 1864 by members of
the Religious Society of Friends as a coeducational
institution. The purpose of Swarthmore College is
to make its students more valuable human beings
and more useful members of society. It seeks to
help its students realize their fullest intellectual and
personal potential combined with a deep sense of
ethical and social concern. While no longer sectar-
ian, the College seeks to illuminate the lives of its
students with the Quaker spiritual principles,

especially the individual's responsibility for the seeking and applying of truth and for testing whatever truth one belives one has found.

For further information, write Office of Admissions, Swarthmore College, Swarthmore, Pennsylvania 19081.

Bates College
Bates College has supported the preparation of this manuscript. Bates is a small, comprehensive, liberal arts institution located in Lewiston, Maine. Founded in 1855, Bates was the first coeducational college in New England. From its beginning the College has admitted students without regard not only to gender but race, religion, and national origin. This proud tradition of egalitarianism continues today—and nondiscrimination in admission, employment, and policy extends to sexual orientation, marital or parental status, age, and handicap. Today Bates is an accredited residential college with 1500 students and 162 faculty members who teach in 27 major fields. Bates is committed to the pursuit of knowledge and the dignity of the individual.

For further information, write:
Dean of Admissions, Bates College, Lewiston, Maine 04240.

Others
The Philadelphia Foundation and an anonymous donor provided significant financial support for scholarships. In closing, we again express our appreciation to The Pew Charitable Trusts for making possible the publication of these proceedings.

Appendix D: Planning
Committee Members

Peter Blaze Corcoran	*Swarthmore College, Bates College*
Penny Colgan-Davis	*Friends Select School*
Suchitra Davenport	*The School in Rose Valley*
Tammy Davis	*The Miquon School*
Lauren deMoll	*The School in Rose Valley*
Robert Kay	*Medical College of Pennsylvania*
Edie Klausner	*The School in Rose Valley*
John Krumm	*The Miquon School*
Kendall Landis	*Swarthmore College*
Jane Miluski	*The School in Rose Valley*
Ann Renninger	*Swarthmore College*
Vladimar Sandberg	*Wallingford-Swarthmore School District*
Dina Seiden	*Swarthmore College*
Steve Smith	*The School in Rose Valley*
Cecelia Traugh	*Friends Select School*
Robert Vitalo	*Media-Providence Friends School*